Sir Philip Sidney at his Old School

THE KING'S ENGLAND

SHROPSHIRE
County of the Western Hills

EDITED BY
ARTHUR MEE

With 242 Places
and 109 Pictures

LONDON
HODDER AND STOUGHTON
LIMITED ST PAUL'S HOUSE, E.C.4

First published July 1939
Third impression November 1948

Printed and Bound in Great Britain for Hodder & Stoughton, Limited,
by Richard Clay and Company, Ltd., Bungay, Suffolk.

The Editor is greatly indebted to
LESLIE B. POWELL
and
SYDNEY WARNER
for their help with this book

For the pictures to
SIDNEY TRANTER, ART EDITOR

and to the following:
Messrs B. T. Batsford, Ltd., E. J. Burrow, J. Dixon-Scott,
Herbert Felton, F. Frith, Photochrom, John Stone, Raphael
Tuck, and A. J. Woodley.

PICTURES OF SHROPSHIRE

*Where the pictures are not on or facing the page given they
are inside the set of pictures beginning on that page*

PICTURES OF SHROPSHIRE

County of the Western Hills

NATURE has made it our most characteristic border county, set in the heart of four English and four Welsh neighbours. So it has had more than its share of the old feuds and rivalries of race—more turmoil than tranquillity this lovely country has known. But, like the fires of the Wrekin, the strife has died down in the hearts of men. There is peace in the countryside as at the top of the extinct volcano, and the Shropshire toast today is "All friends round the Wrekin."

A friendly and delightful land it is, 1346 square miles of little known but never forgotten English beauty. All of us know the Wrekin, but Shropshire has nobler heights; she is, in fact, half plain and half hill country. She has a share of the foothills of the Cambrian Mountains of Wales, and the winding River Severn divides the county roughly into high lands and low lands, the river and the hills beyond forming a natural frontier in the racial warfare of other days. The Severn is, of course, Shropshire's chief river, and the Teme is the only other big one. Into the Severn run the Perry, the Rea, the Tern, the Cound, and the Worfe; into the Teme run the Clun, the Onny, the Corve, and another Rea, all nine small rivers.

The stuff that Shropshire is made of has much interest for our geologists. They have taken the race names of its early people for the labels of their science, and every architect and builder is familiar with Clee Hill granite, Grinshill freestone, and Wenlock limestone. The fire-formed Wrekin is the oldest mountain in England, rising a little unexpectedly above much younger strata to a height of 1335 feet. Cambrian quartzite and the millstone grit of the Age of Coal are found on its slopes, thrust aside by lava beds and volcanic ash. When we look with wonder at the hills behind Church Stretton (the Longmynd rocks rising 1674 feet) we are looking at some of the oldest rocks in England, burying themselves out of sight for a depth of nearly four miles, and this great range also crops out to form Haughmond Hill north of the Severn.

It is one of the most dramatic facts about our Island that we can walk across England down the steps of Time, treading the rocks in the order in which they were made. We may start this wonderful walk in London and we end it in Shropshire. Here we reach the oldest strata of all, the Cambrian, with their successors the Ordovician and Silurian, a fascinating series of rocks in which the naturalist traces the evolution of life from its beginning. All these lie in that part of Shropshire between the Severn and the borders of Herefordshire and Wales, and are rich in the natural life of today, good hunting-ground for those who love birds or insects or plants, yet of smaller value to the farmer than the lower lands and the younger lands north of the Severn, where we found rocks of the Age of Coal, with the Trias and Lias laid over them.

Captivating as are these southern rocks from immemorial time, it is from the northern half of the county that Shropshire draws its wealth. This is the miner's and the farmer's country. It is sad to see the derelict mine shafts and the slagheaps reminding us that Shropshire has shared in the Depression of our time, yet Coalbrookdale has still millions of tons available, and a historic position in industrial England. It was the iron ore so abundant here 200 years ago which brought Abraham Darby from Dudley to rent a small forge in 1709. He tried coke to smelt his ore and cast his iron pots, and the two Abraham Darbys following him developed the process till they were able to use coal itself, producing the first iron rails in England in 1767, and ten years later the first iron bridge, which was opened with a span of 200 feet across the Severn near Madeley. About this time the industries built up on clay began—bricks and tiles, and grandfather's clay pipe, and on finer clay which was brought from Cornwall. Now came the first iron barge, built at Broseley and launched into the Severn to compete with hundreds of

2

barges on that great river and on the canals which were coming into being in this level countryside.

Shropshire, we see, was developing, and was something of a pioneer, and we remember that Thomas Telford, who arrived at Shrewsbury to restore Earl Pulteney's house, stayed on as county engineer and built the Ellesmere Canal, one of the engineering wonders of the West. The railways have dimmed the memory of Telford, but he was a vital factor in the growth of Shropshire and every motorist should give thanks for him, for the road system of the county is largely his, especially the coach road linking its capital with London one way and with his own Menai Bridge the other.

It was Telford who revived Roman Watling Street. From Oakengates to Wroxeter Telford's route was Watling Street. Wroxeter was, of course, Uriconium, the Birmingham of Roman Britain, founded by one of the legions in the first half of the first century and prospering for nearly a century after the last legions had left our shores. It is a remarkable record, four centuries of a great city so long ago. It is probable that what still lies below the cornfields here is not less wonderful than the Uriconium which stands revealed. There is for us to see the great wall of the Law Courts with the baths and the little shops in its shade. There are columns from the Forum lying under a hedge, and in the museum here and at Shrewsbury is a great array of relics from the buried Roman city. Either by tribes from across the Welsh hills, or by Saxon chiefs coming up the Severn, Uriconium was overthrown and burned, and when the next great town in Shropshire rose it was called by a name which meant "the hill among the alder trees," which Offa changed when he captured it to "the town among the shrubs." So Shrewsbury comes on to the map.

Offa built his Dyke from the Dee to the Wye, and we find it well preserved in Shropshire, especially near Clun. With the moated mounds so numerous in this hilly border country, the

Dyke served to protect the county from the Welsh and made it possible for Wenlock Abbey to rise in its green fields. After Offa came the Normans, and the glory of Wenlock Abbey was not alone. A kinsman of the Conqueror built Shrewsbury Castle in the remarkable loop of the Severn within which it lies, and across the river he built the abbey of which something may be seen today, for its great church still echoes to hymns of praise, and here its builder, Roger de Montgomery, lies. Now was built the great monastery of Buildwas, an impressive ruin today, with Haughmond and Lilleshall and others reflecting the grandeur of their time. Now came also that group of border castles which played so great a part in our story: Ludlow, Acton Burnell, and Hopton. At Acton Burnell sat the first Parliament to which the Commons were directly summoned. At Hopton the Parliamentary garrison was ruthlessly butchered in the Civil War. At Bridgnorth Charles Stuart loved to walk, declaring the walks "the finest in his dominion."

As for Ludlow, whether we think of the castle or the town it has no rival in Shropshire. He who would spend a day with the glory of the English countryside about him, and the thrill of English history within him, let him come to Ludlow. The castle walls stand on their hill with the round Norman chapel still appealing in its beauty. From within these walls the little King Edward was taken to be smothered in the Tower by Richard Crookback marching bloodstained to the throne. But the walls have pleasanter memories, for here was Philip Sidney as a boy, the young Prince Arthur who would have changed the course of history had he lived, and John Milton himself, who sat in a room where we may sit, watching the first performance of his Comus.

The great houses which succeeded the castles and abbeys in Shropshire have a charm and beauty which make the county famous among architects. They come as a surprise in country and village and town, and Shrewsbury itself is not to be beaten by any town for the old houses still looking down on its streets. We can hardly walk there without passing a Tudor house or a

Georgian house, and at Ludlow it is the same; the black and white fronts of this hilltop town are wonderful to see. The Elizabethan Pitchford Hall is one of the sights of England, and who does not love the little Stokesay Castle, the fortified manor house with its delightful gateway? We come upon it in the lanes, and it is a thrilling spectacle. There is Bishop Percy's house at Bridgnorth, the Guildhall at Much Wenlock, the many-gabled Madeley Court, the stately Condover Hall, Shipton Hall with its slender tower, Stanwardine Hall with its Elizabethan doorway, and the farmhouse at Upper Millichope which is probably the oldest inhabited house in the county.

The churches are a wondrous group. Among the oldest is the Saxon church of Stanton Lacy, with a rare piece of sculpture over a remarkable doorway. At Wroxeter a Saxon cross is built into the wall among Roman masonry which the Saxons brought from the ruined town. There is a fragment of Roman concrete in the Saxon herringbone work at Rushbury. The carvings of animals on the doorway of Stottesdon tower were probably made by Saxon craftsmen, and the chancel arch at Barrow is Saxon work, doubtless older than Alfred. The Normans gave Shropshire many noble churches, apart from their massive buildings at Lilleshall, Buildwas, Haughmond, and Wenlock. For a perfect little building Heath Chapel is hard to beat (another country lane surprise), and there is Aston Eyre, with Christ riding into Jerusalem carved on a tympanum, Bromfield with its massive tower, Edstaston with its rich doorway, Morville with its early chancel arch and later Norman carvings, and Holgate with the quaint figures on its Norman font.

With the coming of the English builders there were stormy times in Shropshire and the building of churches slowed down, but Chirbury's nave and Cleobury Mortimer's chancel arch are from this time, and so is the church at Acton Burnell, rich in characteristic features and having a rare font. The 14th century saw the rebuilding of Chelmarsh church, with a nave and chancel acknowledged to be the best of their kind in the county.

Neen Solars in its cherry orchards is wholly 14th century, and so is some of the best work at Ludlow. Ludlow's tower shares with many others the glories of the 15th century architecture in Shropshire, where the towers of Claverley, Church Stretton, Edgmond, Shawbury, and Upton Magna stand out boldly against the sky. Battlefield has a most remarkable church, for it is a memorial to those who fell on this spot in 1403 when Henry the Fourth gained his decisive victory over the rebels in the great Battle of Shrewsbury. Its little decorative carvings remind us of the struggles and the combatants for mastery. We may see the same delight in portraying the life of man on Ludlow's stone reredos. Tong church is almost entirely from this time; it has been called the Village Westminster Abbey on account of its numerous monuments. It has a fan-vaulted chapel, fine misereres, and a lovely screen. Ludlow's wooden screen is one of the county's fine possessions, as are also those at Hughley and Bettws-y-crwyn, surely one of the highest churches in the land, more than 1400 feet above the sea.

We find many carvings in these churches expressing the joy of life, as well as its vices and virtues, in the prosperous 15th century. The stalls and misereres at Ludlow are remarkable for their satire on the vices of the age, and the fox in the pulpit foreshadowed the great change to come. Tong's stalls are magnificent. This native art persisted, and we find admirable craftsmanship in secular as well as sacred buildings. The room of the Council House at Shrewsbury takes the breath away by its sumptuous decoration. The Civil War left its mark and led to rebuilding in classical style, the best example being at Condover. The lovely painted plaster ceiling of Bromfield's chancel is covered with heraldry finished in 1672. At the beginning of the 18th century the magnificent church at Whitchurch was built, and before the century ended Thomas Telford tried his hand with a church at Bridgnorth.

Those who look for unusual things in churches will find at Clun a rare medieval pyx canopy; at Condover is the first great sculpture by G. F. Watts, and Shropshire has four of the group of about a hundred wooden figures still lying on tombs in this country; those at Pitchford and Eaton are the best. Most of the brasses are gone, but there is a magnificent one at Tong showing Sir William Vernon with his wife and ten children; and at Acton Burnell is one of Sir Nicholas Burnell in armour. On the wall at Claverley is a Norman knight unhorsing a Saxon at Hastings, remarkable because it is a painting of the great Roger de Montgomery himself, with 12 other mounted men, by Norman artists. There are other striking wall-paintings in this church. For the best glass in the county we must come to Ludlow, with windows rich in 15th century work and a 14th century Jesse Tree in the lady chapel. For the best Jesse Tree in the county, however, we come to Shrewsbury, where it graces the window of St Mary's nearly 600 years after it was made for another church in memory of Sir John Charlton.

It may be said that the traveller who seeks delight in churches, in lovely streets, or quiet lanes, in old houses or old towns, will find no disappointment in Shropshire. Indoors and out it has beauty we do not forget, and there are in some of its little churches monuments which the traveller long remembers.

For men who shine in fame about the world Shropshire has a high place. She gave us Charles Darwin, whose long life-work has affected the outlook of every thinking man alive. She gave us Clive, who more than any other man gave India to the Empire. She gave us Henry Hickman, forgotten till almost the other day, yet the first discoverer in the world to lay the foundation of anaesthesia, the science which saves mankind from pain. She gave us Piers Plowman, the first poet to sing of the heroic spirit of the English peasant. She gave his schooling to Philip Sidney, immortal for the spirit of sacrifice in death, and to that heroic successor of his in our own time, Andrew Irvine, who disappeared in the clouds on Everest, marching to immortality at the top of the world. She gave us Bishop Percy, the grocer's son who found a servant lighting a fire with old manuscripts, rescued them, and put them into the first great collection of English poetry. She gave us Richard Baxter, the saint imprisoned by the butcher Jeffreys, but honoured forever as one of the rarest figures in our annals.

If we want other names for the roll of honour for this fine county we have those of Bishop Walsham How; of William Wycherley the dramatist; of the Tom Brown who wrote "I do not love thee, Dr Fell"; of Ambrose Phillips, the poet whose nickname gave our language the pleasantry of Namby Pamby; Sir Archibald Alison, historian of Europe; the first Lord Acton, great friend of Mr Gladstone and himself a historian; Lord Herbert of Cherbury; Stanley Weyman and Mary Cholmondeley, the novelists; Admiral Benbow who fought the French with mutineers about him until his leg was blown off; Rowland, Lord Hill, Wellington's right hand at Waterloo, who led the final charge which swept Napoleon's Old Guard off the field; Richard Corfield, the soldier-administrator of Somaliland; Sir Herbert Edwardes, known as the Hero of Multan for staving off a rebellion there, of whom Lawrence wrote from India that since the days of Clive no man had done what Edwardes did; and, of course, the spirit of Alfred Housman, author of A Shropshire Lad, though he himself was born across the border. We find 5581 names on the county's roll of honour in the war, so that we may assume with confidence that Shropshire's lads still carry on the prestige of their ancestors. The spirit of Sir Philip Sidney is in its schools, and will not die.

Giant's Shaft

ABDON. Towering above it, eighteen hundred feet above the sea, is Abdon Burf, stark summit of Brown Clee Hill, with a walled enclosure in which the men of the Stone Age fortified themselves. Quarrying is destroying much of this site of prehistoric civilisation, but the great boulder, Giant's Shaft, about which our ancestors and their families gathered in those old times, looks much as it must have looked to them 4000 years ago. The scattered farms and cottages of the village rest on the hillside 1000 feet below the Burf, with billowing hills to look on and Corve Dale a picture in the west.

The little church, with its steep roof and double bellcot, has timbers 600 years old in a gabled porch sheltering a doorway through which nearly 20 generations have come and gone. In the white-walled interior is a chapel with massive walls where men came to pray while Llewellyn the Great was at war with King John. A deep recess has a beautiful window at floor level which has brought the sunlight of six centuries into the chancel. There is no chancel arch, but in place of it a massive old screen reaches like a gable to the roof, in which are timbers set up while America was still unknown. At the font have been christened over 20 generations of Abdon children.

Bishop Burnell's Splendid Church

ACTON BURNELL. We should see it in daffodil time, when its churchyard is a blaze of gold; but at any time it is a place of much charm and fascination. It takes us back vividly to the century of Magna Carta, to the time of Robert Burnell, the Bishop of Bath and Wells who was one of Edward the First's most trusted ministers, Lord Chancellor for many years. Most of this splendid church he built, with the castle rising from a beautiful lawn beside it; and still standing in this park are two grey gables of his ancient house, nicknamed the Parliament Barn, because King Edward's Parliament met here in 1283.

The memory of Bishop Burnell has come down to us as that of a covetous and ambitious man, who collected estates as another man might collect horses. He had possessions in 19 counties, and

9

owned 82 manors; but he built the Bishop's Palace at Wells, left in this village much that has proved fine and enduring, and played no small part in the great reforms of his day.

His castle is ruined, a picturesque shell with embattled towers, but his church stands as a beautiful example of the building style towards the end of the 13th century, its chancel one of the finest in the county, with lovely groups of lancet windows, rich mouldings, slender shafts, and foliage capitals. All about the building, inside and out, are carved quaint heads of men and women, one (over the east window) probably a portrait of the bishop, and another (on an arch) perhaps King Edward himself. Graceful foliage adorns the corbel brackets of the three beautiful arches of the chancel and transepts, and in the chancel wall is a remarkable little window about seven inches square. The low tower with its pyramid roof is modern.

There are traces of old wall-paintings of flowers, a tomb recess 600 years old, a very fine double piscina with little heads under the drains, black and white Tudor roofs, and a collection of medieval tiles almost covering the north transept. Jacobean craftsmanship is seen in the altar table, the pulpit and some of the pews near it, the stalls, and in two small chairs carved with a man and a woman. The font cover is Jacobean too, but the eye is drawn at once to the font itself, an exquisite example of 13th century art, simple and dignified, with delicate shafts separating eight trefoil recesses.

The oldest monument is a finely arcaded tomb to Bishop Burnell's grand-nephew, Sir Nicholas Burnell of 1382, with a beautiful brass portrait of him under a rich canopy. He has a long moustache, and wears armour with a pointed helmet and a collar of mail. Close by is a sumptuous Elizabethan tomb, reaching to the roof and enriched with an extraordinary display of ornament. On it lies Sir Richard Lee in gorgeous armour with a mass of lace-like carving, a tiny dog peeping out of his gauntlet; and his wife in a gown of rich brocade, with a beautiful cloak and a close-fitting headdress. Carved at the top are a helmet and a crest of a squirrel, and at the back of the tomb are nine daughters all in different kinds of dress, for all the world as if they were looking over a balcony. Two sons in armour stand at their father's feet, and a third is at his head. On the opposite wall Sir Humphrey Lee of 1632 kneels with his wife under a canopy, below them being a son and a diminishing row of five daughters.

There is a memorial to an English officer who died fighting for Austria in 1794.

Three lancets in the chancel are filled with beautiful glass in memory of William Serjeantson, who completed 60 years as rector here in 1924. His is one of the longest records in the county. One window shows the Madonna and Child in blue and white, another has Robert Burnell in his robes, and the third is a picture of Edward the First in chain armour with the royal arms.

Close to this fine church stands the great house in its lovely park, which has a lake. The house is in Grecian style, and has a chapel built in the 18th century by French monks who came to England as refugees.

Between this village and Cardington is a stretch of Roman road about 500 yards long, reminding us that Acton lies near Watling Street; and a mile or two away at Langley is a forlorn little chapel of the 17th century, no longer used but equipped with simple benches, a few box-pews, a six-sided pulpit, and a quaint reading desk. The roof is stoutly timbered, with some quaint heads and fleur-de-lys, and the chapel has kept a piscina and a stoup from its 13th century predecessor. Also at Langley is the gateway which led to the old Manor House of the Lees, who lie at Acton. Now part of a farm, it has Elizabethan timbering and a battlemented wall.

The Old Way Into the Church

ACTON ROUND. It has the dark beauty of the wooded hills around it, and a hillside church shaded by a copper beech. The captivating porch of time-worn beams shelters a grand old door with scrolled hinges fashioned 700 years ago and good for many more years of service. Half-hidden by the beams over the door is a tympanum that may be Norman, its carving too worn to tell a story. The walls of the nave are Norman, the chancel 14th century, but the arch between them, although in 13th century style, is modern. Among the memorials of the Acton family of Aldenham Hall, near Morville, is an 18th century wall monument showing Sir Richard Acton and his wife fondly clasping hands.

As Strange as Fiction

ACTON SCOTT. A picture of rural charm, with fertile valleys to the south breaking the line of its encircling hills, it has links with a European romance as strange as fiction, and with history 15 centuries older.

Near the Tudor hall by the church, unsuspected until last century, are the foundations of a Roman villa, a domestic link in the defensive chain drawn across the county when Wroxeter was a centre of Imperial grandeur. There were underground chambers for heating the great house, and (suggestive of a hasty departure) coins left when the legions marched away to Rome. The coins and other Roman relics were at the hall when we called.

Among the fine yews in the churchyard is a grand veteran 21 feet round, out-topping the massive 13th century tower. The church, much refashioned while the old tree has been growing, has a sanctuary window in memory of a rector for over 60 years of last century, G. A. Magee. Here are memorials of two famous families who were destined to cross swords, the head of one to be made a baronet for his loyalty to Charles Stuart, the head of the other rewarded for his devotion to the Commonwealth. One of the families is shown in brass, on which are engraved portraits of Thomas Mytton, his wife, and 11 children. Thomas, who left a reputation for public spirit and high courage, was succeeded by a more famous namesake, one of the few notable Shropshire Parliamentarians, who gained a succession of strongholds in the county for the Commonwealth. He was granted £5000 by the nation. The rival family was the house of Acton, to whom there are two monuments. It was a 16th century Edward who built the hall, but the family had been here over 300 years before Charles Stuart gave it a baronetcy. From this house sprang two remarkable men.

John, the sixth baronet, in an expedition against the Barbary Corsairs rescued 4000 Spaniards from slavery. Entering the service of Ferdinand the Fourth of Naples, he became Commander-in-chief of the Army and Navy as well as Prime Minister. Arriving at Naples victorious from the Nile, Nelson, enslaved by the charms of Lady Hamilton, worked in close cooperation with Acton, who advised the flight of the king and queen, carried out secret preparations enabling them to smuggle vast treasures aboard, and then, with the king, queen, and Lady Hamilton, fled to Sicily. Acton married his niece when she was only 14, and she survived him 62 years. Of their three children one became a cardinal and another was the father of that prodigy of learning Lord Acton, the historian who regarded his grandfather's fortune as tainted and proudly refused to accept it.

The Headless Abbot

ADDERLEY. A market town six centuries ago, it has shrunk to a small village, with Adderley Hall close by in a park of 200 acres.

The church stands by a little green with a mounting-block, and is mostly about 150 years old; but it has two ancient possessions which have seen the decline of Adderley from greater days. One is a Norman font which spent part of its time as the base of a sundial, the other is a fine but headless brass showing the vestments and crozier of a 14th century abbot. There are Jacobean chairs and altar rails, a handsome modern screen with bold columns, and a monument with a carving of a seated woman in memory of Sir Corbet Corbet, who died in 1823. Many of the best things belong to the 17th century chapel, which has a massive panelled roof with rich bosses, panelling round the walls, and a splendid Jacobean screen. In one of the windows are the arms of twelve Earls of Kilmorey, the Needham family, whose memorials here go back to Sir Robert of 1556, shown on a brass with his wife and nine children. By the wall of the church we noticed the gravestone of Sarah Williams, a faithful servant for 60 years.

A King Crosses the Border

ALBERBURY. It crosses the Welsh border, so that England loses a bit of it to Wales. In the great house in Loton Park, home of the Leightons, is a brass tablet recording the fact that George the Fourth, when staying here as Prince of Wales, walked a mile into the Principality and came back wearing a sprig of the first oak he saw across the border. A mile away is what is left of the medieval abbey, now a farm, but still belonging to the Oxford College to which Henry the Sixth gave it. It has traces of its ancient moat, some ancient walling, a window and a doorway of the 13th century, and an old piscina in the dairy. Something of the old vaulted roof of the chapel covers one end of the house and can be seen in the bedrooms.

In a park of 100 acres stands Rowton Castle, with the 15th century tower surviving from the burning down of the place by the Commonwealth troops, who took it after a heroic defence for nearly a fort-night by Lady Lyster. We come to the village through Loton Park, one of three Shropshire manors with which Henry the Seventh rewarded John Leighton for turning to him in time for the Battle of Bosworth Field and the beginning of the Tudor Dynasty, John's son was knighted by Henry the Eighth, and Sir John's son married a cousin of Queen Elizabeth.

The Leightons sleep in the ancient church in which they were christened, but one of them sleeps in the open like the chiefs of prehistoric tribes who lie in the barrows round about. He was Sir Bryan, the ninth baronet, still much loved and remembered, for it was only in 1919 that he ended his days and wished to be laid at the highest point of the park in which he had spent so much of his life.

In the church is a remarkable series of memorials to the Leightons, seven embossed brasses, each with a groundwork of oak and acorn, and all in rich heraldic colours. One is to Robert Leighton, a member of the Restoration Parliament, and on another is a picture of Loton House as it stood in 1756. A third brass has two women guarding a shield, and a fourth a mounted bugler. General Leighton is on another, shown on a battlefield in the Peninsular War, with a little scene of an old man admonishing his son, saying "Remember thy Creator in the days of thy youth."

There are brass portraits of the youthful figures of Forester Leighton in clerical robes, with his wife in a bonnet with the flowing skirt and pointed bodice of the early 19th century, and another brass has the portrait of a widow of the house, a pathetic figure under a great canopy, wearing a lace-trimmed cap and a tasselled veil over her curls. Most pathetic of all is the unusual memorial to a gallant young Leighton of our time, the propeller of the plane he flew in the Great War.

The church itself springs from Norman days, and still has the original massive saddleback tower; it rises just above the gabled roofs. An immense building for so small a place, the church has a fine medieval arcade, sculptured heads on its windows, and some 14th century glass showing angels and a crowned Madonna. The magnificent roof of the nave is 500 years old, its arched timbers finely carved. There are new and old timbers in the roof of the modern chancel. The nave has kept the old squire's pew in which the Leightons sat, and there are many old box-pews and benches with Jacobean ends.

Linked to the church by a flying buttress are the ruins of the castle in which the warlike Fitzwaines lived 700 years ago in the shadow of the Norman tower; and in the churchyard is a medieval cross capped by a modern head with three sundials. The little village green has a striking cenotaph with a plaque of the Happy Warrior; it is crowned by a dome on eight pillars.

Heraldry Magnificent

ALBRIGHTON. Traffic rushes through from Staffordshire, but it keeps its ancient calm uncommonly well. There are fine timbered houses facing the broad highway, and an old timbered inn which may have been the home of the Talbots who lie in the church across the way. Its nave is modern but the chancel is 600 years old, and the tower, which has a fine round-arched window with pillars and capitals, is a mixture of Norman and medieval work. The east window is original with fine tracery, and the chancel has a noble modern arch and an old roof of open timbers. There is a Jacobean pulpit with eight carved panels, a modern font in medieval style, and two grand old tombs. On one of them lies Sir John Talbot, bold in white marble and wearing Tudor armour, with his feet on a lion and his head on a helmet, his wife beside him with small figures of their children. It is thought that the other tomb may belong to the first priest of Albrighton, William de Picheford. It is a magnificent heraldic monument, one of the finest in England, carved with 27 coats-of-arms, and it was found buried under the south aisle last century. George Woodhouse, a 19th century vicar, has a marble tablet recording that he was here for 58 years.

A charming medieval sculpture of two heads close together under a little arch is set in the south wall outside, marvellously well preserved after centuries of wind and rain. Built into the wall round the corner is a stone engraved with the portrait of a gentleman of Elizabethan England, Leonard Smallpece. In the churchyard is a cross with grotesque carvings at the four corners of its base.

ALBRIGHTON. It is near Shrewsbury. Its little church is only a copy of Norman architecture, but it has a real Norman font with patterns of chevrons and horseshoes. A brilliant window by

Christopher Whall shows St George between St Andrew and St David. The canopied pulpit with its deeply sunk panels is the good work of Jacobean craftsmen, and was made about the same time as the timber porch of the hall in the park across the way.

The Medieval Embroidery

ALVELEY. To walk into Alveley is like entering an ancient fortress, so sturdy are its stone cottages, so massive the walls that guard the church, all deep in the shade of immemorial elms. The foundations of the clerestoried church tower, and the four great pillars and arches of the north arcade, are all Norman, but the south arcade is 13th century. The nave has a 15th century roof resting on strange stone corbels, and there are frescoes which may be older still. The biggest and clearest, eight feet square, painted in yellow and red, is a portrayal of the triumph of good over evil, and shows a woman wearing a crown, with a skeleton of sin or death on her right, holding a sheaf of darts in one hand and thrusting a spear through her heart with the other; while on her left is a herald with a trumpet, and a man putting two dragons to flight with his sword.

In the wall of the 14th century chapel is part of a stone engraved with a cross, and there is also an ancient altar stone with five conse-cration crosses, a beautifully carved piscina, and medieval tiles with grotesque animals. On the painted reredos is the Nativity, the Cruci-fixion, and the Descent from the Cross. There is a brass with a portrait of John Grove, who died a few months after Shakespeare, and an inscription telling of his bequest of five pounds to "labouring men of honest conversation."

But the treasures of the church are its old glass and its embroidery. Its altar frontal was embroidered 500 years ago in yellow and green, and is nine feet long, showing Abraham with three tiny figures in his bosom, and angels holding scrolls. The old glass is in two of the 15th century clerestory windows, in which we see a bishop, three saints, and seven smaller figures, all wearing embroidered cloaks, all fairly complete, and brilliant in colour. Three little roundels of old glass in the west window show a Crucifixion and a saint.

A stone figure of Christ is in memory of the 13 men of the village who fell in the war, the inscription asking us to remember them with loving thankfulness. There are fragments of ancient patterned masonry in the outside walls, and on an old battlement by the porch

A Scene near Bishop's Castle

The Longmynd above Church Stretton

THE BORDER HILLS OF SHROPSHIRE

Acton Burnell   **The Ruined Castle**

Acton Burnell   Roman Road

Alveley   Wayside Cross

is a carving of a fox with a goose in its mouth. In the churchyard are stone coffins and the remains of a magnificent medieval cross, and standing alone about a mile west of the village is an ancient wayside cross with a round head.

Proud Lineage

ASHFORD BOWDLER. Its pretty cottages and farms are hidden in the Teme valley, and on the steep brink of the river stands its tiny church, old but restored, with a quaint shingled tower growing from the nave. It has two filled-up doorways through which the Normans walked, and its modern timber porch shelters a medieval doorway and a battered stoup. Parts of old pews line the walls, and there are panels about 300 years old in the pulpit and the reading desk. The fine deep splays of the windows are remarkable, and one of the narrow windows was built into the chancel wall by Norman masons. There is a tiny echo of far-off days in Scotland in a tablet to Thomas Ricketts, whose grandmother was proud to claim her descent from the man who saved King David's life in the hunting field. The king was threatened by an angry stag, and it was on the scene of his escape that he founded Holyrood Abbey.

The Window Like an Eye

ASHFORD CARBONELL. It has an ancient bridge with a single arch and with an old water-mill for its neighbour; it bestrides the River Teme. Black and white houses gather round the hillside and above them stands the long and aisleless church, looking east to the Clee Hills and west to the border. One black and white house has a high yew hedge and arches of yew spanning its garden path, and the churchyard has four yews that have watched many generations come and go.

The church has a timbered belfry and a Norman doorway still opening into it. The Norman priest's doorway remains in the chancel, another doorway of that time has been built-up in the north wall, and there are several Norman windows. The low chancel arch of the Norman builders remains as it was, and the children are still christened at the Norman font.

It is the windows that attract our notice here, for one is extraordinary and two others are of great interest. Above the two slender and deeply splayed Norman windows on the east wall is one of the extremely rare windows called a vesica, shaped like an eye and strangely related to the symbol of the fish which was used by the early Christians because the Greek word for fish contains the initials of Christ. The two other windows of special interest are in the nave, both having the old iron hinges fixed in the 14th century for shutters; probably they were left unglazed. One of these windows has fragments of glass, in which we noticed a rose.

There is an ancient aumbry and an Elizabethan chalice. Old panelling lines the chancel walls, and there are 15th century beams in the nave roof. The modern oak pulpit has the Good Shepherd carved on one of its panels.

On a lawn by the open road above the village is a fine old gabled manor; down in the village is a rough-hewn block of stone set by the wayside in memory of the men who died for peace.

The Tragic Bride

ASTLEY ABBOTTS. Sheltered among noble chestnut trees and stately copper beeches with far horizons seen between, it has Tudor houses and an upland church which takes us back 800 years. The old black and white house looking over the churchyard is charming, linked by a romantic note of sadness with the ancient church. In the north aisle is a maiden's garland, on which hangs a sorrowful tale. It is here in memory of Hannah Phillips, who died at the black and white house on the eve of her wedding which was to have taken place in this church in 1707. With the garland are preserved the dress, the shoes, and the wreath the bride would have worn on the happy May day of her wedding, and her initials and the date are on the side. We have come upon a small number of these garlands still surviving in our village churches from the days when it was the rule to hang them in memory of such tragic maids. It was such a garland as this that Shakespeare had in mind for Ophelia when he made the churlish priest protest against these "crants," whereupon her brother burst out in his fury:

> I tell thee, churlish priest,
> A ministering angel shall my sister be
> When thou liest howling.

Very interesting is the chancel, all Jacobean, with a roof of open timbers resting on carved oak corbels, a phoenix, a laughing lion, a winged horse, and a unicorn among them; and below are brackets quaintly carved with human figures. The pulpit has 12 Jacobean panels richly carved with flowers, and all the panelling round the chancel is of the same age. Fragments of 13th century glass in the east window make up a small complete figure in a cloak of gold against a rich background. The nave has two Norman windows and a blocked doorway of the 12th century; and the plain round font, brought years ago from a farm where it served as a cattle trough, has been used through 20 generations, and more.

On an alabaster tablet are six enamelled coats-of-arms in memory of Colonel Billingsley, one of Charles Stuart's commanders, who died fighting with sword in hand in the churchyard of St Leonard's at Bridgnorth. At a windowsill we found an ancient corbel of white stone gracefully carved with the head of a woman.

Through the Centuries

ASTON BOTTERELL. It lies near the foot of Brown Clee Hill, with all the loveliness of Shropshire round it. Almost every century since the 12th has contributed something to its church, the chancel walls being Norman, the aisle 13th century, the arcade 14th, the nave roof 15th, the porch 17th, and the tower 19th, having been rebuilt with much of its old stone. There is a Norman font, a plain old chest, and an altar table with two grim scenes carved on a panel, showing a man in chains led away by soldiers and kneeling at his execution. On a Tudor tomb lie John Botterell in armour with his feet on a lion, and his wife with a dog at her feet, below them three children wearing ruffs; their canopy is supported on six columns with coloured coat-of-arms and Tudor flowers. A humbler memorial is the worn 15th century stone to another John Botterell, showing him in his armour beside his wife in a long simple dress, with three sons and three daughters at their feet. The old manor house of the Botterell family, now a farm, still has a 16th century ceiling with a frieze of vine. In the churchyard is an ancient yew with two trunks.

The Norman Sculpture

ASTON EYRE. It is among the orchards on the Bridgnorth road to Ludlow, and it has in its church one of the oldest and quaintest stone sculptures in Shropshire. It is the Norman tympanum above the doorway, representing the Entry into Jerusalem. Christ is mounted on an ass, wearing a long plain gown, a palm branch in his left hand; before the ass sits a man with a long beard, laying palm leaves on the road, and on the other side is another bearded man, leading a smaller ass and carrying a garment. The tympanum is deeply carved and the detail well preserved, but its most striking feature is the sense of movement the sculptor gave the figures, as vivid today as eight centuries ago. The door beneath it is a veteran of 300 years, its long iron hinges having the date on them, and leads into a nave with four Norman windows. The chancel has a Norman arch, an Elizabethan doorway, and Elizabethan panelling along the east wall. The pulpit, with two queer human figures carved in oak, is Jacobean.

Among the fine old farms near the church is one, Hall Farm, with part of the walls of a 13th century manor house.

Saxon Saint and Roman Stones

ATCHAM. Its name is shortened from Attingham, which means the home of St Eata's children, and its church is the only one in England dedicated to him. He is remembered as one of the 12 English boys received by St Aidan, as Bede tells us, and he grew up to be the first Abbot of Melrose, the teacher of St Cuthbert, and Bishop of Hexham, where he was laid to rest before they took him on his wanderings and laid him finally in Durham Cathedral.

Atcham has two bridges over the Severn, one modern and one 18th century; and facing each other across the open space are the handsome gateway of Attingham Park, with its great house of about 200 years ago, and the fine church partly built of Roman stones from Uriconium, two miles away. Cut in many of them is a dove-tailed hole for the lewis, a Roman device for lifting still practised today.

The bold tower has a band of ornament, and a Norman doorway with ten white shafts expanding into leaves and supporting a broad red arch like a projecting hood. The porch is dated 1685, and near it are five tombstones carved 600 years ago with crosses. The nave has a Norman window and a 500-year-old roof, and the 13th century chancel has a priest's doorway.

Treasures have come to Atcham from other churches and other lands. Two Flemish panels in the pulpit show the Mocking of Our Lord and the Carrying of the Cross; and four German panels in the reading desk are deeply cut with scenes of the Prodigal Son, his departure and profligacy, the feeding on husks with the swine, and his joyous return. The delicately traceried screen with carving of heads and figures and a tiny cherub is from another village; from St Chad's at Shrewsbury is an engraving on alabaster of a Tudor family, as vivid as any brass; and from Bacton in Herefordshire is some remarkable glass of the 15th and 16th centuries. That in the east window shows the Madonna between St John and a martyr, below being two figures kneeling at a desk with their 12 red-haired sons and seven daughters. Even more interesting is the glass picture in the nave showing Queen Elizabeth with her gentlewoman Blanche Parry, who is said to have served at Court for the whole of her 82 years. There is a sculpture of Blanche on her tomb at Bacton showing her with Queen Elizabeth, and there also we may see a marvellous altar frontal worked by her.

Another nave window has musical angels in 15th century glass, and an unusual Tudor memorial framed on the wall is a stone cut with figures of Death and a corpse in its coffin. Here, in a font now gone, was baptised Ordericus Vitalis, who wrote a celebrated Church History of England and Normandy, beginning it, he tells us, in 1075, the year of his birth. His life was spent as a monk in Normandy, but it is thought he may have gone to school at Shrewsbury.

A Poet by Chantrey

BADGER. There is much to delight us in the green splendour of these wooded slopes, the beauties of Badger Dingle with its running brook, the rich gardens of Badger Hall, and the treasures in the little church. The Norman foundations of the tower are the only relics of the church before this, but the tiny nave and chancel are full of charm and colour. A fine copy of Titian's Ecce Homo is over the altar and at the west end hangs a copy of Guido Reni's Annunciation. The east window has figures of Our Lord and two saints in old Flemish glass, and there are other old roundels with symbolical figures. The marble font is a copy of the font in Christopher Wren's famous church of St Bride's in Fleet Street.

An exquisite screen mostly 400 years old divides the transept from the nave; it is carved with flowers and grapes and has many small bosses, elegant capitals, and tiny battlements. The dark oak of the screen sets off the gleaming white monuments beyond. One is by Chantrey, and shows Isaac Hawkins Browne, a good lawyer but a poor poet, sitting with his books. On another monument sits his mother, welcomed by an angel from the clouds, the work of Flaxman. There are two memorials by the famous sculptor John Gibson, one showing Mrs Harriet Cheney, whose family built the transept and the porch, seated with an angel grasping her hand, the other in memory of Harriet Margaret Pigot, with two ascending figures of women.

One other gem of marble deserves remembrance, for it tells of a woman's long service to the village in recent times; it is a tablet with a charming panel of children poring over their books, set up in memory of Emma Grainger, schoolmistress here for 42 years. In the churchyard are the steps and shaft of a medieval cross.

Saxon Heritage

BARROW. It is a lonely place with a Saxon heritage, one of the oldest and most fascinating churches in Shropshire. Its tower was set up by our first Norman builders, and its west doorway has a tympanum which was probably the work of Saxon masons just after the Conquest. It is carved with three rows of six squares, each with a different pattern. Both north and south doorways are also Norman, and they bring us into a dimly lit nave which fills us with wonder as we gaze on the strength and massive simplicity of the ancient walls. They have stood since the 11th century, and three of their original windows remain, narrow and deeply splayed and hardly touched by time. In the chancel the sense of wonder grows, for its south wall was probably built as long ago as the 8th century, and its crude masonry is as the Saxon builders left it. The north wall has a Saxon window, and the Saxon chancel arch looks sturdy enough to last another thousand years. Over the doorway through which the Norman priest would pass is the arch remaining from a window he would see.

Pausing in the chancel and looking down the nave, we may realise the sense of security the Saxons and Normans demanded in their churches. This one is small, but had it been a feudal stronghold its walls could not have been more solid. Pictures painted on them by medieval artists were found last century, but only a trace remains above the chancel arch. The font is ancient, and in the porch are a few old tiles, but the interest of everything here pales beside that of the chancel walls, which bridge a gulf of perhaps 1200 years and were old in the days of King Alfred.

A brass tablet has a tribute to Ann Hay, a faithful nurse in the Forester family at Willey Hall for nearly half a century. The hall is in the lovely park.

Stone Age Rampart

BASCHURCH. Looking out to the distant hills of Wales, it has a story going back to the coming of the Saxons. A mile or more away is a survival from antiquity, a camp of three acres surrounded by a Stone Age rampart and crowned by a round mound about 50 feet high. A causeway connects this enclosure with another, and still another causeway leads into a deep pool at the base. In the pool a thin bronze water-clock was found.

There is a patriarchal yew in the churchyard, a poor hollow trunk. Above it, on a Norman base, rises a sturdy 14th century tower with massive buttresses and a pyramid roof. The present doorway has been here 600 years. Norman pillars with square capitals carry six arches in the nave and the tower arch has Norman stones. In an aisle are three beautiful recesses carved six centuries ago, one with nearly a hundred ballflowers in its decoration. A doorway from Crusading days has been built up. There is a Jacobean font and an 18th century chest.

Here there have been two vicars with a record between them of 104 years; Robert Jeffreys for 58 years of the 18th century, and William Jones for 46 years of last century. One of the windows shows the Good Shepherd, David with his harp, and Christ at the Sea of Galilee, with disciples cooking fish taken from a net lying by them.

The Battle of Shrewsbury

BATTLEFIELD. It is one of the marvellous places where history comes to life, and not only history but literature, for we walk here with some of the greatest and bravest men in Shakespeare.

It is the field of the great Battle of Shrewsbury in 1403, the victory of Henry the Fourth over the proud rebels who were giving him little peace, lords of the north and barons of the Welsh Marches. We find it all in Shakespeare, the king sad at the wild life of his son, the rash bravery of Hotspur at the head of the rebels, the useless negotiations before the battle began, and Falstaff feigning death to save his skin.

Hotspur fell, his followers fled, and for a little while the king was master. And here, on the very field of battle, he built this noble church, raising it as a shrine in which prayers were to be said for the slain, and founding a college of priests to serve it. Traces of the dwelling of the priests have been found in the churchyard, and the doorway they used is now filled up in the wall; but the church itself, with a gorgeous tower built a century later by a master of the college, is as fine a monument as we could wish. We come to it by a remarkable lychgate, brought from Upton Magna and carved with hearts and other fancies.

Magnificent outside and in, the chancel has 12 pinnacles linked by a lovely parapet, and among the striking gargoyles are knights hauling ropes and fighting; while over one of the windows is a figure of King Henry himself with his dagger at his hip.

Very fine is the hammerbeam roof inside, though it has been nearly all made new. On the beams are 20 shields of the king and Prince Hal and their knights, and among the corbels, which are all different, we see groups of heads and a woman with ivy in her mouth. The modern screen is beautiful, but the treasure of the woodwork is a 15th century carving in one of the sedilia; it represents Our Lady of Pity, and shows the Madonna supporting the head of her Son, who lies across her knees. It is moving and terrible in its simple tragedy.

A 19th century monument has the arms and the elephant crest of John Corbet and his family, descended from one who came to our shores with the Conqueror. It was John Corbet's daughter, Lady Brinkman, who restored the church when it was almost a ruin, adding the vestry as a family chapel. The vestry windows have now some fragments of medieval glass.

King Henry's church at Battlefield took the place of the one at Albright Hussey a mile away, now ruined to its foundations. Many stones from it are in the lovely Tudor manor house which was first the home of the Corbets and before them the home of the Husseys, whose shield with a riding boot is in the roof of Battlefield church.

A Sister's Tribute

BECKBURY. It is a pleasant tree-shaded village with a 17th century timbered hall and an attractive little church, largely rebuilt last century but keeping something of its long past. The chancel is 600 years old, and the east window has fragments of its original glass. There is an engraved stone showing Richard Haughton in his armour, with his wife at his side and elegant little figures of their four sons and six daughters below. He was a soldier in the time of Henry the Seventh. A soldier of our own time is remembered in a beautiful window, showing brother and sister clad in rich medieval dress with the Holy City in the background; it is a sister's tribute to her brother John Lloyd, who fell in Flanders in 1915. On an outside wall of the chancel is a canopied recess which may have sheltered a founder's tomb.

Between Two Rivers

BEDSTONE. Embowered in trees on a hillside between two rivers, it looks across to Castle Ditches, a prehistoric camp a mile away to the west. There are old thatched cottages in the village and the modern house of Bedstone Court with charming grounds. The church, with its black and white bellcot and a little shingled spire, has a deep chancel arch the Normans raised, the charming windows with which they lit both nave and chancel, and some of their masonry still in the walls. The font is also Norman; this village has had its children christened at it for 800 years.

A Church of Charles the Second's Day

BENTHALL. It has a fine viewpoint at Tykes Nest, 400 feet above the Severn; a Tudor hall which was garrisoned in the Civil War but survived with its panelled rooms, carved staircase, and its Jacobean ceiling; and a quaint little church built soon after the Restoration. The church is among the trees by the side of the hall, and we come into it by a splendid old door, with long hinges ending in flame-like ornament. There is a Jacobean pulpit with three carved panels, and on the wall is a curious 18th century monument to Ralph Browne with a coat-of-arms, floral carving, urns, and a skull, a small iron grille protecting it all.

Old Scriven

BERRINGTON. It lies in the Severn Valley with the splendour of the Wrekin beyond, and has a cluster of farms and cottages, with the gabled Manor Farm sturdy and fine after three centuries.

The church, standing on foundations believed to be Saxon, has a 15th century tower, but the building is for the most part 700 years old. A Tudor door swings in a doorway through which 20 generations have passed; and over nave and chancel are black and white roofs which have echoed to six centuries of praise.

Among the treasures of the church is a massive Norman font, carved with seven crude heads, a grim animal from mythology, a cockerel, and a burning candle. High up on the corners of the nave are two ancient stone figures, one wearing a cape with a frill round the face, the other apparently a man with a performing monkey and a tasselled stick. On a wall monument is the kneeling black-robed figure of Adah Greaves, wife of a Jacobean rector.

The oldest and most treasured monument of the church is a rarity, a figure of a cross-legged knight carved from a solid piece of oak, wearing spurs, 14th century armour and helmet, his head on a cushion, his hands in prayer, and at his feet a lion. The identity of the figure is lost, but the villagers call him Old Scriven; he is one of only about 100 medieval wooden sculptures now left. In the sanctuary is a fine chair with angels, cherubs, and canopied figures of Peter and Paul, carved by a craftsman of last century. Most striking of all the woodwork here, however, is the splendid 19th century pulpit, lavishly enriched with carving, with faces at the corners, and so lofty that the floor has been lowered to accommodate it.

BERWICK. It has a small quadrangle with a stone gateway and 16 almshouses with dormer windows, a Queen Anne house in a park and with a little classical chapel belonging to it. The chapel is 17th century and has been refashioned in the last 200 years. It is a neat and cared-for little place; and the walls have fine oak panelling up to the ceiling. One window has the portrait of a knight in armour, Reginald Phillips who died in 1915, and on the wall of the porch is a tablet to William Molton, "an honest and good man" who was born here in 1703 and died in 1803.

The Pedlar's Stone

BETTWS Y CRWYN. It may be said to look down on all Shropshire. On its windswept hilltop, over 1400 feet high, it ranks with the loftiest villages in the country.

Here for seven centuries has stood its little church, ministering to the scattered mountain farms, a belt of firs and chestnuts about it and a sentinel yew in the churchyard. Its chief beauty is its fine woodwork, its crown is its splendid 15th century roof. The beautiful oak chancel screen is the proud work of medieval craftsmen, who carved it into traceried bays and decked its spandrels with roses. The two-decker pulpit and the font cover are Jacobean. On the ends of sturdy benches are the names of local farms.

In the neighbourhood are many earthworks telling of prehistoric wars, and still in this parish, though four miles across country and farther by road, is the Cantlin Stone, engraved "W. C. Decsd. here. Buried 1691 at Betws." It is perhaps unique, for it is a memorial to a pedlar who lies in the churchyard. His strength failing on his last round, he died where the stone is set up. Not for the first time in parochial history a dispute arose as to which parish should bury a stranger and Bettws took him to its churchyard. No more was heard of the matter until 1875, when the Clun Forest Enclosure Act was passed, and then, on proof that Bettws had given burial to the poor pedlar 184 years before, the parish was granted several hundred acres more.

Near the Cantlin Stone is a carved cross, set up by Beriah Botfield, MP, a botanist and bibliographer who sat in Parliament for Ludlow.

Little Neighbour of Shrewsbury

BICTON. In the Severn valley near Shrewsbury, it has a fine modern church standing out among a few cottages and farms. The windows are bright with scenes and figures from the Bible, the best a series in the south aisle, where we see Four Evangelists, Peter, Paul, and James, and Jude with his little boat, all richly drawn and coloured in memory of a lady who saw 92 years of last century. The east window has a striking Crucifixion, and other windows show the Light of the World, Christ with the Children, and the Annunciation. There is a massive font of alabaster. To the north, at Up Rossall, the Severn makes a great loop and nearly forms an island. Centuries ago the lord of the manor lived here in a house protected not only by the river but by a moat and a rampart too. His next home was a timbered Elizabethan house which is now a farm, and after that a red brick house built in Cromwell's century.

Three Merry Heads

BILLINGSLEY. One of the lovely old villages between the Clee Hills and the Severn, it has three groups of neighbours in the farm, the church, and two poor old yews, both of which have been growing by the porch for centuries. The 14th century timbered porch, with three quaint laughing heads in its oak tracery, shelters a 13th century doorway with a Norman arch, and near it is a Norman doorway used no more, with two worn heads, a tympanum, and cushion capitals. But the most beautiful old stone is the 600-year-old Easter sepulchre, which is finely canopied and has under the recess a small arcade. The beams in the nave roof are 500 years old, there is a Jacobean pulpit and reading desk, and a few medieval tiles in the vestry. Here is one of the pathetic wooden crosses from Flanders, set up on the grave of Harold Gibbs, whose portrait hangs above it. He fell as a lieutenant at Arras in 1918, having served from the first day of the war, and being the first son of this village to fall.

The Castle of the Norman Warriors

BISHOP'S CASTLE. A quaint little town of steep streets and old houses, set among the border hills on the edge of the treeless Forest of Clun, it grew up round a castle built by warrior Norman bishops. Three relics of their might and vigilance remain.

To the west is Bishop's Moat, a high conical mound with a dry moat, which the bishops are said to have converted from a prehistoric camp into an observation post. To the east, at Lea, are walls with doorways and windows of the great square keep of their outlying fortress. At the top of the town itself are the remains of the keep of their original castle, the last of the wall, surrounding a mound which is now a bowling green.

Here still stands the little town hall built nearly 200 years ago, with a clock-turret above and the old stone lock-up below, its round windows guarded by iron grilles. Beside it is a black and white house, and not far away the 18th century market house. The pretty cream-walled rectory has a yew hedge, and two splendid trees.

In the churchyard, which has a handsome gabled lychgate and shapely old yews, is an obelisk in memory of 33 brave townsmen who sleep in some corner of a foreign field that is for ever England.

Of the original church there remains only the 13th century base of the tower, crowned in Tudor days; it may have been made new from the old materials after the Civil War, when the church, having become a fortress, was set on fire and ruined. The colour scheme of the interior is effective with cream walls and black roof timbers thrown into relief by blue ceilings. There are graceful arcades on clustered pillars, and a lofty and beautiful arch frames the chancel and the apse. Here is the ancient piscina, and a font which Norman priests may have used; it has a Jacobean cover. The modern font has 16 fine heads and is set on a base rich with ballflower. Sculptors of our own day have carved the stone pulpit with canopies and pinnacles; the oak reredos has a Last Supper in which the Disciples are shown in animated conversation.

A stone figure which was once built into a wall represents Gervase Needham, a vicar ejected in 1643 for his Royalist sympathies; it shows a man clasping a book, his head on a cushion. We noticed that two vicars of the 18th and 19th centuries were here for long periods, Isaac Frowd for 57 years and W. M. Rowland for 50.

Justice Shallow's Grandson

BITTERLEY. Crossed by a rippling stream and shadowed by the hills, it lies among rich orchards and green meadows. Away from the village, in a lonely spot in the fields, the ancient church stands by Bitterley Court, a big old house with plastered walls, a projecting wing, and gables.

In the churchyard is one of the finest treasures of its kind in this countryside, a tall and graceful 14th century cross with slender tapering shaft, complete with base and steps and its weatherworn head, on which are the Madonna and Child and the scene on Calvary.

The church comes down to us from the days when the Norman style was merging into English, and it has the massive tower the Normans loved to build. It is so low as barely to clear the nave roof, and has a turret with a shingled cap and a little spire. Among the old bells is one still ringing which was cast by the monks of Worcester in time to ring for Agincourt. Three bells here have been ringing since medieval days, but the belfry has lost some of its ancient timbers, which have been made into a screen across the tower arch. The arch itself is 700 years old, and looks into a lofty and aisleless nave separated from the chancel by a great screen which is the chief possession of the church. It is the old chancel screen made nobly new, roodloft and all, and it has a wealth of fine craftmanship, linenfold panels in the base, traceried open bays, and extraordinarily deep carving supporting the loft on the nave side. The coving is panelled and has bosses of flowers, one boss having a fine Madonna and Child. Above the vaulting are five bands of intricate carving, and above the loft another rich cornice crowns the traceried bays.

In the sanctuary guarded by this screen Timothye Lucye kneels in Elizabethan armour and puffed breeches. He was a grandson of Shakespeare's Sir Thomas Lucy (Mr Justice Shallow, in The Merry Wives of Windsor); and his monument has the pillared canopy characteristic of those days. It looks down on a stone in the floor to Sir Thomas Walcot, a stone with a story, for on it are carved three chess-rooks, part of the arms given to John Walcot when he was playing chess with Henry the Fifth. John gave Henry the checkmate with the rook, whereupon the King gave him the rook for his coat-of-arms in remembrance thereof. Here it is for all to see.

Rich in treasures is this place, for its beautiful round font, arcaded and carved with a border of foliage, was made by the Normans; a child's coffin stone with a fleur-de-lys cross lies under a 14th century recess, the altar table is Elizabethan, the carved pulpit, two chairs, and the lectern are Jacobean. The linenfold on the reading desk is from the ancient roodloft. The long and narrow chest is a splendid legacy of the 14th century.

There is a window of thankfulness for a rector's golden wedding, a window with two Roman soldiers in memory of the men who did not come back, and a wooden cross brought from the grave of Colonel Holberton, who fell in Flanders in the last year of the war.

Standing by the stream that flows through the village we came upon one pathetic relic of the historic days this place has seen, a crumbling Jacobean house. It is said that when it was new one of the Walcots of Bitterley Court was page of honour to Charles Stuart, and that he brought home with him a piece of the cloak worn by his master as the axe fell.

The Earl and the Village Maid

BOLAS MAGNA. Here time flows as peacefully as the River
Tern beneath its summer sheen of white water flowers. From
here six men "with smiles and gallantry went forth to serve," and
their memorial is in the red Georgian church, where are a few stones
in the east window 700 years old, some massive medieval seats in the
17th century chancel, two carved Jacobean almsboxes, and the rest
as it was made new 200 years ago—the pulpit with the sounding-
board over it and the squire's pew below, the box-pews for the
villagers, and the gallery for the choir.

It was in the summer of 1791 that Sarah Hoggins, the village
beauty of Bolas Magna, lost her heart to the sad-faced man who had
come as servant to her miller father. Gentleman Harry they called
him in the village, and only the vicar knew that he was the Earl of
Exeter's heir, left broken-hearted by a wife he had divorced. Sarah
Hoggins and Gentleman Harry went up to London that autumn to
be married at St Mildred's in Bread Street (where Shelley married his
second wife Mary), and for the first two years they lived a simple life
at the villa now called Burleigh Farm half a mile away.

When the ninth Earl of Exeter died, the tenth earl set out with his
village bride to the ancestral home in Lincolnshire, the magnificent
Burghley House near Stamford. Sarah was entranced. "It is yours,"
said her husband, "and you are the Marchioness of Exeter." Tenny-
son relates the story in one of the worst poems he ever wrote, turning
the husband into a landscape painter for the sake of a rhyme, and
making Sarah wilt under the shock of finding herself an aristocrat:

> . . . a trouble weighed upon her,
> And perplexed her, night and morn,
> With the burthen of an honour
> Unto which she was not born.
> Faint she grew, and ever fainter,
> And she murmured, "Oh, that he
> Were once more that landscape-painter,
> That did win my heart from me!"
> So she drooped, and drooped before him,
> Fading slowly from his side:
> Three fair children first she bore him.
> Then before her time she died.

The eldest of these three children has a grave at Bolas Magna, and Sarah herself died in 1797, not from the burden of an honour too great to be borne, but because the bringing of a fourth child into the world proved too much for her strength.

BONINGALE. It has black and white cottages making a delightful picture, a tiny church with a timber bell turret, and a 16th century farmhouse, Lea Hall. The church has a Norman window in the nave, an ancient chest in the 16th century vestry, a carved altar table and panelled pulpit that were probably here in Elizabethan days, and old roofs adorned with richly carved bosses and angels. The 14th century east window has a modern picture of Christ appearing to Mary at the tomb, a memorial to Charles Powys Isaac, who had been vicar for 54 years when he died in 1917.

BORASTON. It has massive timbers that we are not likely to forget; they are in the roof of its small church, rough-hewn rafters probably 600 years old, crossing the nave at little more than half its height. The church has been refashioned but this astonishing sight remains, and there are two Norman doorways now walled up and one 14th century window still in place. The oak screen and the pulpit are fine pieces of modern craftsmanship, and there is a screen, as well as a brass exquisitely engraved with flowers, in memory of a vicar of 45 years last century, Hubert McLaughlin.

A King in Hiding

BOSCOBEL. We may wonder if that English king who was flying for his life forgot something of the bitterness of Worcester as he rode through this pleasant countryside. It is a quiet road from Whiteladies Farm to Boscobel House, with lovely country all about us, and well it may be that in this peaceful scene a Stuart could forget the tyranny of the people and the divine right of kings, and envied the simple security of a Shropshire man. Here still is the little wood known as Spring Coppice, where the king hid on his ride, and not far away is Hobbal Grange, home of the mother of the Penderels who saved his life, and where he also called. There are many fine oaks hereabouts, and apart in a field near Boscobel House stands a stately veteran protected by an iron fence which tells us that this tree "under the blessing of Almighty God, the King of Kings, had the honour of sheltering from his foes his Majesty King Charles the

Cardington   Plaish Hall

Boscobel   Historic Boscobel House

Bromfield   **Priory Gatehouse**

Bishop's Castle   Town Hall   **Clun**   Town Hall

Second." But it is not the tree in which Charles hid, for that was cut down by souvenir hunters or perished in due course; but we may presume that this is grown from one of its acorns, and it stands as the symbol of a romantic adventure.

Boscobel House, sheltered by a noble beech which would probably be growing when Charles was here, may be seen by courtesy, and it has still a number of hiding-places, one which is pointed out as the king's being reached by a short stair leading to the cheese room; in the landing is a trapdoor which leads down to a hiding-place most cleverly contrived and lined to deaden sound.

In a field by a wood are the ruins of the 12th century church of the nunnery of Whiteladies, near which stood the house where the king sheltered on his way to Boscobel. There are Norman arches and capitals, but the roof has gone and trees grow from the walls, and where solemn chants were heard the wind now moans and rooks make dismal chorus. In this lonely sanctuary of ruin sleeps Mistress Joan Penderel, and a new stone has been set up recording that "here lyeth the bodie of a friend the King did call Dame Joane." Near it is a stone inscribed to William Penderel, "son of him who preserved the King." There are Penderels here to this day, and still every year they receive the pension awarded them by the king.

The story of those September days in 1651 is one of the most exciting chapters in the Stuart romance. Charles the Second, after Cromwell's "crowning mercy" at Worcester, fled with a beaten remnant of his army, hoping to reach London before news of his disaster arrived. As soon as he could he slipped away from the beaten rank and file, and with some forty men of distinction made his way to Boscobel, which was the property of the Giffords of Chillington, and was tenanted by William Penderel, one of six brothers devoted to the Stuart cause.

The Giffords, being Roman Catholic, had honeycombed the house with hiding-places for priests, but, no one knowing who might be in the place at the moment, it was decided first to try Whiteladies, half a mile away, where Humphrey Penderel was in charge, another brother, Richard, the chief hero of the adventure, occupying Hobbal Grange close by. At Whiteladies Charles dropped all his retinue but Lord Wilmot, divested himself of his fine clothes and jewellery, darkened his face and hands with soot, and put on a coarse shirt, darned stockings, a leather doublet with pewter buttons, a ragged green coat and breeches, a greasy old hat, and rough country boots.

News was brought by the Penderels that troops were in the neighbourhood, and, accompanied only by Richard, Charles crept out by a back way and made for Spring Coppice here, where they arrived at sunrise on the day after the battle. Richard secured Charles a blanket and some food, and at night Charles set out with him in the attempt to make his way over the Severn into Wales, with Madeley, the home of Francis Woolf, as first stopping-place. At midnight they came upon a mill at Evelith, with the miller sitting at his front door. As they refused to stay his challenge, the miller, accompanied by a number of soldiers quartered with him, gave chase, and the fugitives pounded along a dark lane deep in mud till they could run no longer, and lay there in the mire for half an hour, listening.

Reaching Madeley safely, they were housed for the rest of the night and for the next day in a barn, and then, learning that the countryside was full of soldiers and that all the ways over the Severn were guarded, they set out to return to Boscobel by the way they had come. To avoid passing the mill again they had to cross a river in the darkness, and Richard could not swim. Charles helped him over, but his feet were blistered and torn, his boots full of grit and stones, and again and again he lay down declaring he could go no farther. Penderel encouraged him, and at last they reached the wood here, to learn that the Royalist Colonel Carlos had arrived. Charles entered the house, where a woman dried his boots, gave him a change of stockings, and doctored his feet.

Three or four years earlier a great oak had been pollarded, but it had now grown a thick new crown, and into this the two men climbed, Charles with a cushion for a seat and the Colonel's knees for a pillow. During the day he slept, but awoke to catch sight of Cromwell's men hunting in the wood, and to hear them say, as they searched beneath him, what they would do to Charles Stuart when they caught him. That night he slept in a hole beneath a trapdoor in the cheese room, his way of escape to the oak being through the chimney. The next day, while he was being shaved and having his hair cropped close, Humphrey Penderel came in with the dire news that soldiers were still in the neighbourhood and that a price of £1000 was set on the fugitive's head. All the Penderel brothers and their womenfolk knew of it, but not for an instant was there a thought of betraying him, never anything less heroic than a resolve to die if need be to help and succour him. Charles remained here on the 5th and 6th of September, with the Penderels scouting far and near for tidings of hope or of danger, and on Sunday night he set out on the long pilgrimage ending in his arrival in France.

BOURTON. Its peace cross stands in a charming little garden where the road turns, and just below it is the gabled hall with an old studded door. It is now a farm, and uses its dovecot as a storehouse. A simple 19th century church stands on the hilltop, with fine yews for company and a splendid view of Brown Clee Hill. There is Jacobean craftsmanship on the pews, lectern, and reading desk, and on a big pulpit with little grotesques at the angles of its six sides. The Litany desk also has ancient carving; and a curious possession is an old font with a square piece cut away from the bowl.

Like a City of Romance

BRIDGNORTH. It stands like a city of romance on one of Nature's first-class sites. It is good to walk by the river and look over its bridge to the roofs rising in tiers above the face of the red sandstone cliff, or to look down from Castle Hill and see the Severn flowing peacefully through. It is two towns in one, up and down, high and low, and there are few English places like it. One part is by the river, the other 200 feet above, and we rise by steps from Low to High. The traveller's mind will go back to old Italian towns as he climbs up Stoneway Steps cut sheer through the rocks, or as he takes the shortest and the steepest cliff railway in England (with a gradient of two in three), or as he walks about in this jumble of old houses, through the crazy streets which must make this old town a nightmare to an architect, but an antiquarian's delight. It has a tower that leans much more than Pisa's, one of the queerest sights in the town, with a peace memorial standing by at the edge of a precipitous cliff. Nothing is quite usual in this romantic place.

Perched on the crest of the hill which dominates the town, the ruined tower leans over the path into the little park. The leaning tower of Pisa is five degrees out of the straight, the Bridgnorth tower is 17, and so startling at first sight that the stranger thinks it must fall. Yet it has stood 800 years and is perfectly safe. Rising 30 feet and as broad as it is high, this ruined keep belongs to the castle built in the first year of the 12th century by Robert de Belesme, a Norman rebel baron. It is recorded that the castle was set up in great haste, and besieged in 1102 by Henry the First in person "with the army of nearly all England," and again by Henry the Second, who had Thomas Becket with him.

The castle appears to have withstood all its enemies until the Civil War, when it was in peril of being blown up with the Royalist garrison in it, for an engineer of the Parliamentary army appearing on the scene during the siege of the castle had the terrible idea of tunnelling the rock until he reached a spot below the powder magazine. It was not until he reached it that the garrison discovered the secret of what was happening and they then wisely surrendered. It is said that Cromwell narrowly missed being killed by a musket shot aimed at him from the ramparts during the siege so dramatically ended. We may still see the tunnel made by Cromwell's engineers, and we are told that when it was explored in our time they found candles left by the tunnellers. What is certain is that they found cracks in the base of the tower into which we may thrust an arm.

Today the ivy is creeping up the ruined mass, and facing it rises the unusual-looking church, built not by an architect but by an engineer, the famous Thomas Telford. It is the church of St Mary, standing on the site of an older one which William of Wykeham knew. It has a curious tower with a dome set on columns and crowned with a small cross. There is a magnificent panorama from the church, as there is also from the edge of the cliff, where the peace memorial stands, close by. This striking monument of a soldier of the Great War stretching his hand out towards the Severn, with his pack on his back and his bayonet pointing upwards, is the work of a Shropshire man who gave London some of its noblest monuments and set up the famous Quadriga at Hyde Park Corner, where it has become familiar to millions of people. He was Captain Adrian Jones, who took up art as a career after 23 years in the army, and lived to work at his sculpture when he was 90 years old. Some seats in the park here have been given in memory of those who fell in the war, and one of them has on it a plate with the names of three brothers who did not come back.

In this unusual town we find ourselves continually climbing steps or passing under arches. The old north gate still throws itself across the road, a noble-looking structure refaced with sandstone, with three arches, three windows, and two battlemented towers; and the attractive town hall stands also in the middle of the road, with a deep arch through it. It is a delightful little structure with its upper storey timbered, a clock set in its gable, and an elegant little lantern soaring over all. The town hall is a barn which has risen in the world, having been brought here from Much Wenlock and set up on these stone arches in the time of the Commonwealth to replace the old hall burned down in the siege. In its windows are portraits of 14 English kings, and the scene of the meeting of Henry the Fourth with Prince Henry and Sir Walter Blunt before the Battle of Shrewsbury. It is this scene that comes into Shakespeare, when the king arranged for part of his army to meet him at Bridgnorth to defeat the rebels:

> *And, Harry, you shall march*
> *Through Gloucestershire; by which account,*
> *Our business valued, some twelve days hence*
> *Our general forces at Bridgnorth shall meet.*
> *Our hands are full of business; let's away,*
> *Advantage feeds him fat while men delay.*

Two ancient houses in the heart of the town have delightful timbered fronts and historic links with famous men. One is Bishop Percy's house, the oldest house in Bridgnorth, built in 1580. It is a magnificent example of Tudor timber work, with three storeys, three gables, and an extraordinary mass of timber arranged in curves and straight lines, and a porch in which we read the old inscription:

> *Except the Lord built the Owse*
> *the labourers thereof avail nothing.*

In one of the little rooms behind this wonderful façade was born the famous Thomas Percy, remembered as the bishop who found an old manuscript book in a house at Shifnal and was inspired by it to search for more manuscripts and to build up the collection of what has come to be a work of classic interest, Percy's Reliques of Ancient English Poetry. The time came when the bishop sought to prove his descent from the Percys of Northumberland, but he was in fact a grocer's son educated at Bridgnorth Grammar School and sent to Oxford in 1746. He made a big collection of Chinese poems and proverbs, and, having rescued an ancient manuscript from being thrown on the fire at the house of his friend Humphrey Pitt at Shifnal, he began the great work on which his fame is based. His Reliques created a new interest in poetry and gave him a great reputation in his day, so that he was made Dean of Carlisle and afterwards Bishop of Dromore in Ireland. He was there 29 years, during which time he added a new transept to his cathedral. His sight gave way and his last years were pathetic, for in Trafalgar year he lost his sight and the year after he lost his wife. A Percy Society was formed to keep his name alive, and his portrait was painted by Sir Joshua Reynolds.

The other historic house is the house in which lived a curate for the church of St Leonard's, one of the delightful vistas as we walk between the black and white fronts of Whitburn Street. The curate was the immortal Puritan Richard Baxter, who lived in this little timbered house by St Leonard's during his first pastorate. From here he went to Kidderminster for his great lifework, a little discontented with the people of Bridgnorth but dedicating to them the book that has gone around the world, The Saint's Everlasting Rest. He was in Bridgnorth nearly two years, which seemed to him a great thing in those troubled times, and it was here that he began to feel himself a Nonconformist. He would neither make the sign of the cross, nor wear a surplice, nor pray against the Scots. He refused to take an oath that clergy would never agree to the changing of the government of the church by archbishops, bishops, etcetera (called the Etcetera Oath). He wrote in his autobiography that the people of Bridgnorth proved a very ignorant, dead-hearted people, not responding to his preaching, and when the opportunity came for him to move to Kidderminster, where the church had a drunken vicar with a tippling curate, he made the change and "it pleased God to give him much encouragement." It was this good old man who was badgered and bullied by the brutal Judge Jeffreys, who unhappily adopted Shropshire as his home, living at Wem.

St Leonard with his chains looks down from the splendid tower, which was refashioned last century, when the church was rebuilt, into a faithful copy of its 15th century predecessor. It was necessary to refashion the church because it suffered great destruction in the Civil War, when the fighting was fierce even among the gravestones, and Colonel Billingsley, commander of the forces of the town, was slain in the churchyard. There is a group of almshouses on three sides of a little square built in his memory in 1687 and rebuilt last century, and here in the church is his coat-of-arms painted on wood, his actual sword hanging on the wall below it.

The church is one of the widest in the land, spanning 91 feet with the aisles; only a few of our cathedrals are wider. It has an ancient hammerbeam roof brought to light in the Restoration. There is much attractive craftsmanship in the screen and about the altar, and the 19th century font has a wealth of intricate carving. It shows two figures holding a Bible and a chalice to symbolise the church, a mechanic and a merchant, a sage and a soldier, a maid and an old lady, all carrying a small cross and all standing on serpents; and it has a canopied cover adorned with angels which was exhibited at the Royal Academy and is the work of Joseph Philips, whose carving we have seen in Liverpool Cathedral. He carved the figure of a trumpeting angel here, and the delicately traceried screen. The cross and the candlesticks at the altar are by Bainbridge Reynolds, whose metal work is also seen in Liverpool Cathedral. The reredos has lovely figures in stone with the Crucifixion scene in the centre, on the left being St John, Nicodemus, Joseph of Arimathea, and the Roman Centurion, and on the right the Madonna with Mary Magdalene and two women of Jerusalem. The lovely triptych of the Last Supper in the chapel is by Frank Albert Smallpeice, a Shropshire artist of the 19th century, who painted it in memory of his mother; there is a bronze inscription to him. An inscription to Richard Mortimer Thursfield tells us that he was a surgeon on HMS Glowworm, and was killed when the ship was sunk by an explosion in 1919, and one to Colonel Harold Welch tells us that he was killed in action at Amiens on the last Good Friday of the war, after winning the DSO. There is a brass to John Sewell, who played the organ here for 59 years, and an old brass inscription to Dorothy Sheppard of 1706 which tells us briefly that "she was a discreet woman." One of the windows has portraits of two kings, Alfred and Charles Stuart, and four Archbishops of Canterbury: Theodore, Dunstan, Langton, and Cranmer. There is a beautiful Children's Corner with a painting of Christ and the Children, a great chest with carved panels probably Elizabethan, some iron lids of tombs with curious inscriptions, and a lovely east window with a wealth of rich colours and 37 figures, in memory of a headmaster of the grammar school last century, Thomas Rowley. The house which he and all his predecessors knew still stands, a noble Elizabethan home with six gables and five groups of chimneys; it is now the residential part of the grammar school, the school itself having been moved outside the town. A notable scholar of the school, who was here in the 18th century, is remembered in the Stackhouse Library, a building by the church with 1400 valuable books which he left to a reading society of the town. In the library is a chair in which Bishop Heber used to sit, probably writing his famous hymns, and here also is kept a precious chalice 700 years old found in the hands of a skeleton unearthed on the site of the Grey Friars monastery which used to stand on the river bank.

There are fragments of the medieval walls still to be seen (in a yard in Pound Street and near the Baptist church). But older far than any wall in Bridgnorth, older than the ruins of the Norman castle, are the caves in the face of the rock on which the castle stood. Today they are cellars or storehouses, but once they were homes, for there have been cave-dwellers in Bridgnorth. What is called the Hermitage was a cave chapel a thousand years ago, and has a rough-hewn chancel arch and a recess used as a piscina. Here the brother of the first King of All England is said to have lived a hermit's life; he was Ethelward, brother of Athelstan. From the caves a wooded path leads to a high rock where is a point called the Tailor's Stone, because long, long ago (perhaps soon after truth was lost at the bottom of a well), a tailor vowed that he would make a coat while sitting up there, but lost his thimble as he was sewing on the last button, and stooping to find it, fell and broke his neck.

Irish Yews and Scotch Firs

BROMFIELD. Not all the traffic rushing through can ruffle its calm or spoil its beauty; and it has two scenes to remember and a story it should not forget.

One scene is from the gates of the big Georgian house in Oakly Park, and is set with a mill, a weir, and a little bridge over the Teme; the other, seen from the vicarage, is set with a medieval church, a lovely priory gatehouse, a fine three-arched bridge, a row of poplars, and a background of black and white houses. The story is of a

Bridgnorth　　　　**The Town Rising Above the River**

The Town Hall

Bishop Percy's House

The Bridge over the Severn
IN OLD BRIDGNORTH

Bridgnorth   The Castle Keep

Bridgnorth   The Old North Gate

Holdgate

Stottesdon

Berrington

THREE RARE NORMAN FONTS

young doctor who offered a priceless boon to a generation which would not listen.

The church and the gatehouse are between two rivers, the Teme and the Onny, which become one a little farther along. In their waters the monks used to fish, but all that is left of the priory is the gatehouse, with a black and white gable, an oriel window, and a pair of ancient studded doors. There is a wicket hole in the doors and many a musket hole made, probably, in the Civil War 300 years ago.

Forty Irish yews form an avenue at one end of the churchyard, and three stately Scotch firs stand between the gatehouse and the timber lychgate set up in memory of a 97-year-old lady who had an adventurous life as the wife of New Zealand's first bishop, George Augustus Selwyn, who sailed his own boat round his vast diocese (which, by an error, was made to include the Pacific Islands also!). After their far-off adventures they came to settle in Lichfield, where Dr Selwyn was bishop.

The massive west tower has a 15th century top, but is Norman below, where it forms a lofty porch with a rich doorway and a great studded door swinging on hand-wrought hinges 200 years old. Once the church had an older central tower, but this crashed down, destroying the chancel, which the monks rebuilt where the tower had stood. It is this that accounts for the two Norman arches still in the chancel, one blocked in the east wall; but something much stranger accounts for the bedroom window high up in the wall; it came about like this. When the priory and its church were handed over after the Dissolution to a man called Charles Foxe, he used the chancel as part of his new house, making a bedroom of the top half and putting in this Tudor window to light it, surely the only bedroom window in any of our churches. After about a century fire destroyed the house, whose roofless walls still stand beside the church, and perhaps the owners looked on the fire as an act of God, for they promptly gave back the chancel to its proper use and at the same time gave it a most extraordinary ceiling.

This painted plaster ceiling is the most striking possession of the church, and has been called "the best example of the worst style of ecclesiastical art." It is typical of its period, and its clouds and angels, its maze of ribbon texts, and the two angels holding an open Bible on the wall, seem as fresh as when they were painted in 1672.

The spacious church has a wide and lofty nave divided from the north aisle by a 13th century arcade with one deeply patterned capital. Both nave and aisle have steep oak roofs, and we do not wonder that their maker was proud to put his name on one of the beams: "1577, made by me, John Gethe." Old linenfold panels the chancel, and on the other walls and in the vestry are panels from the old pews and the reading desk. The Jacobean pulpit has the Annunciation, the Nativity, the Crucifixion, and the Ascension carved in its deeply recessed panels, and the old oak reredos in the aisle (where is also a Norman shaft piscina) has similar carving of the Evangelists and their winged creatures. The other reredos is a striking modern oak triptych with a copy of an Italian Crucifixion scene painted between saints and angels singing the Te Deum. The brass lectern is a copy of the famous one in Southwell Minster, and the new oak chancel screen with grotesque animals creeping along its cornice is worthy of the medieval craftsmen who made the quaint stone heads in the aisle. Lions and birds appear on some medieval tiles below a canopied 14th century recess in the chancel. Glowing in gold in the old glass of a vestry window are 13 Bible scenes, and others appear in good modern glass, one nave window picturing Paul asleep dreaming of the man of Macedonia.

At the 13th century font there was baptised in 1800 a child who would have helped to take away much of the world's pain had the world only listened to him, for he was the first man to discover the use of anaesthetics. He was born at a farmhouse still standing in the hamlet of Lady Hilton, and was only 30 when he was carried to the simple family grave outside the porch. For years all that he would have done for mankind was forgotten, but on the 100th anniversary of his death a great company of people came to pay homage to Henry Hickman and to unveil a tablet to him in the church which saw his promise and his fulfilment.

A stone in the church bids us "honour a physician with the honour due unto him," the physician in this case being Henry Hickman, the forgotten immortal.

The Forgotten Immortal

HE was born in 1800, the very year when Sir Humphry Davy suggested that nitrous oxide gas might be found useful in deadening the pain of surgical operations. No doctor seemed interested in Davy's hint; no scientist experimented with the idea; the operating-room remained as full of horror and pain as a torture chamber. Surgery could make little advance.

But the baby born at the time of Davy's inspired guessing was to grow up to carry out the experiments the great scientist had called for 20 years before. He started young, almost as if he had known that there were so few years ahead of him. Before he was 21 he was a member of the Royal College of Surgeons. He moved his practice from Ludlow to Shifnal and then to Tenbury, supporting a wife and four children. He gave up every Tuesday from 10 to 4 to advising poor people free, and all his spare time was a search for something that would deaden the pain of the surgeon's knife. Sensitive to pain as he was, he himself experimented on animals, for it was the only way; but when enumerating his experiments to a scientific body he gave only those that were absolutely necessary to prove his claim, for, said he, "the recital of such experiments must be as little agreeable to you as the repetition of them has been to myself."

He seems to have thought out everything for himself, perhaps he had never heard of Davy's suggestion; and though he overlooked the possibilities of nitrous oxide gas he tried others and found the best to be carbon dioxide, which brought about suspended animation and rendered painless and almost bloodless surgery possible. He was only 24 when he thus carried forward the principle of anaesthetics into the realm of the practical.

Overjoyed by his triumphant discovery, he offered his great boon freely to the world. He wanted no reward for himself; his only aim was to make known the principle that others might perfect the method and carry it out. Here was the balm that would bring oblivion to pain and allow the surgeon to cure without torture. *Here it is!* he wrote to the Royal Society. *Here it is!* he cried to the French Academy of Medicine. But nobody would listen. No one knew this country doctor, and he sounded a bit like a madman. His accounts of all-important experiments were hidden away in dusty files. He could get no reply at all from the Royal Society. He went to Paris, then the centre of medical culture, and appealed to King Charles the Tenth to be allowed to demonstrate his discovery; but, though a commission was appointed to report, there is no evidence that the commission met. The young country doctor returned to England ill with disappointment, not so much for himself but because he knew he had a boon for all and none would accept it.

By the time he was 30 he had beaten himself to death against the wall of scientific indifference and incredulity, and the world he would have relieved of pain knew nothing of him. He was laid to rest in Bromfield churchyard and forgotten. Once, in 1847, when four Americans began using ether and laughing gas, a member of the French Academy of Medicine said their claim reminded him of a similar claim made years before by an English doctor called Hickman, and that same year James Young Simpson chloroformed himself in Edinburgh and achieved immortality. Now, instead of one youthful Shropshire voice, there was such a clamour of voices shouting the same truth that they were bound to be heard. Then it was that Thomas Dudley, a disinterested doctor who liked to see justice done, put on record in The Lancet and The Medical Times that Hickman had offered the world anaesthetics 20 years earlier; but even now other names were to the fore and Hickman's was once more forgotten.

Not till 1913, when Henry Wellcome was forming his Historical Medical Museum for London, was Hickman's part as a discoverer made known again. At last he was acclaimed, and on the centenary of his death in 1930 the Shropshire doctor was celebrated in such a way that never again will he be forgotten. Not that he would have cared for himself, for he wrote of his work that if one grain of knowledge can be added to the general fund to obtain a means for the relief of pain, the labours of the author would be amply rewarded. Certainly he will be forgotten no more.

Birthplace of the Iron Ship

BROSELEY. It has put its name on the industrial map, but who would guess how important it has been in the great development of the modern world? We may think the brightest place in it today is the little garden in memory of the men who went out to France and did not come home again; there is another memorial to them in the church with their names inscribed in oak, and a brass lamp to the memory of Wynward Warner, the rector who won the Military Cross. The church is modern, with a grand battlemented and pinnacled tower and with many carved heads about it.

It has a lofty clerestoried nave, a panelled oak roof with carved bosses, a high chancel arch, and a rich west window. The handsome stalls and the oak eagle of the lectern are modern, but in the chancel is a finely carved Jacobean chair with two figures of bearded men.

In the street are several 18th century houses and an inn with a wrought iron sign which reminds us of Broseley's place in industry; perhaps we are reminded of it still more by the elaborate iron tombs rusting away in the churchyard. It was here in 1787 that John Wilkinson, Father of the South Staffordshire iron trade, made the first iron ship. He had had a forge at Broseley for many years, and it is said that the first engine built by James Watt in the Soho works was built to blow the bellows at the Broseley works. John Wilkinson had the idea of building iron barges, and he built one with everybody laughing about him, but on one summer's day in 1787 the first iron barge was launched on the Severn, which already had the first iron bridge (between Broseley and Madeley). The idea of the iron ship was born, and Broseley was its birthplace.

The Deserted Church

BROUGHTON-WITH-YORTON. They are two scattered villages that have come together, linked by two shrines with the history of 700 years between them. One is a shapeless and overgrown mass of ruins, a church 800 years ago, abandoned owing to its low position by the source of a stream; the other is an ivied stone church with a timbered turret standing solitary in a bower of trees. It is not yet quite a centenarian, but in it are two relics from the ancient church, one a font shaped like a round tub, probably by Norman masons, the other a pyx of hammered silver made in the time of Henry the Seventh and now used as a chalice. It has a cover fashioned by an Elizabethan craftsman, who put round it a ring like a serpent.

Captive Before Caesar

BUCKNELL. It is possible, historians believe, that here was fought a momentous battle pictured in the undying pages of Tacitus, the last fight of Caractacus to stem the Roman invasion.

For three days the stubborn battle lasted; then Caractacus was driven out of his position to make his stand on Coxall Knoll, where we may still see the remains of a British camp. The second position being won by the Romans, and the wife and daughter of the heroic

British king captured, Caractacus fled and was betrayed and sent to Rome, where his simple eloquence, and his plea that Claudius should cover himself with honour by setting him free, won him his liberty. Everybody knows Bernard Barton's poem:

> Before proud Rome's imperial throne,
> In mind's unconquered mood,
> As if the triumph were his own,
> The dauntless captive stood.
> None, to have seen his free-born air,
> Had fancied him a captive there.
>
> *Think not, thou eagle lord of Rome*
> *And master of the world,*
> *Though victory's banner o'er thy dome*
> *In triumph be unfurled,*
> *I would address thee as thy slave,*
> *But as the bold should greet the brave.*
>
> *Now I have spoken; do thy will;*
> *Be life or death my lot,*
> *Since Britain's throne no more I fill,*
> *To me it matters not.*
> *My fame is clear; but on my fate*
> *Thy glory or thy shame must wait.*
>
> He ceased! from all around unsprung
> A murmur of applause;
> For well had truth and freedom's tongue
> Maintained their holy cause.
> The Conqueror was the Captive then:
> He bade the slave be free again.

The truth as to this battlefield can never be ascertained, for although Tacitus describes the scene he does not know its name, but Bucknell has the support of instructed opinion as well as local tradition, and as we wander here we picture the heroic chieftain delivering the impassioned speech preserved for us by the Roman historian, reminding his countrymen how his ancestors had turned back Caesar, and fiercely impressing on them the indignity of tribute and slavery.

The churchyard has two great yews, one perhaps 500 years old, with a trunk 19 feet round. The church built by the Normans was made new when the yew was a sapling, but has kept its splendid Norman font. There is ancient masonry in the walls and in the chancel is the doorway used by the priest 600 years ago, and an arched recess which may have been an Easter sepulchre.

The Ruined Abbey by the Severn

BUILDWAS. Some of us may think there is nothing like Fountains Abbey in Yorkshire, or like Tintern in Monmouthshire, and yet we are held spellbound at Buildwas in the Severn hills. This ruined abbey standing in the meadows by the river is one of those majestic spectacles that make this country unmatched for its long unbroken thread of history. For 800 years these arches have stood where the crusader Bishop of Chester set them. He was Roger de Clinton, builder of one of the noblest Cistercian monasteries in England, with a nave and chancel and a massive central tower, crypt and chapter house and cloisters, which were one of the chief sights in England for 400 years, and for 400 years more have been among our ruins.

It is not many years since these splendid pillars and some of these great walls were hid for nearly half their height by the accumulated growth of centuries, but the Office of Works, the custodian of our national monuments, has rescued this glory from a rubbish heap, and something of its old magnificence remains. Everywhere the ground has been levelled and clothed with turf. The pillars and the walls have been cleared and cleaned, sculptured stones have been brought to light with fragments of tiled floors. The stone seats for the priests remain, and the piscina, the chapter house with its finely vaulted roof, the head of a crusader, stones richly wrought with floral patterns, and fragments of stone coffins, on one of which we see a cross with floral branches and a queer human face.

The great tower rises above the central Norman arches, broken in two but still rising so high above the clerestory windows that one of its own high windows is complete; the highest point of the tower is only about a dozen feet less than when the abbey was in all its glory. Running westward from it is the great nave, in which without a roof, stand 14 of the grandest Norman arches in England the small clerestory windows still above them. The great pillars are 14 feet round, each set on a stone base, and each with its scalloped capitals complete. Here still are the east and west windows, the east wall with its three narrow lights 18 feet high, and the west end with two. We can walk into the crypt, can trace the cloisters where the monks once walked, and can see the guest house walls. The 13th century abbot's house, between the ruins and the river, is now a private house with its old hall and a floor of old tiles; it escaped the destroying hand of Thomas Cromwell and his royal master and is lived in now as it was lived in 700 years ago.

There are the foundations of a chapel near the nave, the burial-place of the ancient Burnell family, and here are memorial stones with their names engraved on them. Buildwas also has a graceful modern bridge, which stands where the old bridge stood in the days of the monks, and by the bridge is an ancient timbered house with a fine old studded door. There is a small 18th century church built with the stones from the ruins, and in it an old carved pulpit. In the grandly wooded grounds of Buildwas Park is a fine modern house in Elizabethan style. But in Buildwas is nothing so impressive as the abbey that has fallen from its high estate, unless it be the everlasting hills that keep it company with the everlasting river flowing past.

The Rare Triptych

BURFORD. It should be seen by all who come to Shropshire, most of all for the many rich possessions of its church, but also for its trees and orchards, its great house in lovely grounds, and its charming setting in a fruitful valley looking across the Teme to Worcestershire. It owes much to the Rushout family from the great house, who cared lovingly for the church and founded the alms-houses in the village. A fine oak lychgate brings us to the church-yard, where a beautiful medieval cross stands, restored in memory of three of the Rushouts, its canopied head having sculptures of the Crucifixion and the Madonna.

The church is a delightful blend of old and new, its story running from Norman days to a fine restoration last century by Georgiana Rushout, whose memorials are the handsome lectern and a window shining in gold with a Jesse Tree. Battlements adorn the exterior, and the tower is splendidly enriched at the top with windows and panels and many little carvings. The lower part is 14th century, except for the west window and the finely decorated doorway.

The Norman walls of nave and chancel were partly refashioned 600 years ago, when the north and south doorways were made. The

Buildwas   The Ruined Abbey

Buildwas   The Severn Near the Abbey

In the Valley of the Onny

Cardingmill Valley, near Church Stretton

priest's doorway is 12th century, and has a door perhaps 700 years old, with a crescent hinge and a closing ring.

Many modern windows fill the interior with a subdued light, and a beautiful rose window keeps company in the chapel with three of the 14th century. But the glory of the church is the chancel, a wonderful place crowded with treasures from floor to roof, including fine memorials in brass and wood and stone. There are remains of a very ancient doorway, a perfect aumbry, a charming piscina, and medieval sedilia with modern canopies. The altar is beautiful with Wise Men and angels, and the reredos is a very fine mahogany triptych with the Annunciation, the Resurrection, and the Adoration, all under canopies and gleaming with gold. Both are in memory of a rector for 40 years last century.

Fine, too, is the chancel screen with its traceried bays and vaulted top, a tribute to a later rector for 44 years, whom we remember again as we look at the east window showing Our Lord in a glowing company of angels. The canopied pulpit is in the rich style of the screen, with figures of saints and bishops; and a delicate side screen brought from Louvain has angels on its arches and crowned heads on its pillars.

The monuments are a rare collection, mostly to the Cornwalls who were lords of Burford for about four centuries, tracing royal descent through one of the sons of King John. The oldest is a fine brass of Dame Elizabeth who died in 1354, a lifesize portrait showing her very severe face and graceful mantle. Under a 14th century arch lies a slim and dainty 15th century figure with a crown, a dog at her feet and two angels at her pillow. She is John of Gaunt's daughter, Princess Elizabeth, whose first husband, the Duke of Exeter, was executed for treason in 1400, and whose second was the most famous of all the Cornwalls, Sir John, created Lord Fanhope for his service to the king at Agincourt. Born at sea, he spent his early years at Burford, and was celebrated as the champion tilter of England. Here he chose that his lady should lie, though she was buried first at Whitefriars in London. We see them both in a nave window set up to one who was 45 years rector, Sir John wearing his armour, and Elizabeth in robes of red and gold.

In the south wall is one of the heart-shrines sometimes found in our churches, that of Sir Edmund Cornwall who died abroad in

E   49

1436 and asked that his heart should be brought home for burial. It is said to have lain until last century in one of the two cavities under this arched recess. Still another rarity is the very fine Tudor monument to Edmund Cornwall, rare because the table tomb and its figure are both of them fashioned in wood. He is believed to have been killed in a tourney when he was only 20, and he lies here in his armour, proud and tall, one of the best wooden figures we have seen. There are only about a hundred of these medieval wooden sculptures in England.

But the tale of the Cornwall monuments is not yet told, for most remarkable of all is a great Elizabethan triptych in the sanctuary, said by one writer to be the finest ancient triptych in the country. Painted and signed by the Italian artist Melchior Salaboss, it has two panelled doors painted outside with the Twelve Apostles and inside with coats-of-arms. They open to show lifesize portraits of three of the family, Richard and Jenet in long gowns and ruffs, and their son Edmund resplendent in coloured armour, his plumed helmet at his feet. Edmund is said to have stood 7 feet 3 inches. Two doors at the foot of the triptych open to show him lying full length, ghostly and shrouded, and an inscription tells of the sweet harmony of his nature, the great strength of his body, and of his dainty touch upon the lute. At the top of the monument is a pediment with the scene of Doom.

Wall monuments show two Thomas Cornwalls of the 17th century kneeling in armour with their wives; a rare memorial on the floor has a portrait engraved on a lead sheet of Elizabeth Devroke in Tudor costume, with six children; and looking down on all this fine array of riches from the past are 12 angels in one of the most beautiful modern roofs we have seen in a village church. Richly panelled it is, and lovely enough for Sir Aston Webb's original drawing of it to have been shown at the Royal Academy.

There is a fine wagon roof over the nave, a 15th century tower arch over a 14th century font, a pair of old stone crosses in the floor, and a small marble plaque with sculptured figures of Mary and the children Jesus and John, said to have been made in Italy about 300 years ago. Below it stands a huge old chest, its three divisions corresponding to the three parts of Burford's big parish.

No one should leave this treasure-house without taking a peep at the cornice outside the chapel, which has a very odd little collection of carvings. Two of the best are a woman with a besom and a little man with a hammer. Others show the sacred pelican, and a savage dog on a man's head; and the quaintest of gargoyles has the grinning face of a long-nosed man, with the body of a winged animal, wearing a tiny clown's hat and crouching over a little monk who seems to be greatly enjoying the fun.

Looking on Fifteen Counties

BURWARTON. It is an ancient and stately village looking out on the richly wooded slopes of Brown Clee Hill and a magnificent panorama of meadowlands. From here we can climb to Abdon Burf, 1792 feet high, and may look out from there, if the day is clear, on 15 counties. Here the Romans must have climbed, for this was one of their fortified settlements, and long before then there were ancient camps on Clee Burf and Abdon Burf.

The old church and the new stand separated by a tiny brook. The old church is a roofless ruin with ivied walls and a little Norman chancel arch still with its carved capitals. It has given its Norman font (with crude patterns on the bowl) to the new church built by Viscount Boyne in 1876. It is a handsome place designed by Anthony Salvin, the architect whose work we find at Windsor Castle and the Tower of London. One of the windows, in memory of the 8th Viscount Boyne of Burwarton Hall (the modern house set among noble trees), glows with bright flowers, a group of people in Oriental costume, and the vision of Christ in Glory. A window in memory of his wife has a lovely figure of Charity with a golden-haired child in her arms, and there is an alabaster tablet with five exquisite cherubs in memory of one of his grandchildren, Michael Russell, six years old. There is a striking iron chancel screen with panels of elegant scroll work, a peace memorial brass with a finely carved border of oak leaves, and an ancient chest.

CALVERHALL. A pleasant village near Whitchurch, it has a modern church joined to a group of 18th century almshouses. The church has fine panelling round the walls, and a beautiful Morris window of Simeon chanting Nunc Dimittis as he holds the Child Jesus in his arms. An attractive peace memorial to 63 men who died has five figures in canopied niches, a soldier, a sailor, and an airman, with a yeoman and St George.

The Old Ladies of Llangollen

CARDESTON. There are two pictures on the walls of its little red church, a great one of much beauty and a small one with a charming story.

Much of the church is 18th century, and pleasantly surprising it is when we step through the porch in the tiny tower. Its old possessions are a medieval font, two carved chairs and an altar table by Jacobean craftsmen, a little balustered gallery of 1678, and some old beams and kingposts in the roof. Its new ones include a fine window of a purple-winged angel, and other windows of the Crucifixion and the Women at the Tomb.

The great picture is an excellent modern wall-painting of the scene in which John the Baptist proclaims the coming of his Master. Measuring about 12 feet by 9, and done in delightfully soft colours, it shows John with several groups of people by the arid banks of Jordan, and Christ coming towards them as a beautiful figure in white. Among the figures is a child holding a posy by her mother's side.

But more than anything else it is the small picture that attracts us, for it is an engraving of the celebrated miniature by Lady Leighton of the Ladies of Llangollen. We see them sitting at the library table in their cottage, the scene of their retirement for half a century. They were two cultured ladies from old Irish families, Lady Eleanor Butler and Miss Sarah Ponsonby, and at Plas Newydd in the Vale of Llangollen they set up house together, far from the world and society, clinging to each other in romantic friendship.

Scores of famous people and thousands of tourists came to see them, and many stories are told of their odd ways. In all their 50 years together they would never sleep away from home for a single night, and only once did they break their rule of not allowing a man to sleep in the house. Their friends and callers were freely discussed between them, and after a visit Lady Eleanor's invariable question to Miss Ponsonby would be, "Sally, do we like them?" and Sally's opinion decided the matter.

It was only by subterfuge that Lady Leighton was able to paint their portraits, having to hide behind the table while someone engaged Miss Ponsonby in conversation. The engraving was not published until after their death, and the sale of it realised large sums of money. Lady Leighton gave much away to charity, and £500 she gave towards the cost of this quaint church tower, which was built in 1844 several years after the famous Old Ladies were laid to rest.

About three miles from Cardeston stands Wattlesborough Castle, a fortified house which has kept among its farm buildings a square Norman tower with old fireplaces and a stone stairway.

The Judge and His Sons

CARDINGTON. Its old stone houses cluster round the long-roofed church with its massive tower. The tower has been as we see it 600 years, but we come into the church through a great Norman doorway with a door that has been opening and shutting since Cromwell's time. There are other witnesses to the handiwork of the Normans, a crude blocked doorway in the north wall with a huge tympanum, traces of another in the south wall, and a small window on each side.

The 700-year-old chancel has no arch, but it has its original priest's doorway and the aumbry which all its priests have used. Some of the pews have been made new from the old ones, and have the names of farms on them. There is much old timber in the black and white roof, and the Jacobean pulpit has at the top of each of its five panels a merman holding his tail.

On one of the elaborate monuments the 17th century left for us, under a painted and gilded canopy, lies William Leighton, Chief Justice of Wales in Elizabethan days. He lies stiffly on his side, his head on his hand, wearing a black-buttoned coat with his red gown, ruffs at his neck and wrists, and a black tam o'shanter kind of hat. Kneeling on a panel below are his wife and three daughters in black, all with ruffs, and with them is a baby propped up in its red christening robe and white bonnet, its head resting on a skull. On another panel kneel the judge's three sons, one in armour and two in black capes.

It was Judge Leighton who built the fine Tudor house (Plaish Hall) which we found for sale. Here was still the old fireback he put into it, the open timber roof and the minstrels gallery, and the rings by the fireplaces for the servant to hold on to when putting the great logs on the fire. It was from this house that there went out in 1914 one of our young heroes who is remembered in the east window of the church. He was Captain S. H. Christy, and he had won the DSO before he perished in the bitterest adventure the British army has had to face for a generation, the retreat from Mons.

A fine ride from the village over the hilltop, rising till we are 1100 feet above the sea, brings us after two miles to Chatwall Hall. The lonely gabled house of stone and timber is 17th century, with some parts older still, and is still the home of the Corfields, who have been hereabouts for over 500 years.

Corfield of Somaliland

RICHARD CORFIELD, a member of this Shropshire house who fell on a battlefield for his country just before the Great War, was a Marlborough schoolboy who went out to Somaliland when he was 23, and used his influence as a political officer there for making peace and building up goodwill among the natives.

He was one of only about six white men in the interior of this great country, which 20 years before had become a British protectorate. From Somaliland he went to Nigeria, but in a few years more there was trouble among the Somalis, for the religious fanatic known as the Mullah had stirred up his followers. Richard Corfield was summoned back to Somaliland to command a Camel Corps of 150 natives and three English officers. In eight months the Corps established peace and order among the protected tribes. Old feuds were settled and new ones nipped in the bud, caravans set out again, and traders returned to Berbera for the first time in three years. Suddenly one night Corfield was awakened by the news that the Mullah's Dervishes were raiding again, and he set out and reached a place from which their fires could be seen. Soon after four in the morning he marched off with his Camel Corps. The Dervishes could be traced by a long cloud of dust rising from the herds of looted cattle, and the little force set out in pursuit where the bush was thick.

Corfield had left his camels and ponies in hiding, and his men were spread in a long line with a maxim gun in the middle. Suddenly the Dervishes appeared, opening fire without warning, and half the excited natives ran away while the other half confronted the enemy in disorder. In that critical moment Corfield fell shot through the head, the maxim gun was put out of action, and only a miracle saved a great disaster. The miracle was apparently the giving-out of the enemy's ammunition, for they withdrew after being repelled in five or six attacks. Corfield was censured for his defenceless heroism, but the defeat so shattered the Mullah's prestige that he never returned, and the attention drawn to Somaliland in England brought about a strengthening of the garrisons to protect the country. Still among the Somalis the name of this Shropshire man is like the name of one of their brave chieftains; his memory is beloved by them all.

Cromwell and Caesar

CAYNHAM. It straggles with wayside orchards above a brook and looks out to the scarred tops of the Clee Hills. It has at one end a great house in a park and at the other a church made new last century. The church has 13th century work in its low massive tower crowned with a pyramid roof peeping above the nave, and there is a Norman doorway and two Norman windows. Its chancel has two rare treasures, the modern stone roof resting on the original 13th century corbels, and a striking triple chancel arch looking like three open lancets, a tall one and two dwarfs. The 13th century font has been refashioned, its octagonal bowl resting on eight shafts round a tapering column.

Crowning the hill is the ancient British camp which may have been used by Caesar and Cromwell; it has a fosse and a rampart 20 feet high, supposed to have been occupied by the Romans, and also to have served Cromwell as a base in the siege of Ludlow Castle.

Medieval Masterpiece

CHELMARSH. It is an unspoiled village by the Severn, with old timbered cottages and a 14th century church which has been described as one of the finest pieces of medieval architecture in Shropshire. There are documents giving 1345 as the date when it was largely rebuilt. The nave has a saddleback roof of that time, but the doorways come from an earlier church, and there is still Norman masonry in the west wall. The aisle has also a blocked Norman doorway, and the bowl of the font is Norman. The windows are 14th century, the piscina is set on a 14th century pillar, the communion table is Jacobean, and the pulpit has Jacobean panels. The tower is 18th century, and the modern porch has three old fragments built into it: part of an old cross, a Crucifixion carving, and a piece of a 13th century coffin lid. Some of the modern woodwork has been carved by village craftsmen. The chancel screen has fragments of the old screen worked into it, and delicate tracery painted green and gold. The choir stalls and the chancel panelling are beautiful with intricate carving of flowers and patterns.

Shading the churchyard are two splendid copper beeches.

Post-haste to be Gone

CHESWARDINE. A hill village with long views over two counties, it has a refashioned church with a 500-year-old tower. On one of the buttresses is carved a lion, and outside the tower is a worn tablet to little Francis Butler who lived for two years in the 18th century, telling us in the formal language of its time that this short-lived flower and portion of innocence post-hasted to be gone.

The north chapel, rebuilt with stones of 700 years ago, has a 15th century roof with carved bosses and contains two medieval gravestones, one with a plain cross and the name of Ralph Tilston, the other with a very elaborate cross, two fishes, and a lamb. In a corner hangs the sanctus bell, used for 150 years to call the children to school. There is a medieval chest, an attractive pulpit, and a huge painting of the Stuart arms, enriched on either side with a picture of a child, one with a red rose and the other with a thistle. The altar has a richly coloured triptych of the Nativity, the Flight into Egypt, and Jesus in the Temple; and a good window of Simeon and Jesus is in memory of a vicar who died in Berkswell church, Warwickshire, while the choir was singing, in one of the darkest years of the war, the Nunc Dimittis, Now lettest thou thy servant depart in peace.

Lady Godiva's Church

CHETTON. It is said that Lady Godiva, whose husband was lord of the manor, founded a church here, but the oldest parts of the church we see are 13th century. It has a charming south doorway of that time, and across the 13th century chancel arch two great stone faces of a man and a woman stare at each other, faces shaped like an egg and as expressionless, the woman with a fan-like mass of hair and wearing a Tudor headdress. There are four more ancient heads in the chancel, one of a man with a bandage over his mouth. There is an aumbry, a shallow piscina, and a plain font, all from medieval days.

The village with black and white farms and cottages, a 400-year-old inn by the churchyard, and fine yews, is on a spur of Brown Clee Hill, from which we have wide views.

Here Slept a King

CHETWYND. It is called Chetwynd Rural, and with much truth, for we see it against a background of woods on the road north of Newport. The trees belong to the big park of the Elizabethan great house, where they still point with pride to the room in which Charles Stuart slept. In the park is a lake covering 23 acres.

A lovely tower and spire watch over the 19th century church, which has a handsome screen traceried in medieval style, a fine lectern with angels and an archangel at its base, big marble columns dividing the nave from the chancel, and a peace memorial window with a kneeling figure in khaki. The pulpit is in memory of a lieutenant.

The road northward passes through the wild-looking plantation called Chetwynd Heath and comes to Sambrook, a hamlet with part of its medieval preaching cross, known as the Butter Cross.

CHILD'S ERCALL. It stands high, with a fine avenue leading to the Hall and a pinnacled tower of which it has been proud for 500 years. A quaint elephant swings in the wind aloft. Other parts of the church are older than the tower. There is a chancel doorway of the 12th century, an arcade of the 13th, and an aisle of the 14th with a canopied piscina. The font is 600 years old, curiously shaped with sloping sides. Two windows are in memory of John Noble who preached here 20 years; one shows the Ascension and the other, given by village children, shows Christ with the little ones. On the battered churchyard cross is a sundial.

The Gay Adventures of a Poet

CHIRBURY. It stands at a meeting of valleys, looking away to the high crest of the Berwyn Mountains of Wales. An inn covered with creeper, a group of black and white cottages, and a church with its 600-year-old tower, make a pretty corner of the village. The church itself comes from the 13th century, and its nave arcades seem to be tumbling over, so greatly do they lean outwards. The black and white roofs of the nave and aisles are apparently 16th century; the chancel was rebuilt in the 18th. The shallow bowl of the font is 600 years old, the brass lectern with the lions is a copy of the old one, the square of tiles in the chapel with men and griffins on them is ancient. There is a fine blue window with Gabriel bringing the good news to Mary, both clad in rich raiment, a Bethlehem scene in red, blue, and gold, with the ox and the ass and adoring angels, and a window with saints in memory of John Burd, who was vicar here for 49 years and died during the war. At the old font was baptised in 1658 a man remembered on a tablet by the chancel arch, Thomas Bray. In 1695 he was invited to take charge of church affairs in Maryland, where the descendants of the Pilgrims were settled, and he was asked to supply the colonists with clergy. As only men too poor to buy books would go, he set himself to supply their needs, providing libraries for them. Out of this grew the Society for Promoting Christian Knowledge, the SPCK, and Thomas Bray was its founder.

There lies in the church Richard Lloyd who built the fine black and white Elizabethan house we see on the road to Church Stoke. It is Marrington Hall, about a mile away, and it has a remarkable sundial on its lawn. It is dated 1595 and is a square stone pillar with seven dials decorated with heraldry, mottoes, and the figure of a man; and the inscription running round says:

> From dai to dai these shades do flee,
> And so this life passeth awaie.

At the vicarage is a fine library of chained books left to the village in the 17th century and now kept in two cases, one with 115 books of which 83 have chains, the other with 89 books of which 81 have chains. Chaining books was unusual in a private library. It is believed that the books came from the library of Lord Herbert of Cherbury, a Shropshire man who took his title from this village with a slight variation of the spelling. He was born in the hamlet of Eyton near Wroxeter, the elder brother of George Herbert, and married as a boy of 15 while still at Oxford. He had a remarkable career for a poet, full of adventures in France and in the Netherlands, in Spain and in Italy. He was involved in a duel arising out of a drunken quarrel, and was thrashed by the husband of a lady with whom he had flirted. Yet he had great esteem wherever he went, for he was a man of wide learning, great wit, and undoubted valour, and in 1619 he was sent out as our ambassador to France. It was he who suggested the marriage of Charles Stuart to Henrietta Maria, and he carried out the negotiations for it. He came home heavily in debt, and was rewarded with an Irish peerage. Half-hearted in Royalist support at the outbreak of the war, he surrendered Montgomery Castle to the Parliamentary Army, and received a pension from the Commonwealth. His fame rests on his writings, chiefly on his autobiography and his poems. The poems, though often rough and obscure, have sometimes a lyrical sweetness; the autobiography is a dashing tale of valour and gay life, and his prose works include remarkable speculations on knowledge and religion. He was a friend of all the leading scholars in Europe, and at home was on friendly terms with Ben Jonson and his circle, so that he may possibly have known Shakespeare.

Old Yew

CHURCH PREEN. We seek it in the narrow lanes and find it almost lost in the hillside. The church is tucked into the hill, screened by towering trees and with ferns creeping up its walls. One of the trees which shade it is among the noblest yews in England, about 50 feet high and 200 feet round the branches. It is flourishing, green and shapely, with great iron bands round its hollow trunk, which measures 33 feet round the base and 23 feet at four feet up; it must have been growing before the days of Joan of Arc.

Extraordinarily long and narrow is the aisleless church, 70 feet from end to end and only 13 wide. It was made new last century, but has kept some of its 700-year-old windows, and has blocked up the doorway through which the monks of Wenlock Abbey used to pass. Still here also are the old piscina and the deep square bowl of the 13th century font. The pulpit and reading desk are Jacobean. A touch of colour on a drab wall is a mosaic of Christ with the woman of Samaria. Still hanging in the modern bellcot is a bell which rang out in this countryside before the Reformation; and almost touching the church is the house on the site of the old priory; it is charming, like a little castle with a lookout turret rising above the battlements.

A Noble View

CHURCH PULVERBATCH. It looks out on lovely scenes, and has a surprising sight not to be missed, a hedge of clipped yews, shaped as a deep arcade of ten arches running round three sides of a square, the fourth side being a mellow farmhouse from 18th century England. A quaint tower has been looking down on these village roofs for 150 years, made of dark and light stone, with a large ball at each corner of the parapet. The church has few attractions; but it has a Jacobean chair, and woodwork of the 18th century, including an altar table with dainty fluted legs. A rector for 42 years is remembered in the sanctuary.

The twin hamlet of Castle Pulverbatch is half a mile away, with one of the best of all Shropshire views from a mound marking the site of a Norman castle. To the south we can ride for several miles, sometimes at 1000 feet above the sea, looking out on the glories of these Welsh and English hills.

Ancient Strongholds

CHURCH STRETTON. This happy place draws people to it like a seaside town, for health is in its air and a thousand delights in the little streams and green hollows of its sheltering hills.

More and more houses dot the wide valley and start to climb the slopes. To the west the great moorland ridge of the Longmynd rises nearly 1700 feet, with the lovely Cardingmill Valley scooped out of it and the prehistoric Portway running along the top. To the east are the rugged Caradoc Hills with Watling Street at the foot, and the banks and trenches of Caer Caradoc's old stronghold 1500 feet up. Some think Caractacus used this fortification, and the cave below bears his name. Other ancient camps and tumuli hump the hilltops; but since history has been written the story of Church Stretton has been fairly uneventful, and all the happier for that. We read of the life on its hills in Mary Webb's books, for this is her country. She spent her honeymoon in this town, the Shepwardine of her stories.

There are few old houses, but the cross-shaped church with crazy stone walls goes back 800 years, its oldest inhabitant being a worn little man with arms akimbo over the old north door, here, perhaps, before the Normans who made the doorway, and the other to the south. At the end of the 12th century a tower was added to the

Norman nave in place of their chancel, and the chancel and transepts were built. There are angels and grotesques round the tower, to which the 15th century gave a new top; two struggling figures make a gargoyle at one corner, a little man clings for dear life to a water spout, and St Lawrence holds his gridiron in a corner niche. It is the four inside arches to this tower which strike us first on entering, whole groups of 13th century folk appearing on the delightful capitals.

Shropshire has no older roofs than these beautiful rafters, 700 years old like the walls they cover. The striking black and white roof of the nave is 14th century. The font is 15th, and the corner where it stands is panelled with Jacobean carving from the old pulpit. Elaborate Jacobean panels cover the sanctuary walls with sea serpents and little watching heads, and a medieval panel here has a very queer medley of animals, one a robed ass holding a bishop's staff. The Jacobean reredos has four carved pillars and a panel of the Pieta. It is odd to see, high up in a windowsill, a piscina which belonged to the altar of the vanished roodloft.

A little green-robed Jessica in one of the lancet windows recalls a best-seller of long ago, for she is here in memory of Sarah Smith, who wrote Jessica's First Prayer, and took her pen name of Hesba Stretton from this town, in which she spent her childhood.

A shapely yew shades the churchyard where a stone of 1814 to Ann Cook tells us:

> *On a Thursday she was born,*
> *On a Thursday made a bride,*
> *On a Thursday broke her leg,*
> *And on a Thursday died.*

If we expect to find old black and white houses in this town half-way between Shrewsbury and Ludlow we shall be disappointed, for, apart from the 16th century Talbot Inn which is now part of Stretton House, there is nothing much in its streets; but a little to the north is All Stretton with three fine old houses, including a Tudor manor house with a grand black and white exterior, several panelled rooms, and a fine oak staircase, while to the south is Little Stretton, a delightful village etched in black and white. There is the old manor house, and behind an oddly shaped hedge by a little bridge over the brook is Tan House with rich timbering, a thatched porch and quaint gables, and memories of a writer of the last generation almost forgotten in ours—Ian Maclaren, who often stayed here.

On the way to Little Stretton, overlooking Watling Street at the foot of Ragleth Hill, are the remains of Brockhurst Castle, an earthwork with a dry moat and some stones from the fortress here in Norman days; and beyond Little Stretton the hamlet of Minton looks down on the happy valley from its perch on the Longmynd, its cottages clustered round a green and its old manor houses side by side with a moated Saxon mound.

A Picture From the Conquest

CLAVERLEY. Its timbered vicarage with quaint heads on the ends of the beams, its charming group of black and white houses, and its gabled inn have been here for centuries, and with them the cross in the churchyard, which has for company a magnificent yew with a hollow trunk 30 feet round, in which four men could sit round a table. It is the king of a churchyard made delightful with small rock gardens.

The church is Norman and medieval. The Norman stones are in the base of the tower as they have been 800 years, and the great arches of the north arcade, resting on four massive columns, are also Norman. The south arcade, with dragons, leaves, faces, and graceful figures of women on its capitals, is 13th century. The chancel is 600 years old and the porch and the upper part of the tower were added 500 years ago. There is a Norman font with richly carved arches and foliage, and another font bowl with two ancient iron bands.

Red roses glow in old glass in the chancel windows and a transept window has fragments of glass probably 500 years old, showing an angel and a charming head of a girl with golden tresses. The splendid tracery of the east window is filled with prophets, saints, and angels. Masses of dark colour and a few faint lines are all that remain of the medieval paintings on the walls of the tower and above the Norman arches, but the vicar has copies of them. The most important painting showed horsemen in the style of the Bayeux tapestry, and are thought to have represented a scene at the Battle of Hastings, perhaps the dramatic incident of Roger de Montgomery, founder of the church, defeating a stout Saxon warrior.

There is graceful woodwork old and new. In the north aisle are remains of an ancient screen, the pulpit has panels 200 years old, and the medieval roof of the nave rests on queer heads carved in the 18th century. The chancel has a Jacobean roof with leaves and shields on its bosses, a modern screen with saints, and choir stalls with beautiful panels.

Hollowed out under one of the arches of the tower is a great cavity which is believed to have been used as a penance seat, and certainly it would be very uncomfortable to sit in; near it, through a gap, can be seen crude masonry probably older than anything else in the church, with the marks of the mason's tools still visible.

In the two chapels lie the notable folk of the village. On the oldest tomb, an alabaster monument of 1408, are the engraved figures of Richard Spicer and his wife, both greatly worn. There is a 16th century figure of William Gatacre in his armour with his wife and 11 children; Francis Gatacre, probably one of their sons, is engraved on another monument with his wife. Sir William Forbes Gatacre, who commanded a division in the march on Khartoum, has a marble tablet, and there is a wooden cross from the grave of Captain Gatacre, who fell in the Great War.

General Gatacre was one of the brave soldiers of the second half of last century and shared in dramatic adventures in India, South Africa, and the Sudan. His troops were in Bombay when plague was carrying off 300 lives a day and his energy in fighting it brought him the gratitude of Christian, Mussulman, and Hindoo. He took part in the advance up the Nile for the recovery of Khartoum, and his army was in such fine condition that it could march 140 miles a week; his men called him General Backacher. He went out to South Africa and there met with disaster, losing nearly 700 men out of 3000. He was relieved of his command a little later for failing to relieve a British detachment, but it was no stain upon his honour, though he retired from the army in 1904, when he went out to explore rubber forests in Abyssinia and caught a fatal fever camping in a swamp.

On an elaborate tomb lies Sir Robert Brooke in the robes he wore as Speaker of the House of Commons in 1558, with elegant figures of his two wives beside him and an exquisite procession of 18 children as weepers round the tomb. In the porch is a stone tablet to 198 men of Claverley who left their village homes, as the inscription tells us, in defence of the liberties of Europe, thirty of them never coming back.

Time was when a friend of this village left eight shillings a year for a man to drive dogs out of the church and rouse the sleeping people. The man carried a long rod with a knob at one end and a fox's brush at the other, and we are told that he would tap the heads of sleeping men with the knob and touch the faces of sleeping women with the tail.

East of the village is Tinker's Castle, a ridge of sandstone hollowed out in many places, marking the site of an ancient fort.

The Turbulent Clee

CLEE ST MARGARET. It lies remote and tranquil among the orchards on the slope of Brown Clee Hill. Through it runs the Clee, a turbulent brook which for 50 yards claims the whole width of the road before disappearing to plunge over a steep bank. Near the church is a timbered manor house now a farm, with a dovecot in one of its gabled ends. A mile away, connected by the Devil's Causeway with Roman Watling Street, is Nordy Bank, an imposing prehistoric earthwork surrounded by a deep fosse, and wonderfully preserved.

The village has a Norman heritage, a little church in a churchyard glorified by two immense beeches, and a yew 14 feet round. Over the sharply pointed roof rises a quaint wooden bellcot. There is herringbone in the outer walls of the Norman chancel; at the east end it takes the odd form of a fish, an emblem which has its place in early Christian art for the slight reason that the initial letters of the Greek words of a sacred phrase form the Greek word for fish.

In the modern porch, with an old door on strap hinges, is a tiny Norman doorway, the top of its arch only six feet high. The narrow chancel arch, with a square peephole on each side, has doors in place of a screen, with panels from a Tudor chest. The priest's doorway is the one through which Norman monks would come to watch and pray. There is a chancel window of their day, and the bowl of the font is that to which children were brought for baptism. Nine stout old pews have bench-ends older than the Reformation; there are ancient beams in the black and white roofs; and the pulpit and the chancel seats are Jacobean.

The Home of Piers Plowman

CLEOBURY MORTIMER. We shall all be told here that it is the home of Piers Plowman. Here in 1332 William Langland

The Massive Tower

18th Century Lychgate

The Ruin on the Hilltop

THE CHURCH AND CASTLE OF CLUN

Tong 15th Century Miserere with Quaint Faces

Tong Old Miserere with Annunciation and Crucifixion

Stanton Long
Medieval Door

Atcham
Norman Doorway

Morville
Ancient South Door

is said to have been born. Along these roads a hundred years after
he had left them they brought the body of Prince Arthur whose
death was to change the course of English history, bringing Henry the
Eighth to the throne and so ushering in the Golden Age of Queen
Elizabeth. In the pavement near the church is a fragment of the
medieval cross by which the sad procession paused to rest on its
way from Ludlow Castle to Worcester Cathedral.

The village lies in lovely country that must have delighted Piers
Plowman. From here to Bewdley in Worcestershire stretches Wyre
Forest, once the preserve of kings and now the delight of all. It was
the wild cherry of Wyre Forest that yielded the first cultivated stocks
in England, and still the valleys are wonderful with their pink and
white blossom in the spring.

The street is lined with charming doorways of timbered cottages
and Georgian houses, and in the churchyard wall which overlooks
the street is a curious figure with arms akimbo which must be older
than all these houses except that fragment of Woodhouse, much
restored and now a farm, which is said to have been part of a dwelling
of the Austin Friars where Langland received his early education.

This grand church tower has stood nearly 800 years, and from it
rises a crazy spire of oak. It has been twice repaired in the last two
centuries, but again the wind and rain have warped and twisted it,
and it curves in the middle as if it is about to fall, but it is safe. The
church porch is 700 years old and has beautiful doorways carved with
heads and foliage. Here is a stoup with a remarkable sculptured head
looking rather Egyptian with hair falling on each side and slanted
eyes; it was found in a garden and is thought to be 500 years old.
The impressive tower arch has in it the oldest stones in the church,
laid by the Normans; they are in the outer order of the arch, the two
inner orders being restorations. The chancel arch with fine mouldings
and groups of capitals adorned with heads and foliage is 13th
century, like the south arcade; the north arcade and the chapel are
14th. The roofs have grand oak beams carved with roses and quatrefoils, and there is an ancient dug-out chest, and another with Tudor
ironwork on it. The 16th century altar table is remarkably interesting
because it has five plain bits of oak set in it where Cromwell's soldiers
are supposed to have cut out the consecration crosses.

There are medieval stone fragments including a complete coffin,

F   65

and a holy lamb carved in white stone, and among the interesting woodwork of our time is some by the vicar we met here; he fashioned the peace memorial triptych.

William Langland's memorial is the east window, a lovely tribute paid by a 19th century vicar to the poet's childhood. Beautiful with crimsons, greens, and blues, it shows Piers Plowman lying in a brown cloak dreaming his dreams, with the Malvern Hills in the background, and the River Rea in front. On each side of him are Truth and Falsehood, both with masks, and above are figures of Christ in Glory and scenes of the Last Supper, the Crucifixion, and the Ascension. The inscription dedicates the window to the poet "who sang of Jesus Christ in the allegory of Piers the Ploughman."

The Poet of the Western Hills

TRADITION assigns to Cleobury the birth of William Langland, whose Piers Plowman, next to the writings of Chaucer, was the most important contribution to our 14th century literature, the Pilgrim's Progress of Medieval England; but there are other claimants for this distinction. Practically all we know of him we deduce from the poem, together with a note or two found on 15th century manuscripts, written by unknown hands, stating that he was the son of Stacy de Rokayle (an aristocratic follower of the Despensers), and of an unknown peasant mother; that he was probably educated by the Great Malvern monks, became a deacon but never a priest, married and lived in London, and died about 1390 when he was 60 years old.

The poem appeared about 1360, but during its author's lifetime two other versions of it were written, the length of the three varying between 2500 and 7300 lines. First printed in 1550, the poem has remained a classic, giving rise to unending controversy. Half a century ago Professor Skeat published an edition of the three versions which accepted the dreamer as himself the poet and author of all three versions. This view was afterwards challenged by Professor Manly, who thought he saw many hands and many minds at work in Piers Plowman.

With opinion thus unsettled, the task was taken up afresh by Mr Allan Bright, a notable Malvern antiquary, whose inspired researches leave Langland undisputed author of the work, but assign to him possibly a new birthplace some miles away. That the poet passed his days in sight of the Malvern Hills is common ground;

now Mr Bright, accepting the story of the poet's paternity, has traced the mother, as he believes, to the parish of Colwall, five miles from Malvern Priory, where there was an ancient manor farm lying along the parish of Ledbury and named Longlands. Denied his father's name, this theory holds that the poet took the name of the place at which he grew up. According to this notion Langland, an acolyte of the priory, roamed the Malvern Hills, a shepherd hermit known to the neighbourhood as Long Will; afterwards making his way to London, where he wrote his poem and where he died, the three versions of the poem succeeding each other as new ideas and inspiration stirred him.

We may never know the truth of it, but his place in history, dim and shadowy as is his identity, is as striking as Bunyan's. That he is an undeclared disciple of John Wycliffe is obvious. He sees the ills in Court and Church, the cruelty of the nobles, the rascality of the lawyers, the suffering of the serfs. But he sees also the laziness of some of the poor, the senseless discontent of peasants where industry might improve their conditions.

With John Ball's pamphlets, his writings had an enormous influence on the opinion which blazed out into the Peasant Rising of 1381, but the violence and cruelty accompanying that upheaval were a flat denial of the noble teaching of William Langland, for his work was touched with sublimity of faith and he idealised the suffering peasant as Our Lord Himself.

By Candlelight

CLEOBURY NORTH. It has one of the candlelit churches of these haunts of ancient peace, and in it is ancient wood and stone and glass preserved throughout the centuries. Most of the arches in the church are 700 years old, and the font perhaps a century older; and in one window are fragments of 15th century glass. But it is the woodwork that we must count chief among the old treasures of the church. The 15th century screen in the aisle is lovely with borders of roses in quatrefoils; it has two doorways. The 17th century pulpit has 14 carved panels and four quaint figures of men and women with flowing hair. In the nave are two 17th century oak seats with tall backs, columns, canopies, heraldry, and Tudor roses. The roofs are old—the oldest of them all in the south aisle, a 16th century roof of open timbers on carved brackets in the chancel, and 17th century timbers in the nave.

A Hero and a Ne'er-Do-Well

CLIVE. One of Shropshire's beauty spots, its tall spire and stately tower are a landmark for miles. They were raised in memory of his wife by a man who helped to rebuild the church last century; he placed an inner shell within the Norman walls of the nave, and preserved the two Norman doorways. One doorway is now filled up, but both have sculptured heads above them.

Much handsome woodcarving adds to the charm of the church, the roofs having angel figures and the altar table a richness of ornament. There is a Jacobean chair, and an alabaster reredos copied from Leonardo's Last Supper. A white angel in the tower is carrying a child in memory of the builder's little grandson; and a tablet tells of Captain Percy Thorniley, whose death in 1917 brings home all the misery of war, for he was shot by snipers while talking to German prisoners. A colonel who won the DSO is remembered in the churchyard, where a big marble obelisk stands in memory of the Wormald family.

The village gathers about its ancient hall, a house of 600 years ago made bigger and more beautiful in recent years. It was the birthplace of one of our most famous Restoration dramatists, William Wycherley, whose first play, Love in a Wood, brought him recognition in fashionable circles at Court. He was an extraordinary character, who started life in the Army by receiving £500 from Charles the Second to meet his expenses, and spent most of his life in writing coarse plays and comedies in keeping with the dissolute life of the Court and the Age. At 40 he married a countess who could not bear him out of her sight and with whom he was unhappy; at 75 he married to thwart a nephew, and died 11 days after. Always in poverty, sometimes in prison, and never out of trouble, he was yet a writer of great vigour; his masterpiece is The Country Wife.

A Quiet Place Under the Sun

CLUN. Mr Housman, in A Shropshire Lad, thought it very quiet, and wrote: *Clunton and Clunbury,*
Clungunford and Clun,
Are the quietest places
Under the sun;

and indeed it is quieter now than in its olden days, when border warfare made it a strategic point. It still keeps the old seal and the old maces with the prehistoric relics in the little town hall museum.

Away beyond its boundary stretches the wild moorland crossed by the great dyke Offa built to defend his kingdom from the Welsh. Here are five ancient camps, one of them a thrilling place if we are to believe the things we are told, for Gaer Ditches, with ramparts 25 feet high, enclosing 12 acres with a well in the middle, is said to have been the camp of Caractacus, whose last battle was fought not far away at Bucknell. In the middle of a field at Pen y Wern an immense monolith towers above the ruins of a Stone Circle, a solitary witness to a dim past farther still down the corridors of time.

Romantic and impressive on a height washed on three sides by the river, stand the gaunt ruins of a Norman castle, with part of the keep and its windows, three faces of the old tower, and fragments of two round bastions. It is believed to have been the fortress of one of Scott's novels (Garde Doloureuse in The Betrothed). Scott describes it as so strong by nature and so fortified by art that the Welsh prince found it impossible to conquer it either by force or stratagem.

But it is the almshouse corner of the town that will seem more attractive to most folk. The houses were founded while Shakespeare was still alive, built by Henry Howard, Earl of Northampton, and known as Holy Trinity Hospital. The quadrangle is alive with colour in summer, and the houses form a delightful picture round the lawn. The chapel has its original bell and the original oak seats, and the arms of its founder are in the east window.

The clerestoried Norman church is at the other end of the town, reached by a flight of steps with a lovely 18th century lychgate at the top. Like the old castle, the church had a Saxon ancestor, and the work of the Saxon craftsmen is still in its massive low tower. The Normans built the great walls with the flat buttresses and the west doorway, and the 17th century gave it its pyramid roof and hung the studded door on its elaborate hinges. The great north porch with a gabled room over it (long used as a schoolroom) is also 17th century, but it has a simple Norman doorway with two heads over it.

The spacious interior marks the change from Norman to English. A Norman arch has been rebuilt from its old stones, but the splendid nave arcades have the English pointed arches. On one capital is a grim carving of a man with a cord through his nose, and above is a little man on all fours who seems to be in search of his missing head. The font is 13th century.

There is much fine woodwork, old and new. Three angels look down on the altar from an old medieval canopy in which the pyx was hung, and in the north aisle roof are 22 angels with outspread wings, all old. The continuous roof in the nave and chancel is modern; so are the towering chancel screen, the canopied stalls, the Bishop's Chair, and the charming sedilia with the fine figures of the Madonna, St George, and St Michael. The pulpit is Jacobean. The north chapel has a reredos made from old pews. The chancel reredos is richly carved with figures of Mary and John in memory of a rector of 30 years, and he is also remembered in the east window, which has portraits of George Herbert the poet, St Ethelbert and St Chad attended by monks, Oswini the martyred king, and other saints.

A heraldic brass in the chapel has a coat-of-arms held by two little men in smocks, being in memory of Sir Robert Howard, who was laid to rest here in 1653 after an extraordinary career. He loved Frances Coke, daughter of the famous Chief Justice, and, though her father had married her to a man she loathed, she still loved Howard, and in the end their story brought him to the Star Chamber and led her to the Savoy, where she was made to stand in a white sheet.

Among the Orchards

CLUNBURY. Above it all towers Clunbury Hill, crowned by a prehistoric stone upright; in the valley two rivers run as one, the Clun and the Kemp; and deep among the orchards lies the tiny village, with houses clustered about a church the Normans built.

Its sturdy embattled tower, with evidence of Jacobean restoration, has still its original west door, and in an outer recess is a stone with a floral cross carved when men were still excited over Bannockburn. Here is the great font the Normans made, three of their windows are in the nave and chancel, and something of their work is in two doorways, one blocked. The handsome black and white porch is modern. The odd shape of the medieval windows is curious, each being peculiar and unlike its fellows. Two of them have attractive and unusual glass with sepia tones and red skies, tracing the life of Paul.

The long and aisleless church is spanned by a roof under which sat congregations for a century before the Reformation; the handsome chancel screen is the work of craftsmen of our own time.

The Romans Marched This Way

CLUNGUNFORD. Sheltered by hills and lying in the broad valley of the Clun, it was known to the Romans, whose legions marched along Watling Street half a mile away. A prehistoric barrow by the church, which has yielded bones, pottery, and bronze weapons, reminds us that there was a British settlement here before the world had heard of Rome.

The church near the river has been here 600 years, but its embattled tower, almost detached, is 19th century. Over the old south doorway is a porch with open arcades, crowned by a fine figure of St Cuthbert as a bishop, with two swans at his feet.

The cheerful interior, its rose-coloured walls pierced by three ancient doorways, is lit by old windows, one in the chancel with the hinges of its original shutters. In another are roundels of medieval glass, with two heads in black and gold. The priest's doorway has still the massive oak bolt which many generations of priests must have drawn; it is four inches square and was made by a carpenter 600 years ago. Panelling from old pews lines the walls of the nave; the choir-stalls have Jacobean carving; and there is a Tudor chest.

A Town of Iron

COALBROOKDALE. It is one of the busy neighbours of Ironbridge, sharing with that town the distinction of having seen the iron trade grow from its infancy. The great ironworks of the Coalbrookdale Company are here, and industrialism has claimed much of the beauty of the wooded valley in which the river flows, yet here, as at Ironbridge, are ancient timbered cottages wedged between the houses and the shops. The modern church, with its imposing tower, looks down from a high ridge. It was built in 1851 by Abraham Darby, to whom there is a white marble tablet in the porch, with a bronze portrait of Matthew Webb, who swam the English Channel in 1875; he was born not many miles away, at Dawley, and died at Niagara Falls.

The chancel is beautiful, with a star-spangled roof resting on stone corbels delicately carved with leaves, and a fine east window of the

Crucifixion notable for its rich background of trees and its brilliant figures. The oak pews have carved ends and the oak pulpit has figures of three saints. There is a brass inscription to Michael Fletcher, 42 years a chorister here. The rarest possession of the church is a window of 16th century Flemish glass showing the Last Supper. Many of the figures in it are ugly, Judas (who is taking a wafer from Christ) having a shock of red hair and teeth protruding from his leering face. At one side is a panel showing Christ washing the feet of the disciples, and above are eight small painted panels of the Annunciation and Old Testament scenes.

COCKSHUTT. It straggles along the road and its little ivied church is by the wayside in a churchyard with trim yews and an 18th century sundial. Set in the apse with walls of veined marble and a canopied reredos, are three lancets showing the Crucifixion with a background of a city of tower and turrets; Simon with a book and a saw and Jude with a boat; St Helena with a cross and St Chad holding the church he built at Lichfield.

COLD WESTON. It has little but its magnificent views of the country round, with the bare green heights of Brown Clee Hill and its rolling foothills dotted with trees. For the rest, it has a few scattered farms and a small church almost lost in the hills. Only a field path brings us to it, but it brings us to a curiously misshapen Norman doorway leading into the nave. The chancel has a Norman window left, and there is a plain old font.   •

The First Sculpture by G. F. Watts

CONDOVER. It has memories of a just judge and his courageous son, of one of our great artists, and of a laughing rustic who came to know Spenser and Shakespeare and to cheer the heart of Queen Elizabeth in hours of gloom and peril. Also it has much of its oldtime charm, for the village is delightful as we come to it. Here in its 300-acre park, laced with the silver Cound Brook flowing through it, is the Tudor hall Judge Owen built; at the other end of the village, linked with the hall by a winding road, stands the 15th century home of the Gosnells and the house built for a schoolmaster in the days when Shakespeare was a boy at Stratford. The house has tall chimney stacks. The great stone hall stands in a lovely setting of lawns, and its avenue of clipped yews, in a uniform pattern, is a wonderful sight from the wayside gates. We found a peacock strutting in his pride on the churchyard wall, and proud a peacock might well be of this place with its fine array of monuments, and its marvellous roof. We come to it through a lychgate which is a thanksgiving for 30 years of happy life.

Of the Norman structure there remain only a narrow doorway and a transept of mottled stone with three deeply splayed and richly moulded windows. The tower fell in 1664, and nearly all we see was set up then. The Jacobean builders combined the nave and aisle, and threw over them a noble oak roof which, covering a space 52 feet high and 37 feet wide, is borne on six huge hammerbeams and fine supporting arches, still apparently perfect in spite of the stress of so wide a span. Older than the roof is a fine parish chest with seven iron bands and three locks which may have been here 700 years. On a lofty painted monument, surmounted by heraldry and draped figures, are four portrait statues under canopies: Dame Norton in a gown, veil, ruff, and lace cuffs; her husband in Jacobean black and gold; Judge Thomas Owen in his red robes, embroidered cap, and ruff; and Sir Roger his son in red breeches and armour. It was Judge Owen, father of Dame Norton, who built the hall. A famous lawyer and friend of Bacon, he was the son of a Shrewsbury merchant, and after he had won the esteem of the queen she gave him a family motto bidding him remember his origin. He was buried by her order in Westminster Abbey, where he has a magnificent monument. His son Roger so stoutly opposed the attempt of James the First to exact money without parliamentary authority that he was dismissed from the bench.

Other Owen memorials are a Jacobean medallion showing Martha Owen and her baby, the mother with long curls and wide collar; and a rather theatrical monument by the fashionable Roubillac, with Roger Owen holding a book, his only child sitting at his feet.

An ancient monument brought here from the ruined church of St Chad at Shrewsbury is the canopied tomb on which lie a bearded man in armour, a woman in a rich gown and ruff, three daughters in Tudor gowns, and four sons in long robes.

Much more beautiful and of much historic interest is the monument by G. F. Watts to Thomas Cholmondeley, who took the name of Owen. We understand that it is the first sculpture fashioned by our great Victorian artist who made his subject a lifelike bearded soldier of Crimean days, kneeling in prayer, his clasped hands on his sword. On the monument is the familiar inscription:

What I spent I had: What I saved I lost: What I gave I have.

The sculpture has a special interest because of its relation to the monument beside it. The Watts statue is to the brother of one of the sculptor's fellow pupils at an art school, Reginald Cholmondeley, and side by side with it is his friend's pathetic monument to his own bride, who died in bringing a little one into the world—her "pitiable daughter" she is called on the tomb. The heartbroken husband carved her figure in white marble with this in the inscription:

> *Reginald, always standing by,*
> *Carved me with his own hand.*

The sculpture shows Alice Cholmondeley in a simple dress with slashed sleeves, lying as if asleep on a pallet, her hair flowing over the pillow. Nestling under her arm is the baby with its tiny hand outstretched; at her feet is its empty cradle, with the clothes turned down, as if the child had crept out of it up to her. The mother was married but a year, and the child followed her to the grave.

On a tablet are the names of 18 who did not return from the war, one of them Katherine Harley, killed by a bomb while nursing stricken Serbians at Monastir. The oak screen was erected across the fine tower arch in her memory.

A Fellow of Infinite Jest

CONDOVER'S most famous son was Queen Elizabeth's favourite comedian. In the 16th century Richard Tarlton was tending his father's pigs here when his wit attracted the notice of the Earl of Leicester, who took him to Court, where he played jester to Queen Elizabeth, and formed one of her company of actors. It is said that her cares were never too great for her to be charmed to laughter by his wit and drollery.

Foremost comedian of his age, he was unmatched in the skill with which he improvised comic verse. His face was disfigured by an accident in a bear-fight, but he turned the injury to profit as an aid to merriment. Dying in 1588, he was too early to appear in a play by Shakespeare, who seems, however, to have known him well during the closing years of his life. Shakespearean scholars agree that it is to Tarlton that Hamlet refers in the graveyard scene, where he exclaims, " Alas! poor Yorick, I knew him, a fellow of infinite jest and most excellent fancy," and recalls the jokes with which he would set the table in a roar.

Tarlton has another title to fame, for he is identified with the "Pleasant Willy" of Spenser's Tears of the Muses. Pleasant Willy was a term of familiar endearment common to the time, applied, regardless of his name, to a favourite. This is the significant stanza:

> And he the man whom Nature self had made
> To mock herself, and truth to imitate,
> With kindly counter under mimic shade,
> Our pleasant Willy, ah is dead of late:
> With whom all joy and jolly merriment
> Is also deaded and in dolour drent.

The clue to "Pleasant Willy" was discovered in the 1611 edition of Spenser, where the identity of the hero is declared in early 17th century writing. Everybody, even Ben Jonson, who despised most actors, honoured Tarlton and enjoyed his gaiety. His name and features figured on inn-signs; publications not his own were issued under his name before and after his death, and for a century his memory was dear to England. Adding innkeeping to acting, he died in Shoreditch, where he sleeps in St Leonard's Church.

CORELEY. It has a fine gem which may be as old as anything it possesses, a fragment of ancient glass in the lancet window of the tower, showing a charming child angel in a purple robe with green wings and golden hair. It is believed that it may be as old as the tower itself which has stood with its grand arch and its wooden spire for 700 years. The church has a Jacobean lectern with small heads and grotesque animals, and the pulpit has 17th century carving.

Beauty Old and New

COUND. It is charming, with an ancient church, a delightful timbered post office, and a Queen Anne hall in a lovely park. The pinnacled tower has white angels for gargoyles, and a white lamb among its red stones. It is 500 years old, but much of the church is older. The doorway is 13th century and has a door carved with roses 600 years ago, still with its old hinges and one of the two or three great closing rings left in Shropshire. The chancel arch is also 13th century; and so are the arches marking off the 14th century south aisle, which has a fine canopied piscina resting on a carved head. A Norman font decorated with big sunflowers is the oldest possession of all; but almost as old is the ornamental ironwork on the parish chest.

On the floor, on the walls, and in the windows are sights to draw the eye. Medieval tiles lie near the altar, and a group of 64 are under the tower, one showing a man standing between plants. What is left of an ancient Doom painting shows the heavenly mansions in dark outline, and a crowned head; and in an aisle window is the head of Our Lord and a golden-haired saint in a green robe, both in 14th century glass. In a lower pane are 13th century flowers.

A lovely window of the Annunciation is to Augustus Pelham who was 44 years rector, and a very bright east window has figures of disciples and of Anne teaching the Madonna to read. The handsome carving of Jacobean craftsmen is seen on the pews, the pulpit, and the panelling round the chancel. Part of a 14th century screen, with its original door, stands under the tower arch.

Fixed on the wall are copperplates to 18th century people, beautifully engraved with skulls and musical angels. A monument of 1775 has a crook and a mitre in memory of a Bishop of Llandaff, and kept here in a frame are the mitre and pastoral staff of a Bishop of Salisbury in our own century.

Christ's Oak

CRESSAGE. In Domesday the name of this Severn village near the Wrekin was Cristesache, or Christ's Oak, and it is one of the places which claim to have had an oak under which Augustine preached. That oak, if ever it existed, has gone, but the ruined trunk of another about 20 feet round, said to be the last relic of a forest famous in medieval times, is in a field off the Shrewsbury road, protected by a wooden fence. It was practically destroyed by fire last century, but out of the old trunk new life has sprung, a young oak thrusting itself up through the centre. The 19th century church has a Norman font, a row of 27 medieval tiles at the chancel step, and a Jacobean pulpit with panels of flowers, scrolls, and linenfold, and a prayer carved on it by the craftsman who made it in the days of Charles Stuart, craving God's blessing on his work.

A Strange Spire

CULMINGTON. Withdrawn from the busy highway, it rests by the river Corve, its farms and black and white houses gay with flowers and creepers, its little church with a Peter Pan of spires which has never grown up. The massive tower was built 600 years ago and the spire, which has dormer windows in it, ends abruptly as if disaster had overtaken its builders. So it must have remained for 400 years, looking a little ridiculous; and still it looks queer, for a lead spire like a clown's cap was added to it in 1796. The walls of the long church lean, and are held in position by an iron brace across. In the chancel is a beautiful 14th century recess with fine ballflower in its rich decoration, and at either end of its arch a crowned head. The striking canopied piscina has another crowned head, and a face smiling through the centuries. There is no chancel arch; in its stead is the best possession of the church, a low 15th century screen with delicate bays and a charming cornice of fanlike leaves, crowned by Tudor flowers. The cornice is reproduced in the modern reredos, at each end of which kneels a finely carved angel. There is Jacobean panelling in the choir-stalls; some of the pews are dated 1641; and over all is an old black and white panelled roof with a window in the top. We noticed that last century a rector was here for 52 years.

The Man Who Leapt Into Niagara

DAWLEY. It has a fountain with a small bronze portrait of one of its sons who made himself talked of all over the world, Captain Webb, first man to swim the Channel. He was a Dawley man, and learned to swim in the Severn.

The 19th century church has one old possession from the church before it, a font which has come down to it from Norman days, with the Norman craftsman's zigzag round the base, a band of curious shell-like pattern round the middle, and a border of trefoil leaves round the rim of the bowl. There is a window in memory of three friends of the church in which shines a beautiful figure of St Cecilia with her pipes; she is in a blue robe with figures at her feet, an angel listening to her music, figures in blue raiment on either side, and a model of the church against the background of the hills. The east window is less attractive, but it is in memory of the first bishop of New Zealand, the famous Dr Selwyn who was patron of the living here.

Matthew Webb, a doctor's son born here in 1848, could swim like a duck while he was a small boy, and while he was still a midget he saved a brother from drowning and saved a second life in the Mersey. When serving as mate on a merchant ship he was awarded a Royal Humane Society medal for jumping overboard in a heavy sea to rescue a comrade who had fallen from the tops.

At 27 he was captain of a little ship sailing from Liverpool, and for the rest of his life was known as Captain Webb. It was as a swimmer, however, not as a seaman, that he made his name familiar to the world. First he created a record which stood for a quarter of a century by swimming in less than five hours the 20 miles between Blackwall Pier and Gravesend.

The feat that made him famous was his swimming of the Channel. So many have followed him of late years as to make the achievement almost commonplace, but he was the first man to do it, swimming from Dover to Calais in less than 22 hours. He delighted great crowds with his skill as a diver and swimmer, and his endurance of long spells in the water. In 1883 he undertook for a small wager to swim the rapids below Niagara Falls. Experts implored him not to do it, but he was reckless beyond reason and, plunging into the rapids, thrilled the crowds for ten minutes and then threw up his arms, sank, and was seen alive no more. His body was recovered some days later seven miles down the river.

The Saxon Tower

DIDDLEBURY. It is dominated by a church of rare interest, one of the oldest in Shropshire, with a splendid legacy from the Saxon builders. Their work is best seen in the north wall of the nave, which has a big stretch of Saxon masonry, a simple narrow doorway now filled up, and a little window splayed inside and out. The doorway, seen from outside the church, has crude capitals and is framed all round with a hood-mould. The outer Saxon masonry is built of square stones, large and small; but inside it is a very fine example of the arrangement of stones in herringbone pattern, which covers the high wall for a length of 40 feet and looks as strong and perfect as it did about a thousand years ago.

The striking tower, very low, is thought to be mostly Saxon at the base, where part of its original doorway can be seen like a flattened horseshoe built in over the later entrance, a 12th century doorway four feet deep. Higher up, the tower has a red stone parapet, Norman belfry windows, and a Norman stringcourse with three animal heads and a muzzled bear. A 12th century arch with three stepped mouldings opens into the nave, where an arcade of five bays has been standing for 700 years. In one of the windows is an ancient stone with knotwork, and set in a blocked Norman window is an old relief of little figures in the branches of a tree, a crude representation of the Stem of Jesse. There is an old font, and a modern roof above old wooden corbels of bearded men, some with their tongues out.

In the chancel are two Norman windows and two 14th century recesses, that on the north being richly moulded and adorned with ballflower. A 14th century window has some fine glass as old as itself, showing flowers and a Crucifixion in black and gold and red. There is a wall memorial to Thomas Baldwin, who was imprisoned in the Tower of London for helping Mary Queen of Scots.

An Astonishing Roof

DITTON PRIORS. Its wooden spire thrusts out of the wooded slopes of Brown Clee Hill and old black and white houses cluster round it. We found the village mourning the loss of one of our little railways, for the last passenger had travelled by rail from Cleobury Mortimer to Ditton Priors. The distance is 12 miles and the journey took 78 minutes, four trains a day puffing along through charming country. The motor-car has beaten it and the little railway is no more. A stone on the north-east corner of the church takes us back to the days when neither motor-cars nor trains disturbed the quiet of this place, for it has on it the marks where the marksmen of bow and arrow days sharpened their arrows.

The church has the tower arch built by the Normans, but the chancel, nave, and aisle are 13th century. The chancel has still the doorway the priests would go through before Agincourt. The chancel screen is partly 15th century, with delicate carving of quatrefoils and roses. There are richly carved pews of the 17th century and a pulpit

79

of the same age, panelling round the chancel, and old choir-stalls. A small brass to Thomas Jenks, a 17th century vicar, is engraved with the heads of three boars and a long inscription which would suit some of the writers of our day who do not like good English, for it has no punctuation or capitals; on either side of it is a skull and crossbones carved in wood and painted.

The most surprising thing in the church, and a truly astonishing sight, are the ancient roofs of the nave and aisle, two roofs in one, a mass of beams rising in the most intricate way, so that, looking up through truss and strut and purlin, we have something like the impression that we get in looking up at the Forth Bridge.

Thomas Twigg's Signature

DONINGTON. It has a small and pleasant church with a little precious glass five and six centuries old. In a chancel window is a beautiful queen or Madonna in robes of green, white, and gold, and with her a king, a woman, a bearded man, and a winged angel. In another window are two faces and fragments of leaves, acorns, and flowers, and there are also heraldic shields and small heads among other rich fragments. Except for its modern arch, the chancel, including the charming little priest's doorway, is 700 years old. The 17th century nave has its original hammerbeam roof, with quaint heads on its brackets, and the name of the carpenter is on one of its beams; he was Thomas Twigg. There are 16th century seats with tracery on them in the aisle, and in the churchyard is part of an old cross with carving on the base and a sundial on the broken shaft.

John Boydell and His Pictures

DORRINGTON. It lies on a busy highway, and boasts two remarkable sons, one giving it the church, the other exercising an influence on English art.

The church, built last century, has a profusion of wall-paintings. In the chancel are nine angels in panels; over the arch is Christ in Glory, with Mary and John; and by the arch are St George, and David with his sling and the head of Goliath. The stone reredos is touched with gold and sculptured with Nativity scenes; the Magi offer gifts while a man holds their camels; at one side stands a king, at the other St Andrew, and in the stable the ox and ass are eating,

Edstaston   Rich Decoration on South Doorway

Ludlow   Doorway of Castle Chapel   **Edstaston**   North Doorway

RARE NORMAN CARVING

Ellesmere   The Church and Mere

Oswestry   The Memorial Gates

while two doves look down. The richly carved oak pulpit has angels sounding trumpets, and is in memory of a lieutenant killed at Ypres.

There is a marble tablet to John Thomas Hope, who founded the church in the year of revolutions 1848, and died six years later when he was 93. He would know John Boydell, the most illustrious son of the village, who passed to his rest on the eve of Trafalgar, an honoured European figure. The son of a land surveyor, he reached London on foot, and for pure love of art apprenticed himself to an engraver, beginning his career by engraving prints which he sold to toyshops in sets of six, investing his returns in new plates.

Until this time English art was unknown in Europe, and all our engravings came from abroad. Boydell succeeded as an engraver, but did better by opening a shop for the sale of prints, and in 1751 he produced an engraving of Wilson's Niobe, the first important work by an English artist ever engraved. He founded a brilliant school of engravers, and commissioned such artists as Reynolds, Romney, Opie, and Angelica Kauffmann to paint for him. He built a gallery in Pall Mall for exhibiting Shakespeare in pictures painted for him, and created an immense trade with the Continent, which now for the first time began to buy English art.

Successively Sheriff and Lord Mayor of London, Boydell was eventually impoverished owing to European wars, and, proving that he had spent nearly £400,000 in furthering art, he was allowed by the Government to dispose of his stock by lottery, which enabled him to end his days free from debt.

The Lonely Hamlet

DUDLESTON. A lonely hamlet across the rolling hills, it lies on the edge of the park of Kilhendre Hall. Its 19th century church has a fine medieval chest cut out of a solid block, a pulpit carved in Jacobean days, a sculptured Crucifixion with John and the three women at the foot of the cross, and a lovely east window with the richly robed figures of the Madonna and Child and Peter and John. There are old yews in the churchyard and a fragment of a cross. We noticed that one of the rectors was here for 50 years.

Old Things and New

EASTHOPE. It nestles in a green hollow but has glorious views from the top of the hill at Wenlock Edge, where we see the

Wrekin in the north, the Welsh hills closing the horizon on the west, and the lovely Ape Dale below.

Down in the hollow are a few old houses and farms, with the rectory and the church in a field; it has two fine yews for company. A trim little place, it has a black and white turret and a black and white roof, all new, for the interior and the roof of the 13th century church were destroyed by a fire in our own time. A fine relic surviving the fire is the Jacobean hourglass stand, and on the new door is the ancient closing ring. The 14th century east window has been saved, and in it shines modern glass of the Annunciation and the Cruci-fixion. The oak chancel screen was made just before we called, but was already four centuries old, for its oak is from the timbers of an old house in Herefordshire. It is lofty and graceful and beautifully made, with delicate tracery in the bays and a cornice of oak leaves and acorns. Over the entrance is a rich canopy with two angels.

Hiding in the Woods

EATON. With a pretty brook flowing under a little stone bridge, it lies secluded in Ape Dale, almost enveloped by the great woods reaching down from Wenlock Edge.

Connected with the rectory by a slender iron bridge spanning the deep hillside track, the ancient church crowns a high bank in the churchyard. Above it rises a tower with pinnacled battlements five centuries old, resting on a base which has stood firm since Normans and English combined to build it. The Normans did no levelling when they built, but followed the line of the hill, and the interior slopes gently up to the altar. Norman windows remain in the nave, and there is a doorway little younger. The sanctuary window has three lancets, unusual in being all one size. In them are scenes from the life of St Edith.

There is a memorial to Captain Friederichs, who was killed while succouring a comrade in the Somaliland campaign of 1901. The old font has a handsome oak cover six feet high, carved with grapes and wheat, the fine work of a 19th century craftsman. He was a successor to medieval carvers who left the church rich treasure of wood-carving, chief of them all being the perfect oak figure over six feet high of a man in robes and a close-fitting hood, lying in a 14th century recess under a chancel window. There are only about a hundred of these medieval oak figures in the country, and this one is believed to represent a lord of the manor of six centuries ago.

The chancel, with old oak gates, is lined with decorated panelling from an old manor house. Over it is a 15th century roof with richly carved bosses, some with strange faces. Very striking are the combined pulpit and reading desk, the pulpit with a canopy dated 1670, and some of the pews have Jacobean carving. There are two handsome 17th century chairs, and an old chest with three locks.

At Upper Millichope, a mile and a half away, is one of the oldest houses in England, a Norman farmhouse which eight centuries ago was the home of the king's forester of the Long Forest. One of its doorways has a Norman arch decorated with ballflowers by a mason of the 14th century. In a gable is a window with two lights divided by a stone pillar which has still the old socket for a bolt. Very thick at the base, the walls thin considerably towards the first floor, and a staircase is within the wall.

The Boyhood Home of Richard Baxter

EATON CONSTANTINE. An upland village near the wooded slopes of the Wrekin, it is famous as the home of Richard Baxter's boyhood. Its ancient church has been made new, but it has still its Norman font, chairs with old oak panels, a 17th century oak strip with the names of the churchwardens let into a pew, and before the altar some medieval tiles from Buildwas Abbey.

The black and white Baxter House, where Richard Baxter lived as a boy, stands as in Stuart times with grand old tiles and a little porch, a glorious spectacle. He was born a little way off in his mother's home at Rowton, but this was the Baxter home impoverished by the father's gambling. In such a home this saintly man began his life, and his early education was received from drunken clergy. He had happier fortune at Wroxeter, and at Ludlow had the free run of the Castle Library. He was advised to seek his fortune at Court and at 18 went to London, but in a month he was back again, sadly disillusioned. At 23 he became a schoolmaster and went to Dudley grammar school, and a year later was ordained as assistant to a clergyman in Bridgnorth, where he spent two years.

But he was not happy. Living through 76 years of the tragic 17th century he was one of the men who felt deeply and were of liberal spirit, but could not fit in with the violence of the age. The great work of his preaching life was at Kidderminster over the Worcestershire border, where he transformed the life of the people so that a traveller riding through the town would hear the people singing hymns. He preached moderation to soldiers and civilians alike, and though he became a chaplain in Cromwell's Army and was present at four great sieges, he always sought a middle course. He found himself opposed to extremists in Church and State, and wrote with great power and persuasiveness in the hope of reconciling the rival parties. His motto was: "In things necessary, Unity; in things doubtful, Liberty; in all things, Charity." In the end he welcomed the Restoration, but refused a bishopric, and finally left the Church in 1662. He had been forced by study and conviction into Nonconformity and suffered much persecution, his goods being seized and stolen, and he himself imprisoned.

Macaulay's picture of Richard Baxter before the foul Judge Jeffreys still fills an Englishman with shame; this monster on the bench, unfit to clean Richard Baxter's shoes, called him a dog, an old knave, and a villain, and declared that he should be whipped through the streets at a cart's tail.

At the trial of this venerable Puritan the court was filled by those who loved and honoured him, and Baxter pleaded for time to prepare his defence. "Not a minute," cried Jeffreys, in a storm of rage, "not a minute to save his life." It was on the day on which Titus Oates was pilloried that Baxter made his appeal, and Jeffreys went on, "I can deal with saints as well as sinners. There stands Oates on one side of the pillory, and if Baxter stood on the other the greatest rogues in the kingdom would stand together." Two well-known barristers appeared for Baxter, and to one of them Jeffreys said, "Pollexfen, I know you well. I will set my mark on you. This is an old rogue, a schismatical knave, a hypocritical villain." He then mimicked Baxter in the pulpit, and his fury rose to madness. To the other defender he said, "You are in all these dirty causes, Mr Wallop; if you do not know your duty I will teach it you." Baxter himself tried to speak, and the judge burst out, "Richard, thou art an old knave, but by the grace of God Almighty I will crush you all."

Baxter was fined a sum he could not pay, and was sent to gaol for nearly two years. He came out with his health broken, but went on

preaching and writing, and when he died in 1691 he left behind him
an immense volume of work. His autobiography is a moving and
beautiful story, and his Saint's Everlasting Rest is only second to
Pilgrim's Progress. Coleridge, in summing up his character, says
that under accursed persecution Richard Baxter feels and reasons
more like an angel than a man.

As in the Medieval Days

EDGMOND. Its church and rectory make a remarkable group,
the church most impressive, and the rectory a beautiful embattled house of the 15th century. It was a home of the monks, and
their hall and chapel are still within.

The church tower is also 15th century, but the chancel is a few
decades older and was made unusually long for the use of the
monks. At the sides of its arch are heads of a man and a woman.
The nave has arches 500 years old rising from 13th century bases
and reaching up to the roof; and round the aisle outside are many
striking gargoyles and heads. There is a 15th century doorway with
its original door still swinging on its hinges, a carving on the porch
of children arm in arm, a vestry window with heads and shields in
medieval glass, an elaborate 19th century pulpit with the Four
Evangelists under canopies, and an attractive modern screen. The
Norman font is one of the most interesting in Shropshire, richly
adorned.

Here in brass are Francis Young of 1533 and his wife, he in a
shroud and she in Tudor dress, with nine sons and four daughters.
About them are the symbols of the Evangelists, and a shield with the
Wounds of Our Lord. Two rectors, nearly 500 years apart, are
remembered within these walls. The sill of the tower window is the
tombstone of Nicholas de Peshale, who came here as parson in
1384; and the east window of the Annunciation is to Charles
Pigott who came in 1867. Below is another tribute to him, a reredos
carved with Moses and St Paul and the Crucifixion.

EDGTON. It is happy in its fine view of the countryside, and has
kept some fragments of the past in the little rebuilt church. An
old studded door hangs in the west doorway, and above is a lancet
fashioned when the Norman style was passing away. Another old
lancet is in the nave, its splay filled by two slate memorials from the

time of Cromwell. A third slate is to one of the Sandfords of the 18th century, whose family held the lordship of Edgton for 400 years. Their arms are cut on a stone behind the altar. There is a chair carved 300 years ago, but the oldest possession is the simple bowl of a Norman font.

Norman Smiths and Norman Carpenters

EDSTASTON. Let all who come along this highroad turn aside to see the church in the lane, for it is a gem of Norman building. Its east wall is 14th century and its west is 19th, but the two side walls are of Norman masonry, with a corbel table, Norman windows, splendid doorways, ancient doors, and rare old ironwork. The south doorway has been ranked the richest in Shropshire. Three of its arches are patterned with zigzag, the fourth has a carved head and is supported on other heads, and the capitals are adorned with leaves and little heads peeping out. The wide doors were made by Norman carpenters, and Norman blacksmiths fashioned their ironwork of crosses and foliage and capital C's. The north doorway is also enriched with four arches, one having dragons and heads and the figure of a woman. The capitals are carved, and the door is a medieval one with Norman ironwork. The priest's doorway is Norman too, and has Norman ironwork on its modern door.

All over the walls within are traces of ancient paintings, though no scene is easily recognisable. Two consecration crosses can be seen, one behind the remains of a Norman sedilia, and there are traces of arcades painted on the wall by Norman artists. The roof is medieval, the pulpit is 17th century, and in the vestry is a Jacobean chest. A little 15th century glass shows Christ with a golden orb.

In one of the Norman windows is glass shining with the Madonna in memory of Judge Honyman who died in 1875, and the west window shows the Three Marys in memory of a Mary whose husband commanded the City Imperial Volunteers in the Boer War; above and below the figures are delightful studies of animals and flowers. There is a window to Admiral Bowen and his daughter of Coton Hall, a partly medieval house which is interesting because it was the ancestral home of the famous American Lee family. One of the great-grandsons of a Shropshire Lee made history when he moved the Resolution of American Independence, and with his brother he

was among those who signed the famous Declaration. From the
same family, too, sprang Abraham Lincoln's great opponent in the
American Civil War, Robert E. Lee.

Remembered in this church by the altar is an old lady of 74 who
was for 56 years a faithful servant at Ryebank a mile away.

Shropshire's Lakeland

ELLESMERE. It is the capital of Shropshire's Lake Country,
standing on the biggest of seven delightful meres : Blake
Mere, Kettle Mere, Newton Mere, Cole Mere, White Mere, Crose
Mere, and the biggest of all called just The Mere, a noble sheet of
water with Ellesmere on its western shore. The castle which stood
by the Mere in ancient days has vanished, but the church is still a
noble spectacle crowning the view across the lake. Blake Mere lies
in a deep hollow, giving us a splendid peep as we look down.

The naturalist is much interested in these lakes because of an odd
natural phenomenon occurring every year, as it does in a few lakes
in the North of England. It appears that at a particular time in the
life of the millions of tiny water plants we call algae something about
them disturbs the water for two or three weeks, so that the lake
becomes thick like soup. Occurring once every year on these seven
lakes round Ellesmere, this curious occurrence is known as the
Break.

It is fitting that in this country of delightful waters there should
begin one of Thomas Telford's greatest engineering triumphs, the
Ellesmere Canal, which, reaching away to link the Severn with the
Mersey, crosses the Vale of Llangollen by an aqueduct 125 feet
high and 1000 feet long, and is in places as beautiful as any of
Nature's own rivers.

Fringed by trees and rushes, the Mere, covering 116 acres, is the
home of swans and a happy haunt of oarsmen. To one side of the
lake is a black and white house whose terraced lawns add a grace to
the tree-decked slope ; here are the Cremorne Gardens, and by
courtesy of Lord Brownlow we may all wander here by the lake, a
lovely walk of three-quarters of a mile. Beyond the water is charming
Oteley Park, the only place in the county which has been a deer
park continuously since Tudor times. The modern house has still
a chimney of the old home of the Kynastons, and treasures a Prayer

Book given to one of the house by Queen Elizabeth. A little way out of the village, near White Mere, is the old hamlet of Lee with the Elizabethan Old Hall, a delightful timbered house of many gables.

A fine bowling green above the church marks the site of the Norman castle, owned by a sister of Henry the Second and by a daughter of King John. We may stand where the old keep stood, and see beyond the lakes into seven counties. Here was a garrison faithful to the Empress Maud in her bitter conflict with King Stephen.

In the churchyard is a stone to a man who saw seven kings of England and the two Protectors, and who served "Mr Stephen Hatchett, his son, his grandson, his great-grandson, and his great-great-grandson" before he died at 104 years old.

Only a single pier is left of the Norman church, but the fine central tower has a base 700 years old, and a pinnacled top with gargoyles, heads, and shields, which has been for five centuries a background to the mere. One of the transepts has a doorway old enough to have admitted men of the last Crusade, and there are three canopied seats with black marble columns 700 years old. A north chapel window has sculptured heads of kings, queens, bishops, and civilians. In the south chapel, with part of the medieval chancel screen, is a magnificent oak roof with carved beams, 192 quatrefoil panels, and 144 bosses, delightful work by men who may have fought in the Wars of the Roses. Here is a 16th century altar tomb with the figures of Sir Francis Kynaston and his wife both wearing ruffs. It was he to whom Queen Elizabeth gave the prayer book; he was her cupbearer.

On a wall of the chapel is a stone figure of a man who might have come from one of Chaucer's Tales. At his waist are the scrivener's inkhorn and pen-case, attached to a girdle falling to his feet, where it is gripped by the teeth of a little dog lying on his back in play. In each transept is an oil painting. One of the Holy Family, the other a Crucifixion attributed to Francisco Zurbaran, a Spanish labourer's son who won immortality in the 17th century with such pictures as we see of his in the National Gallery.

The church has a fascinating medieval chest nearly nine feet long, hewn from a solid block of oak. The vestry has a 15th century roof, a Jacobean table, a three-legged chair of the same age, and a small oblong window which, looking into the Sanctuary, is thought to have belonged to the cell of an anchorite, one of the queer folk who immured themselves in churches in the manner of the Indian fakirs. The chancel has a fine old bishop's chair carved with a castle, a mounted man, and a battle scene. Modern poppyheads of the panelled choir-stalls are carved with swans, eagles, angels, foxes eating pheasants, men peeping out of foliage, two quaint little fellows holding their feet, and a man blowing a fire with his bellows.

This old town, so delightful for its lakes, its irregular streets, and its timbered houses, has for its peace memorial a copy of a 15th century lantern cross, and has in its town hall a little museum in which we found an ancient canoe dug up last century at Whettall Moss, and a fine English cup with seven handles which has been recovered from Cole Mere. Ellesmere has a high name in education, for not only has it one of the well-known Woodard schools, but also a college for girls. The Woodard school is housed in a striking block of buildings, and is run on the lines of the three colleges in Sussex founded by Canon Woodard in the middle of last century.

Lord Herbert's Village

EYTON-ON-SEVERN. A tiny hamlet nearly two miles south of Roman Wroxeter it has little but the memory of a famous man. Here was born Lord Herbert of Cherbury, a learned and accomplished figure in the England of the first Stuarts. Diplomatist, philosopher, and historian, he became the close friend of Ben Jonson, suffering imprisonment in France when he helped the Protestants, and in England because he spoke out for the king in Parliament. The modern hall, approached by an avenue of walnuts and chestnuts, stands where his birthplace stood.

EYTON-ON-THE-WEALD-MOORS. It lies among the wild moors north of Wellington with a small church rebuilt in the first half of the 18th century. But still working in its tower is a 200-year-old clock, and still in its windows ard two fragments of Tudor glass, one of St Catherine with her wheel and the other of St Christopher with the Christ-child. There are brass tablets to the Eytons of Shropshire, one of whom was the antiquarian Robert William Eyton, famous last century as an authority on Domesday Book and Norman England.

The village children of this small place come to school in a black and white building partly from the 16th century.

FARLOW. Half of it clusters round the church and half round the old smithy, with about a mile between. From the churchyard are grand views of Titterstone, Abdon Burf, the Wrekin, and all the slumbering meadows. We come into the church under the Norman arch of the south doorway, which has capitals carved like owls and three rows of carving. There is a plain font, probably 12th century, and an Elizabethan silver chalice.

The Rector Craftsman

FITZ. We were privileged to meet here a true descendant of our medieval craftsmen, one who beautified this church, the rector Waldegrave Brewster, who in his younger days did the very fine carving in wood and stone at Middleton-in-Chirbury. We found him in his charming rectory with the work of his hands all about him, chairs and chests and dressers made lovely by his genius. He had been rector 36 years, and he talked to us from a wonderful oak rocking chair which he had made in his forties to give him rest as he neared his nineties. Almost unique it seemed to us, an ingenious composition of four great snakes, grandly carved. All who peep inside the church will notice his handsome bench-ends, fashioned as a Jacobean carver might have done them. Much of the building is 200 years old, but it stands on the foundations of a Norman church, and keeps some worn medieval tiles by its modern font. A Norman capital serves as a piscina in the south aisle. The spacious chancel was designed by Sir Aston Webb and has a massive screen. Some attractive glass to a soldier of the Great War shows Christ in Glory, Peter and Paul, and two bishops.

Hardly anything in Fitz is more charming than the approach to it through a wooded glen; but the village has kept its Elizabethan manor with a black and white front and 17th century panelled rooms.

In the Green Hollow

FORD. It has a lovely valley of its own scooped out at the mouth of a brook hurrying to the Severn. The church stands on high ground with the house bigger than itself, both perched above the little stone bridge and a black and white house. By the bridge, in the bottom of the green hollow, four lanes meet.

Except for its wall the neat church was made almost new last century, but we come into it by a Norman doorway, and there is a

priest's doorway 700 years old. Its finest possession is the beautiful
black and white single hammerbeamed roof; it is one of the most
charming roofs with quatrefoils we have seen, and comes from
the 15th century. So does most of the simple chancel screen, and the
reading desk between two of the traceried bays. The oak reredos has
carved Jacobean panels and four figures probably older, one holding
a globe and a sword, one a church, one a skull, and the fourth pulling
a goose out of a tower. There are two Jacobean chairs with carved
backs. The east window has fine glass of the Crucifixion and the
west window an attractive Nativity. One peace memorial is to nine
men who did not come back, and the other to a boy killed while
leading his platoon in France. There is a slender cross to their
memory near the bridge.

A Hero of India

FRODESLEY. A lonely little hamlet with lovely views of the
hills, it is on Watling Street and has seen the Romans. Its
church was mostly built soon after Trafalgar, and is perhaps the
third to be raised here since the Normans came. Neat and homely it
is inside, with a tiny gallery, a panelled pulpit, and box-pews of
which some are old. One of the treasures is an Elizabethan chalice,
but a greater treasure is a fine register said to be the oldest in
Shropshire. It goes back to 1547, and is so perfect still that the
earliest entries can be easily read. With it is the will of a 14th
century rector.

We find memorials here to the Edwardes family, but we look in
vain for a tribute to the greatest of them, Sir Herbert Edwardes,
remembered in Indian history as the hero of Multan, whose signal
service to his country was to secure the neutrality of Afghanistan
during the Mutiny. His chief, Sir Henry Lawrence, said that since
the days of Clive no man had done as Edwardes and his manifold
services to India have won him a well-deserved place on the Empire
roll of fame. Sir Herbert Edwardes was born at the rectory, and as a
child must have noticed the old font still in the garden, for it came
from an earlier church. There is another old font outside the church.

A mile from the village stands an Elizabethan house now a farm.
It has high stone gables, ornamental chimneys, and a semicircular
tower; and among the fine trees on the hillside below is a splendid
oak with a trunk six feet thick.

Kneeling Warrior

GLAZELEY. Its best possession is the 16th century brass in its refashioned church, engraved with the portrait of Thomas Wylde, who must have been a man of importance in this lovely countryside by the Severn. He wears elaborate dress, and his wife is richly clad beside him, with four sons, two daughters, and three shields of arms. One of the heroes of the village is remembered in a window with a warrior kneeling at the feet of Our Lord; it is in memory of Lieutenant Philip Crooke who fell in Palestine, and has a rainbow of celestial beings behind and bright flowers and butterflies in the foreground, with a child angel above. The colours are soft, and the effect at a distance is rather like looking at a rainbow. Another window has a Nativity with hosts of angels.

An ancient stone coffin lies in the churchyard, where two yews have been growing for more than two centuries. Set on a little lawn in the village is a granite obelisk with a globe at the top; it is the peace-memorial and has on it the names of the Fallen and the words, Courage, Endurance, Cheerfulness, Prowess.

Yews of the Centuries

GREAT HANWOOD. Its cross of peace is by the highway, and its church has a pulpit and a fine lectern in memory of two who gave their lives for England. There is Elizabethan panelling in the chancel, two carved chairs perhaps from the same time, old baluster rails, and a little stool of 1683 said to be made from a font cover. But the oldest possession is the round bowl of the font, fashioned 800 years ago in Norman England. The church is sheltered by many old yews higher than itself, one with a fine ribbed trunk.

The Abbey Bell

GREAT NESS. Halfway between Oswestry and Shrewsbury, it has a great house in a lovely park, an ancient church with something from nearly all the centuries, and a medieval churchyard cross with the shaft broken off. The Saxons built a church here, but it is not their masonry we see. The nave is 700 years old. One of its doorways is now blocked up; in the other, an oddly shaped entrance, is a fine studded door of 1618, carved with leaves and a rose, and swinging on two old hinges. The chancel is 14th century.

The church is charming inside, with rosy walls setting off the black and white nave roof, built with heavy timbers by 15th century carpenters. The neat pews and the gallery are 18th century; two chairs and the altar rails are Jacobean; and there is a very old chest with a panelled top. The font and the lectern are tributes to two parsons. From the 14th century tower six bells ring out, one in memory of a soldier of the Great War and his father, and another in memory of a vicar and a schoolmaster. A third is 300 years old; but the most interesting is a bell about 500 years old said to have come from Valle Crucis Abbey in North Wales. On it are grotesque figures, the Sign of the Cross, and heads of Henry the Sixth and his queen.

The Old, Old Man

GREAT WOLLASTON. In a cottage of this tiny village at the foot of the hills, just off the busy road running into Wales, was born a boy who grew up to be an old, old man and to be buried in Westminster Abbey. The memory of him is the one interesting possession of the little church here, which was made new in 1788 and has a fine portrait engraved on a brass plate with the head and shoulders of a bearded man in a pointed hat, buttoned coat, and wide collar. This is what it says:

> The Old, Old, very Old Man Thomas Parr,
> was born at Glyn in the year of Our Lord 1483. He lived
> in the reigns of ten kings and queens of England: Edward 4,
> Edward 5, Richard 3, Henry 7 and 8, Edward 6, Queen Mary,
> Queen Elizabeth, James 1, Charles 1; Died the 13th, and was
> buried in Westminster Abbey . . . aged 152 years and 9 months.

Old Parr is said to be the oldest Englishman who ever lived, and yet he was only just born in England, for the Welsh border is a quarter of a mile beyond Glyn, which we see on the hills from Wollaston. His timbered and thatched cottage still stands at Glyn attracting many travellers who believe the story of Old Parr. We need not believe it, for there is no evidence of the date of his birth, but this is the tale as it has been told for many generations, and as it is accepted in Westminster Abbey (place of great credulity).

He told King Charles that he went out to service at 17, returning here at his father's death 18 years later to farm the little family holding, and that his lease was renewed by four generations of the

Porter family. He married first at 80, and had two children, who died in infancy; and, left a widower, he married a second wife when he was 122. He was 30 years older when the second Earl of Arundel discovered him, and carried him in easy stages by litter to London to see the King and the Court.

Remarking that he had lived longer than any other man in the land, Charles Stuart asked him what he had done more than other men. "I did penance in the church when I was 100 years old," answered the unblushing veteran.

Old Parr became the wonder of the town, and was shown daily at a hotel in the Strand; but, accustomed to plain fare and the healthy life of the country, he quickly succumbed to the confinement and rich diet of his London life. He died in November 1635 and William Harvey, discoverer of the circulation of the blood, examined the body before its burial, declaring all the organs healthy, those of a vigorous man who had died through substituting the air of the city for that of salubrious Shropshire.

There are many portraits of Parr, mostly imaginary. The story of the veteran's immense age stirred the imagination of William Blake, who painted him, but not as an ancient; he pictured Old Parr as a man of 40. Parr is one of a number of rustics to whom great length of days has been ascribed. Their births were not registered; only the record of their death was kept. It was easy for a veteran, vain, and profited by his tale of years, to ante-date his birth, first by a score of years and then by half a century, for he could not be contradicted and there were no documents to challenge his claim.

The Chimney Stairs

GREET. From farms and houses scattered among the border hills its people come to a little church which has been receiving them for 700 years. It is cosy and trim, with candlelight for winter evenings, and sunlight streaming through charming lancets. Some of the masonry has been made new, but much is as the 13th century builders left it. A rare possession is a two-light window of oak, believed to be 500 years old, and with a bracket for a statue in its splay. There is an ancient font with a Jacobean cover, an old panelled pulpit, and a tablet to two men who gave their lives for the peace of the world.

Close by stands Greet Court, mostly of the 17th century, with mellow brickwork and timbers. It has a big chimney perhaps older still, with a little hiding-place lit by a window.

A mile to the west is Stoke House, standing at a corner of the road, a pretty Tudor home with a staircase in a chimney.

Flowers in the Old Font

GRINSHILL. It nestles under a steep hill with wooded slopes, a quarry at the top curiously reminding us of the head of a sheep. In the village is a Jacobean house, The Grange, to which the scholars of Shrewsbury would come when plague drove them out of town.

Most of the church is 19th century, but it has Norman masonry in two walls, with the old windows and great queer heads under the gables. The east window is brilliant with the three figures of the Crucifixion, standing out against diamond panes of clear glass; and in other windows are tiny panels of foreign glass about 300 years old, each showing a robed figure out-of-doors. The screen is a good example of modern woodwork, and so are the pews with carvings of emblems and leaves, and such devices as a pelican and a maze.

In the churchyard are two things from the 18th century, a fluted font bowl within which flowers grow, and a sundial on the shaft of a medieval cross.

HABBERLEY. It lies among green hills with a group of farms and cottages, an old church much restored, a black and white rectory, and a 17th century manor house with two projecting gables of timber and one of stone. The plain little church has a shapely yew for company, throwing its shade over one of two Norman doorways. There is an aumbry under an Elizabethan window in the chancel. The manor house was the home of William Mytton, an 18th century historian of the county who died here in 1746.

Right-Hand Man at Waterloo

HADNALL. It is the sleeping-place of one who played his part in the making of English history, Wellington's right-hand man at Waterloo, General Rowland Hill. Though the house in which he died has gone, the wooded grounds of Hardwicke Grange are still to be seen outside the village; and here under the church tower he lies, with a monument near the screen. The sculptor has fashioned a Lifeguardsman leaning on his carbine, a shepherd with a crook, and the British lion between them; and carved with the General's arms are his three orders and six medals.

Parts of the church were rebuilt 600 years ago, but it has kept two Norman doorways all the time. The tower and chancel are 19th century, the tower having the stones of an old house whose moat is near a delightful roadside pool. The church porch has some ancient woodwork, and there is much handsome modern woodwork including a hammerbeam roof in the nave. Two Jacobean chairs stand in the chancel. The font came here from Malta and is adorned with lilies, its oak cover being carved to match.

Among several good windows is one of Peter and Paul, and another of John the Baptist and James in memory of James Bibby who built the fine tower and spire at Clive. The east window, with its brilliant angels adoring, is to John Peel who died at Black Birches, a lovely timbered house in a park near Hardwicke Grange. There is a tablet in medieval style to one who was rector for 52 years.

Near the churchyard gate lies old Charles Hulbert of 1857, who was first a cotton-spinner and then a keen antiquarian. Having seen his house and writings destroyed by fire, he began afresh and set up a printing works of his own, building cottages for his men and writing as hard as they could print. His books are standard works on the history of Shropshire.

Rowland Hill, one of three famous bearers of that name, nephew of one and no kinsman of the other, was Wellington's right-hand man in the overthrow of Napoleon. The soldier's uncle was the famous preacher; the Penny Post man was of another family.

Born in 1772 at Prees Hall near Hawkstone, he was one of 16 children, of whom five brothers served in the Army. He distinguished himself at the siege of Toulon and in the Egyptian expedition of 1800. Between intervals of active service he was in Scotland and Ireland raising and disciplining men with whom he was to win fame. Throughout the Peninsular War he was the mainstay of Wellington. He was with Sir John Moore at Corunna, where he saw the last of the wounded aboard before embarking himself, an act which brought him honour from Parliament, and a statue at Shrewsbury rivalling Nelson's in Trafalgar Square. During the campaign of 1811 he won a magnificent victory over the French, effected by a night march through storm and mire, to attack in the morning while his High-

White Mere

Cole Mere

SHROPSHIRE'S LAKE DISTRICT, ELLESMERE

The Medieval Church and Ellesmere House

The Canal linking the Severn and the Mersey

ELLESMERE—CENTRE OF SHROPSHIRE'S LAKE DISTRICT

landers piped, "Hey Johnny Cope, are ye waking yet?" and leading to a great haul of prisoners with the entire camp equipment. Another triumph, entirely his own, was the victory of Almarez, which brought him a peerage. He added to his laurels at Vittoria, at the passage of the Nive, at Orthez, and at Toulouse, each a vital blow to Napoleon.

During the Hundred Days of 1815 Hill was early in the field again, helping to lay the foundation of the final victory to come. At Waterloo he covered the right wing of the general line, and when Napoleon's Imperial Guard made its charge he placed himself at the head of his troops and led the crucial attack on the enemy flank. His horse shot under him, he was down and lost for a quarter of an hour and given up for dead. Second in command to Wellington during the occupation of Paris, he exercised over the victorious troops the moderating influence characteristic of him at all times. During Wellington's Premiership he was general commanding-in-chief, and under successive ministries he presided at the Horse Guards. He died in 1842, and among his bequests were annuities to three men charged with the upkeep of his remarkable monument at Shrewsbury, one of the highest columns in the Western countryside.

Old Doorway and Old Window

HALFORD. The great wheel of its old mill no longer turns, but the beautiful work of a Norman craftsman is still seen here as it has been seen by worshippers for 800 years. Tall elms shelter the church, and a vigorous yew has grown to be more than 20 feet round; but the touch of beauty all will admire is the lily ornament on the Norman doorway in the porch. A little window to the west is Norman too, and probably the tapering bowl of the font.

From the churchyard we see the towers and roofs of the delightful little Stokesay Castle; and a handsome lychgate is here to remind us, in simple, touching words, of a husband and "the other dear lads" who gave their lives for England.

Precious Silver

HARLEY. It is memorable for the entrancing view of the wooded slope of Wenlock Edge from the porch of its church, for the treasures in the church, and for the timbered cottages. Near the village the site of a Roman villa has been traced, and there is a tower of an ancient windmill. The old chancel and nave of the church have been transformed, but the crude Norman font is here, and a fine little 15th century chest with iron bands. Very precious, too, is the silver paten, 500 years old or more, with an engraved head of Christ and a little flower on either side. With it is an Elizabethan silver chalice. The east window has three panels of old glass with the Salutation, the Nativity, and the Presentation in the Temple. In the 15th century tower is an unnamed brass of a man in armour, with his wife, eight sons, and five daughters in civilian dress; it is thought to be the memorial of Sir Richard Lacon, Sheriff of Shropshire in 1477. Benjamin Jenks, rector here for 56 years, out of the 17th into the 18th century, has a tablet; he wrote numerous prayers and meditations.

Old England in a Field

HEATH. We found ourselves in a snowstorm in a lonely place and sheltered in a building set in a field. These sheltering walls have stood 800 years and, save for a change in a window, the centuries have not touched them.

Heath Chapel is perhaps the humblest piece of Norman England that Shropshire has, but how thrilling is its simplicity! Within these walls have worshipped 25 generations of village folk living about a few farms and cottages in this rural solitude. Little has changed through all the years while Brown Clee Hill has looked down from its peak 1790 feet above the sea. It is but a nave and chancel. The only artist who has been this way was the Norman mason who made the only doorway the church has, and gave it a good round arch enriched with chevron and roll mouldings, a plain tympanum, and two shafts on each side. But perhaps we should remember, too, the craftsman who made the crescent hinges on the old oak door.

Except for these things the little church is plain and primitive. The high stout walls are all askew and have the shallow, flat buttresses of very early days. A plain stringcourse runs round inside and out, and there are a few narrow Norman windows. The east end has three of them and the west wall has three; the nave had three, but one has been made square and big to give the parson light in his pulpit. It is perhaps the only alteration that has been made in these thick and ancient walls. Two of the windows pierce the buttresses, one to light the altar and one at the west end.

The place has been whitewashed inside and is clearly not rich enough to make itself beautiful, but it has a quaintness and the feeling of age. The Norman font, like a tub, stands on two great blocks. The plain chancel arch stands with its stepped stones as the builders left it, two shafts with faintly scalloped capitals at each side. The chancel has a low stone tomb with a worn cross, and above the tomb is a square aumbry. The walls have fading traces of frescoes.

The pulpit is the familiar two-decker of the 17th century and there are box-pews from the same days; but were ever such pews as the one in the east and the one in the west? The one in the east fills one side of the chancel, a Jacobean box-pew in front, a heavy bench behind it, both looking like some primitive box carriage with the driver's seat behind. The crude seats at the back, with three tiny benches, seem to have been made for children, and their timbers can hardly be less than a thousand years old. There are railings round three sides of the altar, relics of hat pegs on the walls, and four little paraffin lamps; and there is a toy harmonium from Chicago, with three octaves! One small record the church has on the walls; it tells us that Dr Algernon Langston Oldham helped nobly with raising the money to repair this place, and preached his last sermon here at the opening in October 1912.

It is believed that a moated manor house stood in the field to the east of the church; the mounds in the field may mark where it stood, but they are all that is left of the old companion of this little church. Simple and alone, it carries on the old tale of Old England.

A Saxon Horseman

HIGH ERCALL. Its great tower, begun by the Normans and finished by the 15th century men, has on it the mark of a cannon ball fired in the Civil War, reminding us that here was the last Royalist garrison in Shropshire to fall to Cromwell's men.

The upper part of the tower has a carved frieze, and in one of the walls is a royal horseman set over a Norman opening, interesting because it is perhaps a piece of Saxon carving used by the Norman builders. Another fragment, which may be Saxon, is the narrow tympanum inside the north doorway, its ornament showing a band of stars round a conventional tree.

Much of the church was built again in Restoration times, the architects copying the medieval style, and from that time also comes the double hammerbeam roof of the chancel. But there are Norman arches in the nave, one capital having lovely foliage, and another the heads of a ram and a bull with those of a man and a woman. A 17th century capital has hearts among leaves. In the tower is a priestly figure 700 years old, his robes very well carved, but his head unfortunately gone. Still older in the chancel is a sculpture of a Norman knight in armour, one of his feet resting on a lion. From his belt hangs a small bottle, showing that he had made a pilgrimage.

One of the windows is aglow with the angels appearing to the shepherds; and the 14th century east window shows Christ enthroned with English saints and martyrs, the glass being in memory of the 1300th anniversary of the landing of St Augustine on our shores.

Part of a preaching cross in the churchyard has an 18th century sundial telling the time not only here but at Jerusalem, at Rome, and at Plymouth in New England.

The manor house by the church has a Jacobean arcade of four arches, and standing within its wide dry moat is a handsome gabled farm. In the village are six almshouses founded by Lord Bradford in 1694, the old people still using the original tables, which were made with a low rail to keep their feet out of the rushes on the floor.

In the year 1615 Richard Baxter was baptised here. His father was a man who had been converted from a bad life to a good one, and found it difficult to secure a satisfactory teaching for his son.

The Six Trees

HIGHLEY. It is a mining village by the Severn, but it has some ancient and beautiful things. There is a fine old timbered house by the church, and in the vicar's garden is a tulip tree about 40 feet high, one of the biggest and oldest in England. Keeping it company are six old hornbeam trees cut into the shape of the seven-branched candlestick of Jerusalem. There is a fine medieval cross in the churchyard, with queer heads at the corners and cable moulding at the base. The church has one Norman window in the nave and another in the chancel. We come into it by the original door, still swinging on its old hinges and opened with its old iron ring. The nave roof is 16th century and has 33 oak bosses finely carved with Tudor flowers and other devices. We noticed a tablet to a churchwarden for 60 years, William Jordin.

HINSTOCK. Its church is typical of Dr Johnson's England, with pews and a panelled pulpit of the 18th century, and no chancel. A memorial with three cherubs tells of a rector's daughter who died as a girl in 1715, and a vivid wall-painting of last century shows the visit of the Wise Men. The tower is 17th century, and so are three chairs and a panel in the lectern.

A Bishop and His Brother

HODNET. Old and beautiful, it has kept traces of a fortified site used in turn by Britons and Romans, Saxons and Normans. It has groups of Elizabethan houses at the crossroads, a lovely avenue leading to its hall, and a church magnificent with a tower 600 years old.

We think here of two brothers celebrated about a century ago, Bishop Heber and Richard Heber, the first living at the rectory and preaching from the 18th century pulpit still used in the church, the second revelling in the books he had collected on his travels, and visiting London as one of the founders of the Athenaeum Club. He was a great collector, and had three copies of most books, one to use, one to lend, and one in reserve; and he actually left behind him three libraries. A lamp-post at the crossroads reminds us that the bishop lived here; and we think of Richard as we look at the hall, a splendid building designed by John Nash's pupil Anthony Salvin, whose work is in Windsor Castle. In the park are a 17th century barn and dovecot.

Both brothers must have loved this ancient place, and both are remembered in it, Richard having a big monument on the wall, and the bishop a medallion portrait by Chantrey. Close by in the chapel is the lovely tomb of the bishop's grand-daughter, Blanche Heber Percy, her figure sculptured by her cousin Reginald Cholmondeley, who carved a monument in Condover church. Hanging on the wall is the armour of one of the Vernons, who were lords of the manor, and an Elizabethan memorial with three cherubs tells of the last of them, Henrietta Vernon, through whom the Hebers came to Hodnet.

Other monuments on these walls are to the Hills, Richard who was a statesman in Queen Anne's reign, Sir Rowland of 1783, and Sir Richard who is remembered for his controversial writings. A strong supporter of George Whitefield and other evangelical preachers, he defended six undergraduates who had been expelled from Oxford for adopting Methodism, and made his first speech in Parliament in support of a Bill for the Better Regulation of the Sabbath.

Worthy of its great men is this old church in which we think of them. Its parson comes in through a Norman doorway, and its people open a door 200 years old with ironwork older still. Outside the low window of the chancel is a stepping stone for those who would peep inside. There is a Tudor chest with three locks, and a splendid Norman font whose panels are carved with beasts and birds, underneath being a band of carving with heads. Traces of Norman windows and arches are still to be seen in the south wall of the nave.

From the hands of Jacobean craftsmen come panels and arches now used in the reredos, an almsbox asking us to Remember The Poore, a chair, and a desk containing many old chained books. Among them are a manuscript missal, an illustrated Bible printed only six years after Caxton's death at Nuremberg, Erasmus's New Testament of 1522, and John Garbrand's edition of his friend Bishop Jewel's attack on the Papal Bull in 1582.

Among the richly wooded sandstone hills two miles away stands Hawkstone Hall, now a college, near it being a tall column; a statue of a 16th century Sir Rowland Hill the first Protestant Lord Mayor of London, once crowned it, but had been brought down by a storm when we called. In the park are fragments of a castle built 700 years ago, a Giant's Cave cut in the solid rock to a depth of 100 feet, a grotto, and another cavern where one of the Hills is said to have hidden in the Civil War. So impressed was Dr Johnson by a visit to Hawkstone that he wrote afterwards of the awfulness of its shades, the horrors of its precipices, and the loftiness of its rocks. A walk here, he said, was an adventure; to leave this place was an escape.

Three miles to the west of Hodnet is one of the oldest relics hereabouts, known as the Bury Walls, a prehistoric camp with triple ramparts enclosing about twenty acres.

Treasure Above Corve Dale

HOLDGATE. The plain little village is set on a hill above Corve Dale, and is crowned by a red-roofed church standing out finely as we see it from the valley road, its sturdy tower a landmark for miles. The tower is 13th century at the bottom and 15th at the top, its pinnacles carved with panels, crude crosses, and knotwork, and its stringcourse adorned with queer heads.

One of the two rich possessions of the church is a fine Norman doorway with three rich mouldings in the arch, one chevron, one wrapped with flowers, the third with beakheads and grotesques. The hood-mould is a medley of pellets, hearts, and projecting points: there are two slender shafts each side, and a little man's head in a leaf in one of the capitals. The second treasure here is a unique Norman font with a round bowl. Round the rim is roll and cable moulding; round the bottom of the bowl is stem and foliage: while the surface between the two is a curious medley of knotwork, bands of nailhead, a circle, a cross, a tree, wriggling serpents, and a bird upside down. The stem is carved with zigzag and heads.

Bare inside, the church is not without charm. In modern glass in the east window we see Mary and the Child in blue and white, with Christ risen in red and white. The west end has the best window and the fine font, and an unusual arrangement of the wall of the tower, which has an odd doorway with a flat arch at one side, a large pointed peephole at the other, and a deeply splayed Norman window between them. Much old work remains in the oak pews, some of the seats and backs perhaps 14th century and some of the doors 17th. Against the south wall are two 17th century canopied oak seats with three pillars, arcaded backs, and a cornice of berries. On a windowsill is an old miserere carved with griffins at each side, and two huge griffins under the seat biting and clawing each other.

Built into the outside wall of the chancel is a stone carved with the head and shoulders of a human figure, and on what is left of the old churchyard cross is a sundial.

Near the church is a high artificial mound, and beyond it are the remains of a castle mentioned in Domesday Book. It belonged to a Norman baron and was called Holdgate Castle after him. Only the lower part of a tower remains, having been built into an ancient farmhouse. There are traces of mounds and of the moat, which have survived the destruction of the Civil War.

Into the Haven

HOPE. It lies in a wooded vale, set charmingly between the hills, with one of Shropshire's loveliest valley roads winding above a stream. Its houses are tucked into the hillside, and its little 19th century church stands among trees and banks of bracken. The church has a few fragments of old tracery in its pulpit and pews, and a little copper plaque of the Madonna in memory of a child only a day old. The peace memorial is the organ, on which we see an Elizabethan ship making for port, with these words to 21 who died:

They are glad because they are at rest, so He bringeth them into the haven where they would be.

Lying almost across the river, just below the village, is a huge boulder of interest to geologists; and about the countryside are many signs of our prehistoric ancestors. There are signs also of old lead mines worked in Roman days, and relics have been found such as wooden spades and pigs of lead with ancient stamps.

The Monster Yew

HOPE BAGGOT. Its few houses are hidden in deep-cut lanes on the slope of Clee Hill. Its church stands high in a churchyard beautiful with flowers, apple trees and cherry trees sharing the glory of the setting with a border of lace-like firs, and a grand gnarled monster of a yew grappling the steep bank, full of years and vigour, its trunk 23 feet round. By the churchyard runs a wayside stream, and across the way the water of a holy well falls from a rock. To this well came pilgrims from afar, believing that the water had power to restore lost sight.

The tower, with a modern shingled roof just clearing the nave, has been a hillside beacon for 700 years; and older still are two great millstones built into its base. The porch as we see it is modern, but the splendid timbers of its seats and arches were set up as a lychgate 600 years ago. In the porch is a simple Norman doorway.

The splendid possession of the church is the small but massive chancel arch of the Normans, its great thickness lightened by shafts with cushioned capitals, by chevron moulding, and by stones with star pattern which continues beyond the arch across the east end of the nave.

There is a narrow Norman window in the nave, and another in the chancel with an aumbry below it. In the wide splay of a window 700 years old are two seats for priests and a shaft piscina. The curious font, looking like one shallow bowl set in another, is believed to be Norman; the altar table, the nave roof, and the panelled pulpit are Jacobean. A chancel tablet tells how Benjamin Giles, at the age of 31, was "snatched away from his parents, in consequence of a fall from his horse, by the irresistible call of the King of Terrors."

HOPE BOWDLER. Its houses are dotted about the slopes and hollows, and the little modern church looks down the narrowing valley. Coming to it by a tunnel of Irish yews, we find a building with all the charm of simplicity, built in the style of the 13th century with many lancet windows. A fine gallery of modern glass includes the Madonna and Andrew and John, as well as the Good Shepherd, a fine figure of Our Lord on the Mount, and His appearance to the disciples by the sea. The parson preaches from a richly carved pulpit 300 years old; and there is a handsome chest of the same age. Older still are the Elizabethan chalice and a medieval bell.

In Cypress Shade

HOPESAY. It lies in a quiet corner among the hills, the church and rectory charmingly set in a little group of houses. A fine old lychgate with four gables opens on to a churchyard bordered by roses and cypress trees, the trees higher than the church.

The church is of many centuries, aisleless, reached through a Norman doorway sheltered by a 17th century porch. The massive tower was begun in the 13th century and crowned by a wooden turret in the 17th; the priest's doorway is also 13th century, as is the simple chancel arch. The old studded door still swings in the Norman doorway, bringing us into a dim interior.

On the walls are two mosaics of Paul with his sword and Mary with the crown of thorns, a woman comforting her. Two of the windows are in memory of very old ladies, one of St Elizabeth with a child under her cloak, the other with a fine figure in a red robe and a blue cloak in memory of a lady of 97.

The glory of the old woodwork is in the medieval roof of the nave, but there is also fine carving in the pulpit, the altar, and the reredos, and Jacobean panels in the benches of the choir-stalls. The pulpit has a charming little figure of Mary under a canopy, and under five canopies in the reredos are saints, angels, and a scene of Bethlehem.

There are two round stone houses in the village, of which the only criticism we heard was that it was awkward to fit in square furniture!

A mile away at Aston-on-Clun an old elm stands at a point where five ways meet, and we found it gay with flags which are renewed every 29th of May in memory of a marriage here in the 18th century, wedding gaiety long continued.

The Brave Little Garrison

HOPTON CASTLE. Set in a hollow among the hills, it has a fine black and white house which was once the rectory, but its chief sight is the ruined castle at a lonely corner of the village. Here are the gaunt walls of a sturdy keep, some of it perhaps as old as the 12th century and some about 200 years younger, with little window openings and a fine gateway; and here it was, in the Civil War, that a little company of Cromwell's men held out against Royalist attacks for three weeks. Their commander refused quarter when he was offered it, and, by the rules of war in those days, nearly all the brave little garrison were put to death when the end came.

The village church is modern, and has rich ornament on its pulpit, and on the corbels of the chancel arch. Two chairs are 18th century.

The Peace They Left Behind

HOPTON WAFERS. It lies in a delightful valley below the Clee Hills, with some fine old houses and a church made new last century. Remote and quiet, the memorial to its heroes tells of 21 sons of the village who lost their lives in five countries during the war, and of another drowned at sea. The church has 15th century glass of a small angel with flowing hair and wings of gold in the west window, and a modern east window of Christ walking on the sea. The chancel has a delicately carved marble monument by E. H. Baily, RA, one of the ablest sculptors of the Victorian Era, showing Thomas Botfield, of Hopton Court, reclining on a couch and pointing to Heaven, the drooping figure of his wife beside him. There are two beautiful old chairs, and in the chancel is an open book of stone with the Ten Commandments painted on it. The oak triptych, with its paintings of the Crucifixion, the traceried screen, and the gallery with vine carving are all modern.

Windows of Memory

HORDLEY. A cluster of farms and cottages, with an ivied church which has a Norman past, it rests among little rolling hills, and looks out to the sterner splendours of the distant heights of Wales. Near the church is a farmhouse with the remains of the hall, the old home of the Kynastons. In the turret over the timbered gable are two bells which have been ringing since before the Reformation. There is Norman masonry in some of the walls, and a built-up Norman doorway has still a head at either side. The altar table and two chairs in the chancel are Jacobean. Two windows are in memory of a rector and his wife, his with a Good Shepherd, hers designed to remind us that she never refused aid and comfort to the poor, and was a devoted friend of animals. In her charming window are the Madonna in blue and white, St Martin dividing his purple cloak, and St Francis with his little friends the birds and animals, among them a mouse at his feet.

The Major's Leap

HUGHLEY. A lovely village under Wenlock Edge, we come to its 14th century church thinking of A. E. Housman's lines in A Shropshire Lad, where the poet tells how

> *The vane on Hughley steeple*
> *Veers bright, a far-known sign,*
> *And there lie Hughley people,*
> *And there lie friends of mine.*
>
> *To north, to south, lie parted,*
> *With Hughley tower above,*
> *The kind, the single-hearted,*
> *The lads I used to love.*
>
> *And, south or north, tis only*
> *A choice of friends one knows,*
> *And I shall ne'er be lonely*
> *Asleep with these or those.*

Much is there to see in this ancient place, with its little steeple of 1701 and its gable cross above an east window magnificently moulded. From the 13th century it has kept an altar stone with five consecration crosses; from the 14th a pillar piscina and a corbel thought to represent Edward the Third's Queen Philippa in her crown and wimple; and from the 15th a panelled roof with tiny carved bosses, and old glass showing animals, foliage, and figures including the Madonna and Child. The screen is one of the most beautiful in Shropshire, exquisite with grapes and flowers and birds carved by the 15th century craftsmen.

There is a long medieval chest, an elaborate Jacobean pulpit, and a Jacobean chair with a figure holding a cross and a book. A window showing Christ appearing to Mary Magdalene is in memory of a benefactor of the church (the fourth Earl of Bradford, who died in 1915). It was his father, the third Earl, who gave the fine clock when his horse Sir Hugo won the Derby in 1892.

Lying in the sanctuary is William Corfil of the 18th century, whose gravestone tells us that he died by the hand of a hidden assassin. The village remembers a less tragic little adventure at the rock called Major's Leap, from which, in the Civil War, a Royalist major named Smallman sprang off with his horse and escaped his pursuers. The horse was killed, but the major saved himself by seizing hold of a crab tree.

Many-Sided Mainwaring

IGHTFIELD. Looking out on beautiful views, its churchyard has an old cross and is watched over by a 15th century tower with four fine gargoyles. The church has an aisle roof enriched with various devices popular 500 years ago, a medieval chest eight feet long, and a window with two great lions as stops; but chief among its possessions are two exceptional brasses. One of 1509 shows Dame Margery Calveley with her children under a triple canopy, a scroll running from her mouth with a prayer to John the Baptist, who is shown above with a quaint headdress. The other brass is a portrait of her father William Maynwaring, dressed in a fur-lined cloak and standing on a flowery mound. He was a benefactor of the church.

More than 150 years later there was born here the poet Arthur Mainwaring, who went to Shrewsbury School and won for himself a small fortune with his very first poem, Tarquin and Tullia, a satire on William and Mary which was taken to be the work of Dryden. He wrote a vigorous defence of Marlborough, but it is as editor and author of The Medley, which he brought out as a rival of The Examiner, that his name lives. When these two papers ceased Jonathan Swift wrote that Grub Street was dead. Steele owed much to Arthur Mainwaring, and dedicated the first number of the Tatler to him.

A Surprise for Robert Stephenson

IRONBRIDGE. Here the Severn flows through a deep gorge and the town clusters crazily on steep limestone cliffs, looking for all the world as if it might fall into the river any moment. The spoiler has been at his worst in this once lovely spot, and the industrial revolution has made its melancholy mark on a fair landscape; but here is always the beauty of the river, flowing swift and silent. The chief distinction of the town is its bridge, believed to be the first iron bridge ever built, as big a wonder in its day as John Wilkinson's iron boat, which was launched not far away at Broseley. It was built by Abraham Darby of Coalbrookdale in 1777. The bridge is 196 feet long, with one span of 100 feet and two smaller ones, the total weight of iron being about 380 tons. Long after it was completed it won the praise of Robert Stephenson, who was surprised by this development of the iron industry and thought the manipulation of cast iron, then in its infancy, a bold undertaking in a bridge of such dimensions.

A Tragic Testament

KEMBERTON. It is high and lonely, with a view of the Wrekin and the Clee Hills and a wide expanse of wooded country seen over the old clipped yews in the rectory garden. One old treasure kept at the rectory is a small silver chalice and paten of 1520, battered a little on its journey through the centuries.

When the new church was built last century some medieval tiles were unearthed, and reproductions of them are in the floors of nave and chancel, with pictures of a man blowing a horn and a stag with dogs.

The modern stone reredos is in 14th century style, its canopies sheltering a delicate portrayal of the Ascension and four saints; and the pulpit has a figure of St John. The Crucifixion scene in the east window with the two Marys, Christ enthroned above, is a memorial to a rector's son killed in the war.

Kemberton church has a peace memorial tablet, and a Book of Memory, illuminated in medieval style, bidding us remember the love of them who came not back from the war. It contains records of them all, telling of what they did here, how they sang in the choir and tended the fields or minded horses, until they went, in their youth, to the great slaughter. It is a lovely but tragic testament.

The Three Alisons

KENLEY. From its churchyard we see the Welsh mountains, and from the low tower of its little 13th century church we see part of Watling Street in the valley to the north. The church has 500-year-old beams in the roof, and a two-decker pulpit made by

Jacobean craftsmen. Also Jacobean are a chair in the chancel and the carving on the priest's desk. A tablet tells of Archibald Alison, who was rector at the end of the 18th century, and became known as the writer of Essays on Taste, but is still better known as the father of two sons who were boys together at the rectory across the road.

The father became minister of a church in Edinburgh, thinking that there he could give his sons a better chance in life. Although, as one of his sons said, he "had not enough of the devil in him to find the devil out," many of his sermons were masterly, and Lord Brougham thought his sermon on Autumn one of the finest pieces of English composition. One of his two famous sons was Sir Archibald Alison, a shining light of the legal profession but known far beyond its bounds as the author of a History of Europe which became a best-seller. He was highly esteemed as a judge and beloved as a man, and over a hundred thousand people attended his funeral in Glasgow. His brother William is remembered for his great-hearted work in fighting disease among the poor people of Scotland. He brought about a revolution in the system of poor relief in that country, setting it on a State basis and suspending the voluntary system which had caused much suffering and disease in the slums.

The Great Tudor Folk

KINLET. We may owe much of the fame of England to its majestic oaks. We remember that Nelson's right-hand man at Trafalgar, Admiral Collingwood, would write home from his ship and tell them to give a shilling to his old gardener to pop a few acorns in the ground, for he knew not what old England would do if the time came when she had no more oaks for her old walls. Kinlet oaks were prized for building our ancient wooden walls, and still this place is a delight to see with its wooded slopes, and for the great trees in the wooded park about its 18th century hall. We may think the scene as we stand at the church gate a perfect setting for A Midsummer Night's Dream, an expanse of one of our grand old forests not yet spoiled.

It came into history before the Conqueror's Domesday Book, for the Knoll of Kinlet was part of the dowry of the Confessor's wife, King Harold's sister Edith. The church still standing quiet and remote goes back to those far-off days. It has a grand array of monuments, rare old glass, and one of the finest little medieval sculptures. It has a delightful timbered clerestory above the Norman walls of the nave, and there is the hand of the Norman all about—in the fine arcades, and the chancel arch, and in the tympanum of the small 14th century porch with its pointed arch resting on floral capitals. The chancel itself is 14th century, and in the tracery of its east window are small figures in deeply coloured glass which have been here for many generations, some since the church was built. A kneeling knight in armour, St John holding a chalice, and a woman saint, are at least 600 years old, and other old figures are here of a prior and lords of the manor with their heraldic shields. There is more old glass in the transepts, one of the windows having the head of Our Lord surrounded by flowers and grotesque creatures.

The south transept is an unusually complete example of a medieval chantry, having two aumbries and a piscina, and a recess for a tomb; its 600-year-old doorway has ballflower ornament round it. Round the altar are some old tiles. In one of the windows is Tudor glass, and looking down on this ancient place is the remarkable medieval sculpture which serves as a corbel under the east window. It has probably been here 600 years, and represents a seated figure of the Almighty with His Crucified Son between his knees and a small angel kneeling on each side. It is a gem of medieval art.

It is in this chantry also that we find the oldest and most pathetic figure in the church. She is a lady who died in the year of Agincourt, 1415, and secure in the folds of her mantle lies her little one, wrapped in a shroud. The mother was Lady Lychfield and she wears a horned headdress with a sideless bodice and mantle, her head is on a cushion held by angels, a little dog resting at her feet. Angels at her head, a pet at her feet, and a child in her mantle, she is a gracious figure.

There is a striking array of Kinlet's great folk of Tudor days. On a high tomb in the north transept, one of the most imposing Elizabethan monuments in England, kneels Sir George Blount and his wife; he served in the Scottish Wars, and won for himself the name of the Terror of Scotland, but we can hardly believe it looking at him here, a mild-mannered knight with a Bible in his hands, his wife at his side with rings on all her fingers, a prayer book with a long cord, and her favourite little animal resting at her side. Between them kneel a daughter and a curly headed little boy with a skull in his hand in the fashion of the time. He is said to have been choked to death while eating an apple, and was buried in a silver coffin. The great tomb is in two stages, with a series of columns supporting a canopy rich with heraldry; the panelling below is full of canopies and finials, and behind an iron grille is a broken figure which is said to represent the proud warrior knight.

On an imposing tomb of the 15th century lie the alabaster figures of Sir Humphrey Blount in armour, his feet on a lion and his head on a helmet, and his wife at his side. Cherubs support her cushion, a tiny dog peeps from the folds of her mantle, and five of her children are on the enriched sides of the tomb, two small angels keeping them company. Facing them is the tomb of their grandson, Sir John Blount, in his Tudor armour and SS collar, his wife an exquisite figure accompanied by her five sons and six daughters.

Here in the sanctuary is remembered a man who put his name on the map, for the hill where he led the charge of the South African Light Horse is now known as Childe's Hill. The lovely alabaster reredos of Christ the Good Shepherd is in memory of Captain Charles Childe, who fell in South Africa; the sculpture is under a canopy guarded by two angels. There is a tablet of 1824 with a portrait of William Childe, whose exploits as a horseman won for him the title of the Flying Childe, and a brass inscription to another hero of the house who fell for his country at Vimy Ridge in the days when men were really flying over our battlefields.

In the churchyard is the gravestone of a gardener who looked after the gardens of Kinlet Hall for more than half a century, and the curious base of an old cross with four gabled recesses, and standing as high as the porch. It is said to have been here since 1290.

The Strange Text

KINNERLEY. Its low church tower is Elizabethan, with a top added last century, gargoyles and heads looking out from the battlements. Here in the chancel sleeps an old Bishop of Chester, John Bridgeman, with a little brass plate to mark his grave, and a tablet on the wall to his memory. Born under Queen Elizabeth he was one of King James's chaplains, and became bishop in the days when it was a bishop's duty to repress the Nonconformists whose chapels were springing up everywhere. It is to John Bridgeman's

Hopton Castle   **A Village Byway**

Hopton Castle   **The Castle Keep**

Aston Eyre　　　Norman Carving of the Entry into Jerusalem

Lilleshall　　　Arches and Doorway of the Norman Abbey

credit that he disliked this duty; and someone said of him that he "loved neither to threaten nor to strike, but when he did strike he did it as effectually as if he loved it."

The apse chancel has two fine windows showing the Annunciation and the Nativity, the figures being under classical canopies in keeping with the style of the church. In the churchyard a peace memorial cross keeps company with what is left of a medieval cross; and in a garden at West Felton stands the old font, which was rescued when it was cast out of the church. The base may be as old as the 12th century, and on the bowl is a Greek palindrome (reading the same both ways) meaning "Wash not my face alone, but wash my sins as well."

Three Andrews

KINNERSLEY. Great sycamores watch over the gate to its 14th century church, which has a double bellcot unusually placed where the nave and chancel join. The tower was refashioned in 1674, and built into it are a moulded Norman stone and part of a 13th century capital. There is a medieval font. In the fine east window is modern glass showing Our Lord, St Aidan with a book, and St Chad holding a model of Lichfield Cathedral; it is in memory of three Andrews who were vicars from 1841 to 1904, two of them Andrew Burns and one Andrew Ewbank.

Facing the church is a charming black and white cottage, and between another timbered house and the post office is an orchard with a grim past, for it was the burial-ground of the local gallows, reminding us that sheep-stealers must have been numerous on these wide grazing areas of the Weald. Half a mile away, round the buildings of Wall Farm, are earthworks thrown up by some of our earliest ancestors.

Churchyard Walls of Castle Stones

KNOCKIN. A pleasant spot by a busy road, it has a few black and white cottages, a church hidden by trees, and, on a wooded mound, the site of a castle whose stones have fallen from their proud estate.

Knockin Castle was famous when John le Strange set out from here to fight for King John in France and brought home as his bride the widowed Queen of Cyprus. It was still famous two centuries later when the heiress, the beautiful Joan Baroness Strange married a nephew of Warwick the Kingmaker. Another four centuries it stood, and was then pulled down, its stones being used to build the churchyard walls and the little bridge crossing the stream.

The Norman church, which the castle stones now protect, was built 800 years ago as a chapel to the fortress it has outlasted. It has kept its tall and massive Norman font, a striking doorway with zigzag and leafy capitals through which the Norman priest would pass, and (built into the nave wall) four arches and pillars of a Norman arcade which once led to an aisle. The black and white roof is the work of Jacobean craftsmen.

In the porch are the names of all who went from here to help in the war; one was Captain Edward Walker, the parson's son, who joining up on the second day, served in Gallipoli, Egypt, and Palestine, and fell in action in 1917. He has a window with a fine St George in red, white, and gold. The east window, with the Crucifixion and the Women at the Tomb, is to the fourth Earl of Bradford.

KNOWBURY. It has little beauty of its own but borrows glory from afar, for this plain quarry village of the Clee Hills has magnificent views, from a height of 900 feet, of bordering counties and of Wales. One of the hills behind the village, Titterstone Clee, rises 1749 feet and has an old camp, and what is called a Giant's Chair formed by huge boulders.

A 17th Century Inn

LEEBOTWOOD. It lies in a valley, and has kept a few old timbered houses among the new ones. A fine little inn has the year 1650 carved in stone, a room with good Jacobean panelling, and some stout old beams, all sheltering under a beautiful example of 20th century thatch. Away on a hill stands the church, its little tower overhung by stately trees. Much of it is 18th century, including the altar, the pulpit, and many pews; but two doorways and a gable window tell of the medieval and Tudor builders. One of the chancel seats has Jacobean carving, a roof beam has a curious decoration of dragons with arrows in their mouths, and among the memorials to old families is a very ornate one, with columns and heraldry, to Sir Uvedale Corbet, who died in 1701.

From the church there are fine views of the hills, including the

Wrekin and the end of the Longmynd ridge. We see also the top of Castle Hill, a 40-foot mound said to have been a Saxon fortification. Hiding below it are two charming black and white cottages.

LEE BROCKHURST. Its church has a nave built by the Normans, with one or two of their deeply splayed windows, and an example of their favourite zigzag decoration on the handsome south doorway. The ancient door is studded with nails and has a scrolled handle. There is a Jacobean altar table, and among the village possessions is a medieval paten engraved with Our Lord in the Tomb.

The Old Knight Home Again

LEIGHTON. In this tranquil place where the great house and the church stand together, gentle green slopes lead down to the Severn, and clipped yews are everywhere, and everywhere delightful. They are in the garden of the 18th century hall, in the churchyard, and over a cottage gateway, this one 30 feet high, clipped in haystack shape. By a wayside pond is a charming black and white cottage, an old inn, and a mill shaded by a spreading chestnut tree; and there is a row of 18th century cottages. The old stables of Leighton Hall have a little clock tower. The modern lychgate set in a shady corner brings us to a church no older than the hall, but with much interest from a remoter past. It has one of the finest old sculptured figures in Shropshire representing a knight in plate armour with his legs crossed. He is holding a shield and a sword, and his feet are on a lion. The colour has survived in marvellous fashion on the knight's shield, for it is believed to be more than 600 years old, the figure having been brought here from Buildwas Abbey where the old knight, Sir Richard de Leighton, is supposed to have been buried in 1315. The chancel also has a monument with engraved figures of William Leighton and his wife, he in Tudor armour and she in a pedimental headdress with ruffs at her wrists. In one of the modern windows is a picture of a beloved lady of the hall distributing alms.

In the churchyard is a stone to Thomas Jones, an 18th century curate of the village, with a rather singular inscription saying that it was set up by the villagers because a wealthy relative of Thomas refused to bear the expense of a small monument.

It was here that one of the beloved writers of the Shropshire countryside received her first impressions of its beauty, for Leighton was for many years the village of the childhood of Mary Webb.

Proud Ruins of a Norman Abbey

LILLESHALL. It has a great sight to see, the splendid ruins of its Norman Abbey, which was one of the most magnificent in Shropshire. They stand beside a canal and the fishponds used by the monks, a proud group of roofless walls on a green carpet, with old yews for company.

The abbey church is 207 feet long and unusually planned, for its nave of 108 feet was divided by screens into three parts. The wide western doorway is deeply moulded and delicately carved, and enough is left of its capitals to show how beautifully chiselled they were. To the north the wall stands as far as its second stage, a triple arcade remaining from the 14th century. There are Norman clerestory windows, an east window with a beautiful 14th century arch, and a carved stone just as old with something of a figure in a border of flowers.

Leading to the cloisters is a fine Norman doorway with twisted shafts, leafy capitals, and a narrow tympanum under a series of zigzag arches. A Norman vaulted passage runs between the cloister and a place of burial.

For 400 years the black-cloaked monks went their ways in this place, and when the end came Henry the Eighth gave Lilleshall to the Levesons, a Staffordshire family famous since Edward the First's day. In the village church is a huge monument to one of them in the 17th century, with Sir Richard Leveson and his wife resting on shelves one above the other. Like the abbey, the church has a Norman doorway, and in the same wall is a filled-up arch with a double row of zigzags.

The chancel is 13th century, and capitals of the same time were used as stones by the Tudor builders of the tower, which has a band of ornament near the top. Arches 600 years old separate an aisle with its original 14th century roof; and set in a group of 144 medieval tiles is a Norman font rescued from the churchyard, still with remains of the staples used for closing down its cover against witches. There is a modern pulpit with Michael slaying the Dragon, and a peace memorial window of a soldier and a sailor kneeling before their Master.

At the foot of the village is the Old Hall, a grey building decked with evergreens, now a convalescent home; and on the hill above stands a 70-foot column in memory of the first Duke of Sutherland, George Leveson-Gower, a great landowner in the early years of last century, one of whose achievements was to make 450 miles of road and 134 bridges in Sutherland, all within two decades.

The home of the dukes was at the hall, a modern great house in 600 acres, with a balustraded terrace, lovely gardens, and a gateway reminding us of the gates of Buckingham Palace. A curiosity in the grounds is a marble monument of a dachshund which was given to the Duchess of Sutherland by the Tsar of Russia. A handsome screen in the church is a tribute to the duke who died in 1913.

Norman Heritage

LINLEY. It is like walking in a dream through the fine avenue from the Elizabethan hall, with its delightful groups of chimneys, to the little church among the roses which still in this Electric Age is lit by candles. Here before us are the doorways, windows, and arches, and corbels of the Norman builders, with the stately dignity and grotesque fancies of their masons and sculptors. There are two Norman doorways, one blocked up and one still used, each with a tympanum over it. The low doorway through which we come, not six feet high, has a tympanum with herringbone carving, the other tympanum (seen outside) has a grotesque animal with a human face, the eyes glaring and crude branches springing from its mouth, above it all being three rows of stars. The font has more of this Norman carving, with cable moulding, foliage, and grotesque heads round it; the tower arch has deeply carved capitals by the same hands, and in the tower are three narrow Norman windows. The chancel has four more, and is entered through a Norman arch. The narrow nave has an old saddleback roof, medieval windows, and charming iron brackets for the candles. The chancel has Jacobean panelling. There is a marble tablet to Jane Lowndes, in loving gratitude from a number of village pupils who received education in the school she held for many years at Linley Hall.

The Chappell of Lyttell Ness

LITTLE NESS. It is little altered since the Normans built their church by the great tumulus in which lie men slain in a battle of ages past. In the wooden porch a Norman doorway adorned with zigzag has over it a muzzled bear and a grotesque head. The inside walls still bear the mark of Norman chisels; the font is Norman, with heavy cable moulding, and there is the arch of a Norman window.

The sanctuary, with medieval tiles in its floor, has old Flemish paintings of the Crucifixion, the Descent from the Cross, St Christopher, and St Catherine. Above three Jacobean chairs and a Queen Anne table hang two brass candelabra. There is a graceful chalice with gold bands, inscribed "The Chappell of Lyttell Ness, 1565," a Bible of 1765, and in the vestry a panel of 15th century glass. In one window are St George and St Mauritius, with the archangel Michael holding scales, nine people in one pan balanced against five in the other. It is in memory of Maurice Darby, an officer of the Grenadier Guards who died in the war, and is further remembered on a brass which shows St Mauritius in armour. Lying on the windowsill when we called were the drum and sticks of his regiment. In another window to a soldier are our patron saint and our first martyr, and in the sanctuary a window shows St Martin dividing his cloak for the beggar and St Elizabeth offering fruit to a lame boy.

The Splendour Falls on the Hills of Wales

LITTLE WENLOCK. Much Wenlock in the valley and Little Wenlock on the hill! It lies on the southern slope of the Wrekin, lonely and remote, with a church and ancient timbered cottages sharing magnificent views. From the tower mile upon mile of meadows can be seen in an endless vista, and the traveller who goes past the old gabled house facing the farm-gate can there, like stout Cortez, gaze spellbound, for beyond the western side of the Wrekin stand the fantastic peaks of Wales, and he knows the country well who can name them all. It is an unforgettable sight when the summer sun is setting and flooding the valleys with golden mist. Solemnly beautiful rise Wenlock Edge and the Longmynd in their twin majesty with lonely roads running up to meet the sky.

Little Wenlock's church tower is 300 years old, and so probably is the aisle which was once the nave, the present nave being 19th century. The timbers in the roof of the chancel and the aisle are perhaps 17th century like the grey marble font.

Two faithful servants of last century are remembered here:

Benjamin Dawes who, serving one family for 70 years, "lived in contentment and died in peace," and Elizabeth Dolan who lies here with the family she served for 49 years.

The church reveals little of the ancient story of the village, but we know from the barrows that can be traced, and from bronze weapons which have been found, that long before history was written men lived, toiled, and hunted here, and must have stood here to watch the sun going down beyond the hills of Wales.

Looking out of England

LLANVAIR WATERDINE. It looks across the Teme to the hills of Wales, and has a graceful old bridge over the river. Its church was refashioned in the eighteen-fifties, and takes the place of one which was remarkable for a great wealth of timber. Pictures of it are shown here, and a fine relic of the old woodwork is a set of altar rails believed to have been made from a chancel screen. Their carving shows a woman in a long dress, a bearded man, and little figures of pigs and birds and rabbits, a lion and a dragon, and dogs chasing a rabbit and deer. The closing rail has a Welsh inscription said to refer to the original screen, telling how "Sir Matthew and Meyrick Pichgar set it for ten pounds together." There are two chairs and an altar table by Jacobean craftsmen, and near the pulpit lies the bowl of an ancient font. In the churchyard, with its fine row of limes, we noticed a gipsy grave with a Romany inscription.

By the Borderland

LLANYBLODWELL. Its nearness to Wales has bestowed on it a lovely name and in truth it deserves it, for it means that it is a hamlet of flowers. The church, standing on the hillside, is surprising inside and out. The remarkable 19th century tower is almost detached, and is shaped like a cigar so that the spire grows from the tower without any parapet. Very unusual, too, is the modern south porch with its elaborate entrance arch and fine vaulted roof, and a second arch fashioned in oak. Within is the church's oldest treasure, a fine tall doorway of the 12th century, with a door made in 1713. The north doorway is 500 years old, and has a door of 1753. The surprise of the interior is its painted decoration everywhere, texts and fern-patterns on the walls, golden bosses in the panelled medieval roofs, coloured capitals under the very high west gallery, and more colour on the 15th century arcade, on the carved font, and on the traceried altar. An elaborate hammerbeam forms an arch between nave and chancel; and an attractive screen nearly 40 feet long has kept much of its 500-year-old woodwork. In the trailing vine of the cornice are little animals and birds. A massive monument tells of a Sir John Bridgeman of 200 years ago; and a window of the Good Shepherd and St Michael is in memory of Elias Owen, the antiquary who was vicar at the end of the 19th century. Another window is a tribute to 23 men who died for peace.

By the fine stone bridge over the River Tanat is a little black and white inn which has in our own time passed out of the hands of a family which had been here in charge of it for 300 years.

Ancient Defences

LLANYMYNECH. A plain village near the Welsh border, it has a fine stone bridge over the River Vyrnwy, and a magnificent panorama from the top of Llanymynech Hill, where the Romans left behind them the earthworks guarding their copper mines. What is called Ogo's Hole may have been one of these mines; in it Roman coins and other relics were found 200 years ago.

But without climbing to the top the prospect is lovely enough. From the Oswestry road running round the hill we see far over the Shropshire plains, and from the church at the foot of the village we look across the river to the impressive Breidden Hills, crowned by Admiral Rodney's monument.

The church is quaint and unusual outside, built last century in the style of the Normans, with much ornament, a corbel table of faces, and a tapering tower full of windows and arcading. Inside are two Jacobean chairs, a pulpit to a rector who preached 47 years, a font brought from Buckinghamshire, and a colourful window of St Agatha with pincers in her hand.

Running north and south hereabouts is Offa's Dyke, the great entrenchment built in the 8th century by the Mercian king as a barrier between England and Wales; it stretched from the mouth of the Dee to the mouth of the Wye. Still older is Watt's Dyke three miles from it, which starts at Llanymynech.

Ludlow • The Feathers Hotel

The Green Fields by the Teme

The Castle on the Hill

MATCHLESS LUDLOW

The Norman Keep and the Courtyard

The Little Round Chapel of Mary Magdalen
LUDLOW CASTLE

Ludlow   **The Broad Gate**

Ludlow   **Overhanging Storeys**

Links With the Proud Talbots

LONGFORD. Its modern hall stands in 150 acres and reminds us of the Earl of Shrewsbury's old home here, fortified for Parliament in the Civil War and taken by Prince Rupert. Still standing is a barn in which the Royalist Lord Talbot lay in hiding for days.

The old house has gone, and so has the old church, all save a 13th century chapel with a huge classical monument to Thomas Talbot of 1686 and his wife Anne. Surrounded by iron railings, it has spiral columns with Corinthian capitals. The chapel has five lancets grouped under one arch, and its piscina has a well-carved head for a corbel.

The church a few feet away was built in 1802 and keeps the 14th century font from the old building. Its pulpit has carvings of ploughing, sowing, and reaping, done by a 20th century rector. One of its treasures is a very beautiful window of the Crucifixion from the workshops of Christopher Whall; it is in memory of Ralph and Charles Leeke, who went from the hall to die for England.

Master of 18 Languages

LONGNOR. It has still a watermill on the site of one which was working when the Conqueror came; and, divided by a winding brook, it has a splendid 17th century hall which succeeded one of the 13th century, and the attractive little church built as a chapel for it then. In the modern turret is a bell which has rung over the church for six centuries. Two crowned heads by medieval craftsmen are outside the fine east window, and on a wall is an 18th century sundial. Up one of the massive buttresses runs a little open-air stairway leading to a gallery, a remarkable feature; and the west window is remarkable too, for it is a copy of the east window reproduced in wood. The two-decker oak pulpit is 18th century, and so are the panelled box-pews, each with a candle-holder at the end.

On the fringe of the village is a timbered farm-house which still has part of its moat, and preserves much work from an ancient moat house, mentioned in medieval deeds.

The village has known a distinguished son in Samuel Lee, born here in 1783. A poor boy taught at the village school, he was set to earn his bread as a carpenter when he was 12, and while working in Shrewsbury churches he began the study of Latin from the inscriptions. Having learned Latin, he mastered Greek, and Hebrew and other Oriental languages, but not until he lost his chest of tools did he quit his trade and turn schoolmaster. His scholarship attracting the attention of sympathetic observers, he was encouraged to make further conquests and was ultimately master of 18 languages. He translated the Scriptures into Syriac and the Prayer Book into Hindustani, wrote tracts in Persian and Arabic, at 36 was appointed Professor of Arabic at Cambridge, and died famous throughout Europe, one of the greatest linguists of his age.

The Bull Ring

LOPPINGTON. It clusters about a road where traffic passes over a thing unique in Shropshire, a ring fastened to the ground in front of the inn, the only relic of a Bull Ring remaining in the county. From the little bridge over the River Roden we have a peep of the great house in the park. The oldest possession of the village is the Norman arch in the church tower, though most of the tower is 16th century and most of the church 14th. There are black and white roofs with grotesque faces carved on the ends of the beams, a Jacobean pulpit and a Jacobean table, an old oak chest and 18th century pews. The old east window has modern glass with animated scenes of the Crucifixion, in which the Roman soldiers are throwing the dice and others look on mocking.

As Old as Magna Carta

LOUGHTON. It lies in lovely lanes and has two things to see, a stone and a tree. The stone is in the plain little church, which is one of the few that were built in the 17th century; it is a great rough-hewn stone lintel in a filled-up doorway, a relic of the church that has disappeared. The tree has a hollow trunk measuring about ten yards round, it has six main branches. It is probably as old as Magna Carta, quite seven hundred years.

Where Ludlow Ends

LUDFORD. It begins where Ludlow ends, surprisingly hidden behind a rock-hewn road. From the fine old stone bridge between them, spanning the River Teme, high and so narrow that two cars cannot pass, is a pretty scene of rocky weirs and a mill race, the old mill making light instead of grinding corn. There is a charming timbered house which was an inn in Shakespeare's day, with lovely flowered banks by it bordering a path to the river, all a wonderful mass of colour when we called.

The church is in a delightful setting close to its quaint old neighbour Ludford House, with brick and timber walls and overhanging gables. Over its porch is an oratory with a secret passage. The tiny church is much changed, but has kept a narrow Norman window in the west wall of its low tower, and on the sill of a 14th century window is a piscina made from a Norman capital. In a chapel reached by an arch from the nave are the brass portraits of William Foxe, his wife, and their 14 children; he is in armour with a collar and an apron of mail. On an altar tomb in the chapel lies Sir Job Charlton, Speaker of the House of Commons, who entertained James the Second at Ludford House; his painted figure has long hair and he wears a scarlet gown and a square hat. One of his two wives is near him on the wall, wearing a bonnet tied under her chin. It was Charlton, who, having fallen out of favour with Charles the Second, was forced to resign to make room on the bench for the worst judge in history, Jeffreys; though his appointment was afterwards restored.

From the churchyard, which has a grand old yew 15 feet round its trunk, we look down on the roofs of the gabled almshouses of the hospital of St Giles. Near them is St Julian's Well.

The Enchanted West

LUDLOW. It is an entrancing piece of our enchanting West Country, and we have very few towns like it. Its rivers ring it like a moat, and it stands on its hilltop as a magnet drawing travellers from the hills and plains around. If we would feel the thrill of England, let us come to Ludlow on a summer's day, walk about its castle and its streets, and saunter in the hills about it.

Perhaps we may think of the hilltop towns of Italy and France as we stand on the bridge across the Teme and look at Ludlow creeping up from the waterside, but this quaint and ancient place satisfies imagination as we tramp through its streets, and well we know it is a piece of English history. It satisfies imagination, too, as we look down on it from the lovely hills across the river. Here we have many views of it, all beautiful, and we do not forget the noble skyline of this place, with the pinnacled tower of the finest church in Shropshire rising in the heart of it, and the long splendour of the castle walls.

We see the hill rising suddenly for 200 feet from the wooded valley of the Teme. Perhaps we think of Mr Housman's Shropshire Lad who leaves home with a wish of good luck while Ludlow tower shall stand, and then:

> *Oh, come you home on Sunday*
> *When Ludlow's streets are still*
> *And Ludlow's bells are calling*
> *To farm and lane and mill.*
> *Or come you home on Monday*
> *When Ludlow Market hums*
> *And Ludlow chimes are playing*
> *The Conquering Hero Comes.*

The poet who wrote this loved this place so that he wished his memory to be linked with Ludlow, and in this place his ashes lie. Or perhaps we are moved as we walk about these hills, looking across the gulf the river has made for itself round Ludlow's hill, to think of all those ancient English towns that look on to Wales and have seen so much of our Border history.

We are looking at one of the long line of castles from Chepstow to Chester which more or less divide the English from the Welsh; we are looking on the central castle of that defensive line. From this castle of Ludlow the whole of Wales and the frontier line between England and Wales was governed. A formidable hill-fortress was this, whose business was to keep the peace between two countries that will never fight again. Before peace came between them Ludlow Castle had a stormy time, for from those Norman days it had no peace from raiders until the great Welshman Henry Tudor annexed England as its king. Then Wales was quieted, as Scotland was quieted on the annexation of England and Wales by a Scottish king.

Henry Tudor, Henry the Seventh, who had finished the Wars of the Roses with the help of his fellow Welshmen, was shrewd enough to make good use of Ludlow, the stout Norman castle extended from generation to generation, moated and strengthened by one lord after another until it became a royal castle under Edward the Fourth, who sent to it for safe keeping the two pathetic little princes now known to all the world. It was these very walls that we are looking on that came into the mind of an English king, wading through slaughter to his throne with eight murders already on his conscience, as he took his last short step. These two princes at Ludlow must be out of his way before Richard could be king, and so it was that the royal brothers arrived from Ludlow Castle at the Tower of London, one of them a king to be robbed of his crown, both to be slain. It was Henry Tudor who when King Richard was disposed of, when "the day was done, the dog was dead," made the last home of the little princes the home of his own son, Prince Arthur, with his young wife Catherine of Aragon. A walk round the castle was made for Catherine; it is still called the Queen's Walk, and we must imagine that here these two, so young and yet with such a place in history, would walk and talk of the future planned for them. It is one of the saddest chapters in the story of an English Castle that this love-story ended in a month or two, with peace for the prince and the dawn of long bitterness for his Spanish princess.

It is a great chapter of our royal history that Ludlow has seen, for here lived three princes whose deaths transformed our history and led to those events which 400 years ago changed the face of the world.

It was one of the great acts of our first Tudor king that he appointed a Lord President with jurisdiction over all the Border Counties, and his seat of power was Ludlow. Here, as Lord President, Sir Henry Sidney held his court for nearly a generation, and so to this great place came his immortal son. Philip Sidney would know these walls and climb these stairs, and look across the country from these battlements. His sister Ambrosia lies in the church close by, and the heart of their father lies with her. For 27 years the father of Sir Philip Sidney ruled in Ludlow Castle, and still he is a part of Ludlow, for his heart is in its soil, buried in the chancel of this famous church.

No purer names lived in our annals than Philip Sidney and John Milton, and the stones of Ludlow speak of both. In 1634, when the Earl of Bridgewater had succeeded as Lord President and lived in the castle with his family, a masque was performed in the Great Hall, conducted by the famous musician Henry Lawes, and the masque was written by his friend John Milton. We may stand in this Great Hall, come into it through the doorway by which Milton would come in, and look up at the lovely windows through which the light fell on the first performance of Milton's Comus. Here were first spoken aloud those exquisite passages which will not pass away when Ludlow's stones are crumbling into dust.

So these stones of Ludlow would be thrilling if they were not impressive to see, but in truth they are magnificent with their roofless towers, their open windows, and their touch of medieval genius everywhere. It is all as we would have it.

The castle is at the height of the town, and we come into it by the entrance to the outer court, where is a range of stables, a prison, a porter's lodge, and a beacon tower. We walk on to the two-arched bridge running over the moat at Sir Henry Sidney's Gateway. The moat is dry, but in olden days it divided the outer from the small inner gate, being cut deeply through the solid rock. Sir Henry Sidney's arms are on the gateway, and in a room above it lived Samuel Butler while he wrote his poem Hudibras; he was secretary to the Lord President at the time.

We pass into the castle between Norman and Tudor England, for on one side are the gabled Tudor buildings Sir Henry Sidney built, and on the other is the oldest part of the castle, the massive Norman keep. We can climb the stone steps that have been here 800 years until we stand 70 feet up looking out from the battlements across this lovely countryside. There is much architectural interest on the way, original doorways and windows and odd corners.

It will not bore the dullest traveller to spend an hour in this great place, so wide is its appeal, so fascinating its peeps, so surprising its beauty indoors and out. We may climb up steps and down them, we may work our way through narrow passages and find ourselves entranced by glimpses of the river winding down below. Here are Prince Arthur's chambers with a Norman watch-tower projecting from them, the state apartments and the armoury, the domestic quarters, the room of the little murdered princes, and the great council chamber 60 feet long and half as wide, with its floor and its roof both gone but with the doorways and windows as they were when Milton saw Comus played here.

But most captivating of all is one piece of Old England that has stood here 800 years, the little round chapel of Mary Magdalen. It is superb. The number of round chapels in England can be counted on one hand, and this is the only one whose roof is open to the sky. It is pathetic in its beauty, and is the very heart of the little world within these castle walls

Through its great chancel arch are the foundations of the vanished chancel and the site of the altar. The walls are four feet thick and have been crowned by later battlements; they enclose a space about 28 yards round. Above the stringcourse running round the outside walls are three Norman windows, below are two later windows, and along the walls runs an arcade of 14 niches with roll and zigzag moulding in the arches and seats at the base. It is said that in the niches once stood statues of Our Lord, the Madonna, and the Twelve Apostles.

The lovely Norman doorway has rich carving of zigzag and rests on scalloped capitals, and the majestic arch that faces it, now all awry, has rich star and zigzag mouldings and clusters of four shafts on each side. A charming place this small church must have been with its round nave, its lovely chancel arch, and the tiny sanctuary. The only storied relic we can find is a coffin lid with three fleur-de-lys carved under a cross; it covered someone who knew this place in its glory, as it must have been when a poet of Sidney's time wrote these lines on it:

> *So bravely wrought, so fair and finely framed,*
> *That to world's end the beauty may endure.*

We should pass from all this ruined stateliness to Ludlow's second monument, making a twin glory with the castle wherever we look at the town from the hills. It is one of the noblest parish churches in the land, and one of the biggest; there are not half a dozen so big. The tower rises to 135 feet from the middle of the beautiful church, and its spacious interior, 203 feet long from east to west and 125 across the transepts, stands shaped like a cross with the proportions of a cathedral. It has come down to us from our three medieval centuries, and, though the Norman church before it has utterly vanished from sight, the place where we stand was once a Saxon graveyard, and lying about we found a stone with Saxon knotwork carved on it, and a piece of a Roman capital.

If we are here in the dark months of the year we shall hear the curfew ring, and in any week of the year we shall hear a fresh tune every day from the eight bells in the tower. The tower was built about 1470 and has panelled battlements and lofty pinnacles rising from four turrets. It has two tiers of great windows, those of the belfry adorned with saints and the lower one very effective from inside, between the vaulted oak roof with gold tracery and the splendid arches with rich mouldings and clustered pillars on which the tower rises.

We come into this fine place through a porch like no other we remember, for it has six sides. It was built about a hundred years after the 13th century doorway, and has a fine vaulted roof and a room above it reached by a stairway from the aisle.

We are in the presence of all our great building centuries as we stand in the stately nave. The arcades on their slender columns were refashioned in the middle of the 15th century when the clerestory was added. The south aisle has some of the earliest masonry in its walls. The north aisle with its row of six windows was built about 1316, and the arms of its builder are here in original glass. The south transept comes from the 13th century and the north from the 14th, though both were raised in the 15th. The lower walls of the chancel chapels are part of the early church; St John's as we see it on the north was finished in the 15th century, and is rich in treasure; the lady chapel on the south, with the 12th century aumbry and the two piscinas, was finished in the 14th. Though the fine chancel was lengthened eastwards in the 15th century, when its great windows were put in, its western bay comes from the early church, and its next two bays from 1275. It has four stone sedilia with projecting canopies and a medieval reredos of great richness, modernised with 26 canopied niches in which are saints and Bible scenes. In the reredos is a doorway leading into a little chamber behind, and over the door is a medieval fragment of St George and the Dragon. Opening into the vestry is a 15th century door with its ancient ring; in the vestry itself is a fine old chest with four locks, and in the lady chapel the floor has some medieval tiles.

It is the rare and beautiful stalls that are the glory of the chancel. They are exquisitely carved and have over 30 misereres, making up an almost perfect collection. The stalls were made for the Palmers Guild from planks brought from Bristol, and they are all 15th century except for their modern canopies, which continue along the east side of the chancel screen and are adorned with 148 figures of saints and angels. The cornice is old.

The misereres are interesting not only for the humour running through them as a collection, but also because on many of them the

Ludlow   The Reader's House

Ludlow   **15th Century Misereres in the Church**

craftsman has left a small spray of leaves as his mark. Among the carvings are owls and swans and chained antelopes, a mermaid with a mirror, a fox in bishop's robes preaching to the geese, a pedlar with his pack pulling on his boots, a man warming himself in front of a fire with sides of bacon hanging behind him, a scholar probably from the grammar school, two rude boys making fun of a woman with an ugly hat, and the devil carrying off the ale-wife for giving short measure, while a demon reads out her sin on one side and the mouth of hell swallows her up on the other.

Among the fine poppyheads is a beautiful Pieta, the Madonna with Christ on her knee after Calvary; and St Catherine with her wheel, and St Margaret on a dragon while souls ascend to heaven between them.

On every hand this fine chancel is guarded by medieval screens: it has no fewer than five from the 14th century. Very fine is the chancel screen itself, with its entrance archway six feet deep, a vaulted roof with bosses supporting the loft, and two rows of vines in the cornice. It is one of the roodlofts the Reformation did not destroy. The south transept screen is plain and the north transept has trefoiled bays and traceried panels. The screen of the lady chapel has vaulting on both sides and the lovely screen in St John's Chapel has rich carving and a vaulted canopy.

The splendid medieval roofs are by 15th century craftsmen; the nave roof has gold bosses of foliage; the transept roofs rest on corbels of men, women, and angels; the chancel roof has lovely colour and is adorned with angels and flowers and foliage of gold. Over the altar of St John's Chapel is a medieval canopy with Tudor flowers and fruits among its lovely carving. Older than all is the font, claimed as Saxon and at least old enough to be Norman.

Rich in wood and stone, Ludlow is uncommonly rich in its medieval glass. The seven great windows of the chancel glow with a colour that men and women have looked at for 500 years. In it is what is known among stained glass lovers as the famous Ludlow blue. The splendid east window, as wide as the chancel and 30 feet high, tells the story of the life and miracles of St Laurence in 27 compartments, the scenes having altogether about 300 figures. Below this picture story is a row of canopies, and in the tracery are over 30 lights with angels and saints, the Madonna, and the Child of

Bethlehem. A window over the old vestry door has nine 15th century pictures of saints, among which we see St Dunstan attacking the devil with the tongs, David with his harp, St Leonard with the fetters, and St George. Among nine saints in another window are Thomas Becket, Edward the Confessor, and Augustine, and another group looking down on this attractive chancel has 15 figures under elaborate canopies, ten saints, the Three Wise Men, Edward the Confessor, and unbelieving Thomas holding the Madonna's girdle. A series of window subjects we do not remember seeing elsewhere has ten scenes illustrating the breaking of each of the Ten Commandments.

The oldest glass of all at Ludlow is 14th century; it is in medieval fragments in the south transept and in the east window of the lady chapel, which has a fine Jesse Tree. More appealing perhaps is the 15th century glass of St John's Chapel, glowing in silver, red, and blue, with the story of Edward the Confessor and the Palmers—the pilgrims to Holy Land who carried palms with them. There was a Palmers Guild in Ludlow, and one of the things they did for the town was to buy the materials for the making of the choir-stalls and to give the Confessor window in this chapel.

In it we see two Palmers setting sail for Holy Land, the Confessor giving his ring to St John disguised as a beggar, St John giving the ring to the Palmers with a message to the king revealing his identity, the king giving a charter to the Palmers, the return of the pilgrims to the town gate and their reception and entertainment at Ludlow. Two other windows in St John's chapel show the Twelve Apostles seated with their emblems in front of them, and a window by the ancient screen shines with gold and shows the hands of an angel opening the curtains to reveal a lovely Annunciation, John the Baptist with a lamb, Christopher with a child, and St Catherine with a jewelled crown and her wheel.

Two lovely modern windows by A. T. Davies are worthy of their setting, one showing the dream of St John as he lies asleep by the rockbound coast; the other with Stephen being stoned on a mountain road, a saint kneeling among flowers as angels in blue robes come down the hill. The great west window of the nave is interesting only for its portraits of men associated with the castle, among them Prince Arthur, Edward the Fourth, and one of the murdered princes in The Tower.

To this place there have been brought in our time the ashes of one of the rare poets of England and a great lover of Shropshire, a son of a neighbouring county. In the churchyard rests all that was mortal of A. E. Housman, and on a stone set in the north wall of the church are these words in his memory:

> *Good-Night. Ensured release,*
> *Imperishable peace,*
> *Have these for yours.*

A year before he died he wrote these three verses for his funeral, and they were read at his grave:

> *O thou that from thy mansion,*
> *Through time and place to roam,*
> *Dost send abroad thy children,*
> *And then dost call them home,*
>
> *That men and tribes and nations*
> *And all thy hand hath made*
> *May shelter them from sunshine*
> *In thine eternal shade:*
>
> *We now to peace and darkness*
> *And earth and thee restore*
> *Thy creature that thou madest*
> *And wilt cast forth no more.*

For a place so rich this spacious church has only a few monuments. The only Lord President lying here has no memorial, but his wife, Lady Mary Eure, with whom he lies, rules the south transept from her tomb. She has been brought here from the chancel, and we do not wonder, for she lies stiffly on a shelf, resting on a cushion, holding a book, and looking a little comical in her Elizabethan costume with a ruff and a big veiled headdress. A Councillor of the Marches of Wales in the days of Charles Stuart (Edward Waties) kneels quaintly with his wife on a memorial set up in his lifetime; he is wearing black and red robes with a skull cap, and she has a black gown and a ruff. A Chief Justice of South Wales (Edward Walter) lies with his wife on a fine canopied tomb within its original iron railing, both in Elizabethan costumes; she has a Paris hat and bows on her sleeves, and their five children are with them. The Chief Justice of Chester, Sir John Bridgeman, lies in armour with his wife, dressed as in Charles Stuart's day; and another Judge, Sir Robert Towneshend, is with his wife and their 12 children. The mother has a French cap, a quilted gown, and a book on a chain; he is in armour with his feet on a stag, and all are in Elizabethan dress.

It will probably seem to some that the most interesting tomb in the chancel is the plainest; it is the heraldic altar tomb of Ambrosia Sidney, who died at the castle. To others it will seem that this sanctuary is most of all famous because on the left of the altar there lies all that remains of the heart of that Prince Arthur whose death changed the course of history. Arthur was buried with great pomp on St George's Day in Worcester Cathedral and he has a lovely chantry there, but his heart was sealed in a silver box and placed in the chancel at Ludlow, where he had known his happy days with Catherine of Aragon. The box was opened long ago and stolen, but it is believed that the heart was replaced and that it still lies amid all this medieval glory of Prince Arthur's own day.

This famous hilltop town, recalling a Sidney and a Tudor in its church and John Milton in its castle, has distinction indeed, and yet if it had none of these things, if all its stones were dead and did not thrill with history, this would be a stirring and gracious place. Merely to look at Ludlow is a spectacle to bring the traveller from afar. We may stand at the top of a street and see a collection of black and white houses with a mile of timbers in their fronts. We may wonder about its nooks and passages and curious narrow ways and come suddenly upon charming glimpses of our medieval land. The Feathers Hotel has looked as we see it for 400 years, and it is believed that all this time this very door (with 350 iron studs in it) has been opening and shutting. It has a wonderful front, of which we are sure that our famous tramp poet would say that this is a dull world if we have not time to stare at all the wonder of these ancient timbers, with the ancient balcony, the projecting windows, the quaint little heads and faces that have looked down for so long on packhorses and stage coaches and motor cars. Indoors are rooms as rich as any for a hundred miles around, veritable pieces of Tudor England which, we may surely hope, will never be allowed to pass away.

If we pass through the old courtyard of the hotel across the street (noting its ancient beams as we go) we come upon some steps and find ourselves behind the church, standing at the front door of what is called the Reader's House, a charming place which we may see, some of it medieval, most of it Elizabethan, its fine three-storeyed carved and gabled porch added in the year that Shakespeare died. There are black and white houses overhanging the footways, lovely gables and oriels, the Grammar School with a 14th century room in it and something of the old Rest House for pilgrims attached to it; and there is, of course, the old Butter Cross at the heart of the town, which was once the marketplace and is now an awkward monument of which every motorist must beware. Except for the domed Roman Catholic church the town has nothing new to see. Halfway down one of its steep streets is the last of the seven gates of the old town wall, still with its portcullis grooves; it is Broad Gate, and brings us to Ludlow's charming bridge with Ludford on the other side. The museum, with its collection of entertaining things, has many relics of the past, and indeed we feel that the past is all about us here, for Ludlow, love it as we will today, belongs to yesterday.

Doctor to the Slaves

LYDBURY NORTH. Here stands a wayside tower as it has been for 700 years, with walls as thick as six feet in places, and with a Norman buttress helping to strengthen it. It looks down on a cross-shaped church with low plastered walls, the nave Norman, the chancel with three Norman windows, the south porch with an ancient timber roof and an old arch covered by a new one. The door swings on strap hinges 500 years old, and is scarred with the marks of bullets.

Two things impress us as we step inside, the length of the fine medieval roof, with its quatrefoil panels, and the great array of box-pews with Jacobean backs and ends, all in company with a rich Jacobean pulpit and a restored Tudor screen with much delicate tracery. In fine lettering over the screen are the Ten Commandments, painted the year before Shakespeare died. There is a Norman doorway for the priest, a Norman font with a fluted bowl and a Jacobean cover, and an aumbry and a piscina both 700 years old. From the 17th century come the altar rails and the wooden candlesticks beside the altar.

The side chapels are named after Lydbury's two great houses, Walcot and Plowden Hall. An arch decorated with heads of Queen Victoria and King Edward opens to the 17th century Walcot Chapel, which has good benches and panelling, a fine modern roof, and many floorstones to the Walcots two and three centuries ago. A studded door leads to a room above, once used for the school founded by John Shipton, an old servant of the family. The house is big and plain, with 1000 acres of parkland and a lake. It was once among the possessions of the famous Robert Clive. On a hillside is a group of trees half a mile long, planted so as to form the letters of the word Plassey, the scene of Clive's great victory.

A Norman arch with an old oak screen leads to the Plowden Chapel, 14th century as we see it but said to have been founded by the crusader Roger Plowden out of gratitude for his escape from captivity at Acre. The chapel has an old stone altar, and steps which led to the roodloft. Nine centuries ago the Plowdens came to live here, and in a delightful setting two miles away is their beautiful hall of Elizabethan and Jacobean times, looking to the great bare heights of the Longmynd. It has many treasures, rare books and pictures, old tapestries, and a chalice-veil of remarkable interest if its story is true, for it is said to have belonged to Thomas Becket. There are hiding-holes used by priests in olden days, and a chapel with a brass of Humphrey Plowden and his family in Tudor dress.

To Plowden Hall, after a lifetime of adventure, came Thomas Falkner to be chaplain, and here he died in 1784. He had started life as a Manchester surgeon and then sailed as a doctor on a slave ship belonging to the South Sea Company. Reaching Buenos Aires he fell seriously ill, and was so well nursed by the Jesuits that he changed his faith and joined them, determined to be a Jesuit missionary. For 38 years he worked among the native tribes of South America, coming home when the Jesuits were expelled in 1768. He wrote of his valuable observations in the countries he had seen, and spent his last years as chaplain to Roman Catholics in England.

One of the oldest relics near Lydbury North is the ancient British camp known as Bury Ditches on Tongley Hill. It covers about 16 acres, and has three high entrenchments.

The Wars

LYDHAM. Here, it is said, a battle was fought in Roman England; and here by the churchyard wall stands a granite cross to those who fell in the greatest war of all. There is 13th century masonry in the massive leaning walls of the little church, which has an old panelled door, ancient beams in the roof, a simple Jacobean pulpit, and much old panelling in the box-pews. Some of the windows were made in the first year of the Civil War, and the east window shows a richly coloured Crucifixion in memory of a rector. The font is medieval.

Three Men of a Town

MADELEY. What once was fair has been mightily spoiled, but Madeley must be counted an interesting place. There was a king who was glad to see it, for Charles the Second came this way after Worcester, and was glad of the old barn to rest in. He came to Upper House, the home of Mr Wolfe. The house is still here though much changed, and the attic has still its hiding-place. As it was thought unwise for Charles to hide in it he spent the night and part of a day in the barn with the bats and the owls, and the barn so made historic remains much as it was the next morning when the king set off to hide in an oak tree at Boscobel. Madeley Court has lost its Elizabethan glory, and its stately gatehouse, with the octagonal towers, has been made into cottages. The splendour is departed. The relic of a sundial stands in what was once the formal garden and has become a poultry run, and the great block of stone hollowed out on three sides sets us thinking. On summer days it told the time on these three sides, and showed the position of the planets and the moon as well. It must have been one of the wonders of this countryside, and now it stands forlorn.

One good thing has man done in this place to balance the harm that man had done. We are struck by the beauty of two little wooded hills between which the Court stands. They are covered with lovely trees, and old folk remember when there was not a leaf here. A generation since these hills were pitmounds, heaps of rubbish from the mines, a scar on the countryside blotting out the sky from the windows of the great house. Then came the good thought into some-body's head that the mounds might be planted with trees, and the dream has come true. We do not know if the nightingale comes, but few better homes there could be for them than these two little hills of Madeley Court.

A few steps bring us to the 18th century church, and here again is an unfamiliar spectacle, the strange sight of four stone figures, once with an honoured place in the ancient church and now standing battered and exposed to wind and rain in high niches outside. They are four of the great folk of Madeley Court, John Brooke and his wife, and their son Basil with his wife, all wearing Jacobean dress.

The church itself is a monument to that rare friend of John Wesley, "Fletcher of Madeley." He was a Swiss, and his full name was Jean Guillaume de la Flechère. He came here as vicar and stayed for 25 years, and he lies in the churchyard with his wife. His pulpit is here though no longer used, and there is a case of personal possessions treasured as if they were gold. There are books, letters, and photographs, fragments of Mrs Fletcher's wedding dress, medicine bottles, and the pestle and mortar with which Mrs Fletcher used to mix potions for the poor. The chancel itself is Fletcher's memorial, for it was raised to his memory in 1910. It has a beautiful oak screen with six saints, this having been added in memory of the men who died in the Great War. The oak reading desk has an imposing figure of St John, and the oak reredos is carved with the Last Supper. The east window has bright modern glass with the Crucifixion and the archangels Gabriel and Michael.

Two famous men were born at Madeley. Sir Wyke Bayliss the artist and Lord Moulton the great lawyer. Sir Wyke Bayliss was the son of a railway engineer and very early proved to be a clever artist loving greatly the beauties of churches and cathedrals. He painted many of them. He made an intimate study of the traditional portraits of Christ and wrote a book on them. Lord Moulton was the son of a Wesleyan minister and came to London to read for the bar, building up a high reputation by his remarkable knowledge of patent cases and electrical matters. He sat in Parliament as a Liberal and was finally made a Lord of Appeal. Owing to his extraordinary scientific knowledge of high explosives he was called from his work in the Appeal Court to take control of a branch of the War Office which was turning out high explosives. He was eventually given control of the gas works, coke ovens, and fat and oil supplies of the whole country, and his department produced more than a million tons of high explosives and propellants. One spring day when the war was over he sat in his place in the House of Lords apparently in his usual health, but that night a clot of blood killed him in his sleep. He was one of the most delightful and one of the most learned men of our time, with a proud record of public service.

Fletcher of Madeley

MADELEY'S famous Swiss vicar was on a visit to England in the middle of the 18th century when he became tutor at Tern Hall in Shropshire and was moved to give up his idea of being a soldier and to give his life to preaching with the Methodists. It happened that he found himself devoted to the people of Madeley, and in 1760 he became vicar of what was then a very rough parish, remarkable for its profanity and the ignorance of its inhabitants.

He set himself to reform them, and no man ever worked harder. Here he laboured for 25 years sustained by the friendship of the Wesleys. He faced rebuffs and violence from unruly parishioners, and when they would not come to his church he tracked them to their homes and haunts. He would go round with his bell at five o'clock on Sunday morning to wake them up. He denied himself food to give to the poor. He taught the children in the day school and gave them a Sunday School. In the end his health broke down and a rich friend took him to Italy for a change. It is recorded that as they approached the Appian Way by which Paul walked to Rome he called on the driver to stop and stepped down from the chaise declaring that his heart would not suffer him to ride over that ground on which Paul walked chained to a soldier.

He came back to his people with his health greatly improved and went on with his work preaching, visiting, and writing, though for the last nine years of his life he could write nothing but letters and sermons. John Wesley preached his funeral sermon, in which he declared that he had never met so holy a man and never expected to do so again on this side of Eternity.

Between England and Wales

MAINSTONE. Over the hills and far away it sleeps deep down in the valley of the River Unk. Up another lonely valley lies the church a mile away, tucked in the slopes of Edenhope Hill, where we trace the ridge of Offa's Dyke as it comes down from the skyline to cross the road between the church and the solitary cottages.

By the church gate stands a huge boulder from which the village probably took its name; it weighs about two hundredweight and was used in olden times as a test for strength, a strong man lifting it and throwing it over his shoulder.

The simple aisleless church, with a double bellcot, is not old, but it has something old inside—a font bowl which may be 12th century, and, most astonishing of all, a magnificent roof which comes from the 14th century church that once stood here. It is black and white, and has quatrefoil panelling and finely moulded beams with stone corbels carved with kings and a bishop and medieval folk. On the chancel arch two mischievous boys' faces peep out from the foliage of the capitals. The east window has Bible scenes in bright colours on a blue ground, and in the nave is Gabriel bringing the good news and John baptising Our Lord.

If we have time we may go from here to a point at Bishop's Moat two miles away, where we may stand between England and Wales and have a fine view of the countryside from an ancient earthwork.

The Boy Who Climbed the Tower

MARKET DRAYTON. Those who come in autumn to this busy market town may see the manor steward in scarlet robes declaring open the fair, which has been held annually for centuries; and those who quarrel at the fair may find themselves before a court of pied poudre, as in medieval days. An interesting survival is this court, held on the spot to settle all differences arising out of the fair, its name perhaps coming from the fact that disputants appear before it just as they are, without formality, "with dusty feet."

The columned structure known as the Butter Cross takes a prominent place in the scene, still with two ancient fire-bells in its gable; and some steps opposite a group of thatched cottages and high old timbered buildings lead to the grammar school founded by a Lord Mayor of London in 1558. Here Robert Clive learned his lessons; the school has still the old desk cut with his initials.

The boys have moved to more adequate buildings, but this Elizabethan schoolroom remains much as it was when young Clive was cutting on his desk the name he made famous by adding India to the British Empire. Pitt's heaven-born general was a leader of high spirits in those days, and a bit of a gangster in his way, for it is said that he and some others levied small sums on the shopkeepers for the consideration of not having their windows broken. His daredevilry led him to climb the church tower while the people of Market Drayton stood aghast to watch the small figure lower himself from the top to sit astride a gargoyle. So young Master Clive from Styche Hall started to make known the name which an earlier schoolmaster had predicted would one day be known above most others. We tell his story at Moreton Say, where he lies in the village church.

The tower he climbed is a great height, the work of 14th century rebuilders, who left a Norman doorway at the base of the tower and used a Norman capital when they gave grandeur to the interior with their lofty arcades and the fine arch of the tower. The capital is carved round with 15 odd heads, three wearing mitres and one a crown, and all with varied expressions. No wonder the 14th century builders had not the heart to throw it away; we may wish much else had not perished in the restorations of the last two centuries.

Across the chancel arch (where bellrope holes at the top show that once there were two sanctus bells) is a modern rood screen from the Kempe workshops, its loft not quite high enough to meet the medieval doorway to the old roodloft. The east window comes from the same workshops, and pictures the appearances of the Risen Christ in memory of Richard and Eleanor Corbet, whose distant ancestor, Roland Corbet, is pictured on a brass of 1580, a boy on his knees wearing a full-sleeved robe. A couple also from the 16th century appear in a 14th century tomb recess, Thomas Bulkeley and his wife in a fine black hat, their portraits engraved on stone. A row of three Jacobean seats carved back and front serve as sedilia.

The west window, aglow with Old Testament folk, is a memorial to the Victorian Era, and one who died shortly before the old queen is remembered by a big oil painting; it pictures women weeping over Christ's pierced hands and feet. The Madonna and the Child appear in a lovely bit of tapestry. The peace memorial chapel (where a silver bugle hangs over 146 names) has a handsome altar and a richly carved reredos, a triptych with Christ between four of His followers, all in canopied niches, with 12 angels.

The church hill falls steeply down to where the River Tern marks the frontier of Staffordshire, and just across the boundary at Blore Heath a lonely cross in the fields marks where the Lancastrian leader Lord Audley fell in the Wars of the Roses 500 years ago.

The Good Works of Thomas Bray

MARTON. Its tiny hillside church looks out on the heights, above it being the old half-timbered Marton Manor, and below it a farmhouse including part of the old hall. We catch a glimpse of the great sedge-lined mere known as Marton Pool, stretching for more than 30 acres; and between it and the village is a big tumulus which may have been an artificial island for a Stone Age dwelling. An ancient dug-out canoe found in the Pool has gone to Shrewsbury Museum.

At Marton Crest was born Dr Thomas Bray, whose good work is still marching on after more than 200 years. He started the scheme for providing parish libraries which developed into the Society for Promoting Christian Knowledge; and a few years later, having been sent by the Bishop of London to Maryland, he founded the Society for Propagating the Gospel.

Nelly Foster's Wedding Day

MELVERLEY. Perhaps it was a love of solitude that directed the choice of its first settlers. Amid green fields where the River Vyrnwy sweeps in an arc of splendour on its way to join the Severn, they built their extraordinary church and the few farms and cottages, looking over meadow and mountain to the glory of Breiddon Hill beyond the river.

The church, with two fine yews perhaps as old as itself, is one of the quaintest in the county. Built while Henry the Fourth was dreaming of a pilgrimage to Holy Land, it is not of brick or stone but of huge oak timbers, black and white inside and out, an impressive picture of strength and simplicity. With something of the charm of an ancient house, it recalls the wooden structures of our Saxon ancestors.

A porch probably 500 years old opens to a modest vestibule from which a stairway mounts to the oddest of galleries. The chancel, longer than the nave, has a screen of massive timber reaching to the roof. There are sturdy old oak benches, a fine pulpit of Jacobean days, and an ancient font of unusual shape. Into this rugged scene comes the glowing red, blue, and gold of the sanctuary window, in memory of the priests who served here from the Reformation to 1928 and of the men who went from Melverley to the war. In one of the scenes is a model of Lichfield Cathedral.

We found a delightfully quaint entry in the register, telling of the marriage of Matthew Dodd and Elinor Foster on December 17, 1766; this is the parish clerk's little burst of poetic satisfaction on that morning:

> *This morning I have put a Tye*
> *No man could put it faster*
> *Tween Matthew Dodd, the man of God,*
> *And modest Nelly Foster,*
> > *John Lewis, Clk.*

A mile away is one of the natural sights of the neighbourhood, a mound of hard rock sixty feet high, known as Belan Bank.

William Morris and Burne-Jones

MEOLE BRACE. It is just outside Shrewsbury, but it has still something of the seclusion of the days when Mary Webb lived here before her wedding. Here for a while she lived, before she made her home three miles away at Lyth Hill, a famous beauty spot where she and her writing husband built a cottage. Lyth Hill is a small wooded height with glorious views on every side, over nearly all the hills and valleys described in her books. She was away from her county only for a year or two ; the rest of her life was spent within sight of the Wrekin and the smoke of the chimneys of Shrewsbury, the Silverton of her books.

The village owes its fame today to a gallery of sacred art in the church, whose gay mottled walls colour a quiet nook far from the hurly-burly of traffic. Built last century on the site of a vanished Norman structure, the church, lofty and light, rises from green lawns with a massive embattled tower and shapely yews about it. It is its windows that bring us here, for they are nearly all by William Morris from designs by his friend Burne-Jones. The scenes are full of colour, movement, and imagination. The chancel alone has 170 figures, in red, blue, green, and gold. In the centre is the Crucifixion, with Christ in Glory, attended by angels, apostles, saints, prophets, martyrs; at one side are nine Old Testament scenes, from Eden to the building of the Temple; and at the other side the Nativity, the sleeping disciples, the Baptism, the wedding at Cana, Christ with the children, the raising of the daughter of Jairus, the miracle of the fishes, the Last Supper, and Paul preaching.

In the south chapel is a red rose window of Christ in the carpenter's shop with Joseph and Mary. In an aisle window Enoch is clasping a hand coming from a cloud, Elijah is with the ravens and Noah with his Ark, and in the other aisle are Ruth, Miriam, and Devotion. Here also is a window in memory of one who did not come back, showing Christ as Sacrifice, Valour in blue, Endeavour in green, with a shield and broken sword, and St George slaying the Dragon. The village peace memorial is a fine alabaster wall monument, in the canopied niche of which an angel holds a crown, while at either side of the bronze tablet with its 64 names kneel an angel and a knight. The richly carved reredos shows the Resurrection, watched by angels and soldiers, saints attending.

The Old Roodloft

MIDDLETON. In a pretty corner, not far from Ludlow, we come to its church, reaching the door by a charming lychgate and along a little avenue of Irish yews. Its walls are ancient, but much of the Norman masonry has been made new. Two little windows have been in the chancel 800 years, and two more as old are in the nave. A Norman doorway with a crude tympanum is now filled up. The pulpit is Elizabethan, and so is the altar table, above which the Crucifixion shines in attractive modern glass. But the best sight is the chancel screen with its finely vaulted loft, the front of the loft traceried, and the cornice with three rows of foliage. It was here before the Reformation, and is a fine treasure for so tiny a place.

The Magic Cow in the Old Stone Circle

MIDDLETON. The Middleton near Chirbury, only 500 feet below the summit of Stapeley Hill, it shares the height with the prehistoric achievements of the race which gave us the wonders of Avebury and Stonehenge. Here, with their legends, are three Stone Circles; Mitchell's Fold, a 90-foot enclosure with eight stones standing; the Whetstones, with a few monoliths still in position; and, on the other side of the hill, Marsh Pool, with over 30 stones encircling a space of 70 feet diameter, with a king stone in the centre.

The little church, built about a century ago with a cross-shaped bellcot, contains the most surprising treasure found among these hills, the wonderful work of a parson we had the pleasure of meeting at Fitz (Waldegrave Brewster), a dauntless artist then nearing his four score years and ten. His work here sets us thinking of the medieval scholars who combined preaching and writing with the work of the carver, the hodman, and the mason. It was the parson here who carved the ends of 22 benches in the nave, the fine chair in the chancel, and the varied arm-rests of the choir-stalls, adorning them with flowers, dragons, animals, women in bonnets and draped head-dresses, grim bearded men, jovial laughing men, men wearing the fez, and men in medieval caps.

Even more surprising is the parson's stone-carving, the work on the eight sides of the font, and the delightful sculptures on capitals. On the south side are carved in high relief the 12 figures of the Zodiac; on the other the queer village legend is delightfully told on a sculptured capital.

The legend, an attempt of the past to explain the mystery of the Stone Circle of Mitchell's Fold, tells us that during a famine the good fairy of the village, in opposition to the evil spirit, sent the stricken people a wonderful cow, which, appearing daily within the Circle, yielded an inexhaustible supply of milk, until in an unguarded hour the witch milked it into a sieve, whereupon the animal sank exhausted into the ground, never to reappear.

Here is this drama all clearly sculptured; the Circle itself, with men and women hurrying between the stones, coming and going with their jugs and pitchers, while a man milks the cow, the protecting fairy hovering near. Another scene shows the cow and the witch lurking ready with her bottomless vessel.

The legend is precious as an effort of the primitive mind to rationalise the unexplained origin of the scene; its preservation in stone is a merriment for all who come.

From Shropshire to the Holy Land

MIDDLETON SCRIVEN. It loses itself among trees a mile off the road from Bridgnorth to Cleobury Mortimer. The church, made new last century, has a pulpit and a reading desk with 16th century oak panelling, but the font is modern. It has quaint carvings of the Adoration of the Magi, a winged figure with a sword and a bird on the end of a chain, and St George and a three-headed dragon surrounded by a chain with a little scene in each link. A window with a lovely figure of Dorcas in green and gold takes our thoughts to the Holy Land, for it is in memory of Helen Attlee, who died near the Mount of Olives while working for the Church Missionary Society. She was the only daughter of a rector who is remembered in the next window of the Good Shepherd. In a field near the rectory are two venerable yews.

MILSON. Its lonely farms are among the border hills, with lovely views and much beauty in blossom-time. High above the wayside stands its tiny church, the tower on a 13th century base, and a fine old yew keeping company with the 14th century porch. But older than anything are the Norman walls of tinted stone, the Norman doorway with slender shafts, and the Norman windows in the nave and chancel, two of them bright with figures of St Elizabeth and John the Baptist. The font is ancient, the nave roof has old beams and rafters, and a beautiful lancet window in the tower has been admired for 700 years.

Chaucer's Editor

MINSTERLEY. A rippling stream runs through the village on its way to join the Rea. The beautiful black and white gabled house, Minsterley Hall, is tucked away behind the church. It keeps part of the old manor house of the Thynnes, a family which gave Henry the Eighth a Clerk of the Kitchen and Chaucer his first editor.

The editor was William Thynne, who spent many years and much money in collecting Chaucer manuscripts and in 1532 printed the first complete edition. It may well be that but for the scholarly master of Bluebeard's banquets these manuscripts would have been lost to literature.

A Lady Thynne of later days gave the church its fine silver plate, a flagon, two chalices, and patens. The house is the best thing to see in the village and we see it well from the road behind the church.

The church, rare in coming from the 17th century, when so few churches were built, is a quaint little place. The wooden bell-turret crowns the west front where the doorway is carved with skull and crossbones, cherubs, and an hourglass. The nave has a high-pitched black and white roof and an odd, pillared gallery. The gabled entrance to the chancel screen has a sea serpent carved on each side of the doors, and the oak pulpit has a richly carved Jacobean canopy.

Here we found, hanging from one of the beams in the gallery, one

Market Drayton
The Tower climbed by Robert Clive

Moreton Say
Where Clive of Plassey Sleeps

Lydbury North   **Ancient Church with Massive Tower**

Much Wenlock **The Old Guildhall and Raynald's Mansion**

Hopesay **The Church Among the Trees**

of those pathetic survivals of olden days, seven funeral garlands made of paper flowers. They are one of perhaps a dozen sets still left in England, having been worn by a maiden who died before her wedding day; it was such crants as these that Ophelia was allowed to have at her funeral much to the indignation of the churlish priest. Here they hang on the original iron rods from which they were suspended, after being borne in funeral processions at Minsterley in the 18th century.

MONKHOPTON. It lies in country noted for its oaks and yews, but none of its trees are as old as the doorway through which its people have gone to church for 800 years. The doorway has the Norman chevron ornament on its arch, and two Norman windows in the chancel are decorated with bold rows of zigzag characteristic of the Norman mason, while a third is fashioned in great links like a chain. There are two other Norman windows in the nave which were filled in when the church was rebuilt last century.

Uncle Josiah Keeps Watch Over Darwin

MONTFORD. It lies by the Severn, its 18th century church on a hilltop overlooking farms and cottages to a pretty patchwork countryside, and a fine sweep of hills into which comes Admiral Rodney's column on Breiddon.

The church has little to interest us; it is dim with coloured windows, and has a medieval font, and some old tiles in the sanctuary. What will appeal to the traveller is that near the embattled tower rests Robert Waring Darwin, with his wife Susannah Wedgwood, daughter of the great potter, and some of their daughters. Susannah, from whom Charles Darwin inherited the rare kindliness of his nature, died when her illustrious son was still a child, but her husband, son of the famous Erasmus Darwin, lived to see Charles complete his voyage in the Beagle, and publish the famous Journal.

It was only with reluctance that Robert Darwin consented to his son's acceptance of the post of naturalist on the Beagle, objecting that it would be disreputable afterwards to his character as a clergyman, that it was a wild scheme, that it must have been refused by many others before being offered to him and was therefore a worthless post, that it would unsettle him in life, and that it would prove a worthless undertaking.

Fortunately Uncle Josiah Wedgwood, whose judgment the doctor considered infallible, swept away all these objections, and Charles sailed. He venerated his father's memory to the end of his days, in spite of all this, and declared him the wisest man he ever knew, "able to read the character and even the thoughts of those whom he saw for even a short time."

A mile away from the church, carrying the road from Shrewsbury to Oswestry over the Severn, is the lofty Montford Bridge, built by Telford the roadmaker in 1790. It occupies the site of an earlier bridge which often figures in history. It was here in 1283 that David, last Welsh prince of Wales, was delivered to the English as a traitor loaded with chains, surrendered by his own countrymen, who had captured him in a cave. So important was the event that Edward summoned to Shrewsbury the first Parliament in which representatives of the Commons took part by legal authority. They sent the wretched captive to a terrible death.

More and More

MORE. There are fine hills on the horizon of this little place of stirring memories and rich possessions. It has but a few houses, scattered about its old church, one a farm with 1662 on its black and white gable; but here are links with the Battle of Hastings, and something from the grandeur that was Rome. A mile away, in the park of Linley Hall, successor to the great castle of the Mores, is the site of the butts at which the archers used to practise with the long-bow. In the park are larches descended from the first introduced into this country; the park gave its noble company of oaks and beeches to help the country in the war.

The cheerful little church has a tower 700 years old with a 17th century timber bellcot. It is this church which proudly shelters the oldest and most beautiful possession of the village. On either side of the old tapering font is a strip of splendid tessellated pavement from a Roman villa discovered near the old home of the Mores. The black and white mosaics form a star pattern, and are as perfect as when the Roman craftsmen finished their work 1700 years ago. With its cream walls and black and white hammerbeam roofs, the church has old box-pews, a reading desk with a Jacobean cornice and panels, an ancient chest with seven locks, and a library of old books given by

Richard More in the time of Charles the Second "to teach the minister sound doctrine." The Mores were stout Puritans. Many members of the family sleep in a transept built in 1640 in time to receive Richard More, a fearless champion of national rights, whose shield of arms is in the floor, his painted heraldry being on the wall.

According to Camden the Mores came over with the Conqueror, Richard falling at Hastings. As a reward for his valour there his son received lands and built here his "faire house." Our Norman kings called upon the Mores for 200 men-at-arms in time of war. A 14th century Sir Thomas More shared the captivity of Edward the Second in Berkeley Castle; another member of the family was the great Lord Chancellor slain by his imperious master Henry the Eighth. Richard More was one of the few Shropshire men of ancient family to resist Charles Stuart, and his son Samuel turned from his father's funeral here to the command of Hopton Castle, a Commonwealth fortress. With only 31 men he defended his post for a month against 500. He was imprisoned and exchanged for a Royalist, and continued to hold important military commands until he was suspected of conspiring to depose Cromwell from the Protectorate, when he was excluded from Parliament. The Restoration left him unscathed, and he died in his bed.

One of his sons, Robert, was a devoted botanist and a close friend of Linnaeus, and came back here from the Tyrol bringing with him the first larches to be planted in England. He raced home with his friend the Duke of Atholl who was also taking larches to plant, and won the race, getting his trees in one day before the duke.

A Sword from Mons

MORETON CORBET. It is a village of much beauty and friendliness, with a rare group of old buildings not soon forgotten. We come to them through a gateway which bids all wayfarers welcome from an open road to an open church.

On one hand is the lovely black and white rectory with five gables, and on the other are the brick walls of a Tudor castle dismantled by Cromwell's men, side by side with the shell of the stately hall which Robert Corbet began to build in 1606 and never finished. Its gables, crowned with balls, show what a magnificent building he had in mind.

Before us lies the splendid church, across a smooth green with an exquisite bronze sculpture in memory of little Vincent Corbet who died at Eton in 1903. The sculpture is by J. H. M. Furse, a brother of the famous painter Charles Furse, and shows Mercury doing up the latchet of his sandal.

The chief part of the church is Norman, but it was much damaged during the fight for the castle in the Civil War. A Norman sedilia arch faces part of a Norman window in the chancel, and a 14th century arcade separates the nave from an aisle. The tower was refashioned in 1779, and the chapel where the 18th century squires used to sit has become a delightful Children's Corner. The pulpit and the reading desk have Jacobean carving, and in the panels of the inner west doors there is a medley of 15th century glass, the most striking fragment showing a face with tears on its cheeks. The east window shows the Madonna between St Vincent and St Bartholomew, and the elaborate reredos below has graceful figures of the Madonna and Gabriel.

Among much that reminds us of the Corbets is a glorious coloured tomb to Sir Robert of 1513 and his wife who lived without him for half a century. He lies in Tudor armour, his head on a helmet and his feet on a lion; and in the panels of the tomb are six children, all in different costumes, and ten angels. Beautifully coloured, too, is another tomb to Richard of 1567 and his lady, he in armour with two painted shields on his tunic. Other shields on the tomb are supported by owls and elephants, and the centre panel shows a chrisom baby above a squirrel feeding from a tree. There is a bust of Richard Corbet, who died in 1691, the epitaph telling of his devotion to King Charles, and a plaque to Sir Rowland Corbet who gave his life in the Retreat from Mons, his actual sword hanging below.

Primus in Indis

MORETON SAY. At Styche Hall, on a hilltop north of this village, was born the boy whose schoolmaster predicted before he was ten that "few names would be greater than his." Before he was 50 he was brought back to lie in this church, having fulfilled the prophecy by adding India to the British Empire.

Robert Clive's family had lived at Styche Hall for 300 years before he was born here in 1725, and we like to remember that part of the first prize money he received, after laying the foundation of British

India by holding Arcot against the French, went in redeeming this old home and paying his impoverished father's debts. Market Drayton can show his school and the church tower he climbed to sit on a gargoyle's neck; Shrewsbury has put up a statue to him as its MP; but Moreton Say has his birthplace and his grave, as well as the Clive Memorial Hall.

The church where he lies received a new tower with a short leaded spire in the 18th century, and lost its medieval aspect when it was faced with brick last century; but the fine doorway, the wide arch over the piscina, and half the curious font are all Norman, the font having one of the earliest Norman bowls turned upside down as a stand for a 13th century bowl. Good modern woodwork is here in the richly carved screen, the panelled chancel ceiling, and the pierced pulpit. The altar table and the noble gallery are Jacobean, a fine staircase leading up to this gallery fronted with carved balusters and with an inscription telling that Arthur Sandford gave the timber for it and Lady Jane Grosvenor paid £10 for its erection in 1634.

The same Lady Jane, knowing nothing of the man whose simple brass tablet was to take pride of place here, also erected an imposing tomb in the sanctuary for herself and her two husbands, John Bostock and Richard Grosvenor. A fine group these three make, sculptured on top of their tomb, all wearing ruffs, and with touches of colour left on their dress, on the shields round them, and in the arched recess behind. Lady Jane lived for many years to see herself lying here in stone, for the tomb was here in 1623 and it was 20 years later that she put on the wall close by the quaint wooden memorial carved with the kneeling figures of her three sisters, Mary, Elizabeth, and Rachel, the daughters of Sir Thomas Vernon.

Many are the tablets to the Clive family up to our own day, for, though the heir became the Earl of Powis and went to live in Powis Castle shortly after Robert's death, others of the family remained in the neighbourhood, and the Earl's eldest son, as Viscount Clive, also carries on the name honoured on his ancestor's brass tablet with the three words *Primus in Indis*.

The Romantic Lord Clive

THE son of an impoverished squire, he was a fiery, unruly, yet lovable boy. He climbed the steeple of Market Drayton and sat there unconcerned; he thrust his body into a breach in a dam to conduct a stream into a shop. At school he was the hero of everything but study.

He was sent to India in his teens as a writer in the East India Company, and proved as big a handful to his seniors there as he had been to his schoolmasters. His wayward disposition, intensified by loneliness, drove him to attempt his life, but his pistol twice missed fire and he thought again. "I am reserved for something," he said.

He fought a duel with an officer he had accused of cheating at cards. Clive fired and missed, and his antagonist placed a pistol at his head, and bade him retract or die. "Fire!" retorted Clive; "I said you cheated," and the other dropped his pistol. The incident, varied in the telling, forms the subject of Browning's poem on Clive.

Within a year of Clive's arrival the hostility between the French and English, allied to rival native powers in India, came to a head. The French were esteemed as warriors, the English contemptuously regarded as traders; and but for Clive it would have been France and not England who established an Indian Empire.

When Madras was seized in 1746 Clive obtained a commission and at once revealed his military genius. In order to relieve Trichinopoli he obtained permission to lead an expedition against Arcot. With only 500 men he drove out the garrison, entered a city of 100,000 people, and prepared to defend his gain. With only a low and lightly-built wall, a choked ditch, and crumbling towers of defence, with food short and forces sadly reduced, he sustained a seven-week siege by 10,000 men, and put them to flight after a final battle of 18 hours. By that memorable feat the prestige of British arms was established in India, and the whole course of history altered. Success followed success; Trichinopoli was relieved.

Broken in health, Clive returned to England in 1753, to marry and to enter Parliament, and in 1755 he returned to India as Governor. One of his first tasks was to avenge the tragedy of the Black Hole of Calcutta, where the brutal Surajah Dowlah, Nabob of Bengal, had seized the city, thrown 146 English captives into a room 20 feet square, and left them during one of the hottest nights of the year, only 23 remaining alive in the morning. Clive quickly took Calcutta, but to his disgust the Company made terms with the Nabob.

Clive now planned to overthrow Surajah and set up Mir Jaffier in his stead. A willing and necessary agent in the conspiracy was Omichund, a wealthy Hindu banker, who late in the negotiations, unexpectedly demanded £300,000 for the treacherous part he was to play. Countering him by unblushing mendacity, Clive prepared two agreements, one in which Omichund's claim was admitted and one from which it was omitted; and when the hour came he produced the second and repudiated the first. It is the blackest spot on his fame.

His preparations made, he marched to Plassey with 3200 men, of whom only 650 were English, and with this little force he routed Surajah's army of 68,000 men. He then installed Mir Jaffier as Nabob, and accepted from him £300,000 and land-rents worth £30,000 a year. This is the other blot on his fame, yet when accused before a Parliamentary Commission of rapacity and exaction, Clive, remembering the wealth spread before him, exclaimed, "At this moment I stand astonished at my own moderation!"

He came home leaving an empire where he had found only a trading settlement. Raised to the peerage, he was sent back once more to reform the civil and military services, suppress a mutiny, and establish British rule over a vast area. Returning to England for the last time in 1767, he faced his enemies who were attempting to impeach him, and the affair ended in a resolution by the House of Commons that he had rendered "great and meritorious service to his country." But his health was now ruined, and the vexation of this ordeal completed his undoing. A few years more, and he died by his own hand as he had meant to do before his career began.

A Great Historian

MORVILLE. The old whipping-post still stands at the crossroads, and a fieldpath near it leads on to peace and beauty. It leads to a fine 18th century hall on the site of Morville Priory, and to a church of an age-old loveliness with the murmur of a stream for an anthem, and a wooded hill as a background for its splendid tower. In this tranquillity the Normans raised a church 800 years ago. Their tower, chancel, nave, and aisles remain, and the south doorway is a faithful copy of the one they made; the beams of the door, stained and scarred by time, are clasped by great scrolled hinges which are among the finest ironwork in the county, the centre one probably being Norman.

The six fine arches of the nave with their clustered columns and grotesque heads, the chancel arch with its carved capitals and ornamented moulding, and two of the windows, are as the Normans left them; the chancel also has its original doorway for the priest, but its tympanum of scrollwork is almost worn away.

At the sides of the west doorway are massive quatrefoils which probably belonged to a medieval screen, and above the doorway are three curious heads carved in wood, looking down with strange grimaces. Even more curious are four panels on the walls of the nave, carved and painted long ago, showing the Four Evangelists as grotesque figures with huge faces. The choir-seats have carved Jacobean panels, and there are two ancient chests, one being a dug-out about six feet long bearing the marks made by an ancient axe. One of the north aisle windows has a gem of 14th century glass, showing the Crucifixion in blue, gold, and brown. The big font is a mass of carving, its cable moulding probably being Norman, but the seven queer faces round the bowl and the leaves and medallions are later additions. The handsome pulpit of grey and green marble is modern.

Sir Edward Acton, an 18th century lord of the manor, has an elaborate marble monument adorned with cherubs. A mile away, in a park with magnificent iron gates and a half-mile avenue of limes, is Aldenham Hall built by him in 1697 and incorporating mullioned windows belonging to his ancestral home. In its little chapel is a marble monument to Sir Richard Acton, with a weeping woman and child delicately carved by Westmacott. Here also is an exquisite Madonna in white marble, a memorial to Gabrielle Acton, who died while returning from a pilgrimage to Lourdes in 1930, when he was in his teens.

Aldenham Hall was long the home of the first Lord Acton, the famous 19th century historian. He was born at Naples of a German mother and received a cosmopolitan education. His happiest years were the six spent at Munich, where he learned under Professor Dollinger never to be afraid of the truth whether it happened to conflict with the doctrine of his Church or not. He was all his life a member of the Roman Catholic Church, although openly disapproving of the papal claim to infallibility. He travelled widely and built up an immense library which Mr Andrew Carnegie ultimately bought for Lord Morley, who gave it to Cambridge University. In Parliament he began a friendship with Mr Gladstone which never ended; the Liberal leader rarely failed to consult his younger friend on any important matter. He wrote and lectured on history and religion and became Professor of Modern History at Cambridge, where he was a great success, stressing always the moral side of politics and the necessity of liberty in Church and State. He was unhappily stricken with paralysis at the beginning of this century, and the last few months of his life were spent at his wife's home in Germany.

The Ages Pass

MUCH WENLOCK. It has been said that it sleeps in the hills dreaming of all that it has been, stirring with the memory of warrior kings and the ancient strife of the Border valleys, and inspired by the natural spectacle from Wenlock Edge with a marvellous range of little vales and copses, running brooks and rambling paths, green meadows and winding lanes, and, most impressive of all, the wild peaks of Wales. The Severn flows two miles away, near the Wrekin, eternal yet ever changing with the light. Buildwas is close by, enshrined with all the wonder of the past, and Wenlock town itself has a noble pile of ruins still standing where its Saint Milburga ruled in the days before King Alfred. It has its ancient Guildhall with all its lovely oak, and in the streets are fine old houses and little timbered fronts which must always give it a charm to the traveller who would know our matchless countryside.

It is, of course, the ruined priory which brings the traveller here; it was founded by the granddaughter of King Penda of Mercia, and was destroyed by the Danes, restored by Lady Godiva, destroyed again soon after the Conquest, and finally restored to greatness by the Norman baron Roger de Montgomery, who found Milburga's tomb. It then became the great Cluniac centre for England, and was a proud and prosperous place till Thomas Cromwell destroyed it for his royal master. It remained a neglected ruin until our own century, when excavation brought to light vast masses of masonry, windows and doorways, and a remarkable group of decorated arches. The walls of the chapter house have rich Norman carving showing that it must have been a noble room. The three rich western doorways leading to the cloisters are the most interesting survivals, for the walls of the west front are covered with delicate arcading and groups of tiny capitals in twos and threes, all delicately carved. In one corner is a great lintel with a crude horned face between two writhing dragons. It is astonishing that all these intimate details should have survived so many centuries of wind and rain.

The most substantial relic of the priory church is the 13th century south transept 70 feet high, still with the spacious corbelled vaulting shafts and the stiff-leaf foliage. There also remain parts of the west wall of the north transept with beautiful arcading. Within the cloisters is a circle of broken columns, surrounding a fragment of the monks' lavatory, of which two striking panels of sculpture remain. One has two vivid figures of saints enclosed in arches within a greater arch; the other has five figures under a trefoil arch, and may represent Our Lord asleep in the boat. Under two alcoves near the chapter house we came upon many fragments of sculpture exquisitely carved, as well as medieval tiles, urns, and bits of carved oak. The Prior's House still stands in a garden of clipped yews, much as it was 500 years ago, but it is not shown; it has a long storeyed gallery on one side, fine windows and buttresses, and a steep roof of ancient tiles.

Wenlock's old Guildhall is a timbered building resting on the stout oak arches of the butter market, and we may see on one of the pillars iron rings which mean that it was used as a whipping-post. The gabled front of the Guildhall, with the battlemented church tower beyond and the timbered front beyond that, make a fine spectacle at a street corner. The end near the church is stone, and older than the timbered structure; it was built as a prison. It is on record that the timbered frame of the Guildhall was put up in two days, all the timber having been cut out and numbered so that the carpenters had merely to peg it together. Upstairs is the magistrate's room, and the council chamber, both panelled with oak and with open timber roofs, and with a wonderful collection of carved chairs and fittings. Over the seat of justice are the arms of Queen Elizabeth, and on the timber roof is a Latin motto urging the magistrate to judge justly and have mercy. Here are kept the old stocks made for three and remarkable for being fitted with wheels so that they could be taken round the town.

The church has a 14th century porch with a room over it, and the interior belongs to all the medieval centuries and later. Most of the best Norman work is hidden from us, for the west front is covered by the tower added by the Normans after the rest of the church was finished. It seems an odd thing to have done; only the lowest arch of the front was left uncovered, it having been the main entrance. In the walls of the tower hiding this Norman façade are two quaint little heads.

The plain chancel arch is Norman, and there are remains of Norman windows high up in the south wall, and crude Norman masonry over the medieval arch to the lady chapel. The arcade is 13th century, eight stone corbel heads are 15th, and the nave roof 17th. The chancel has a fine 15th century east window, with an elaborate canopied niche on each side, one still with its medieval colours. Two corbels on the north and south walls of the chancel are believed to represent Henry the Third and his Queen Eleanor, who came as guests to Wenlock Priory several times. Both the chancel and the lady chapel have 15th century sedilia, those in the lady chapel having panels grotesquely carved with animals and shields. On the Jacobean pulpit are five queer women with outstretched arms, and heads of lions between them.

A 16th century brass in a stone frame shows Richard Ridley kneeling at a table, and there is a brass inscription to Robert Grainger, who was killed in a desperate engagement with a French ship in 1813; he remained at his post terribly wounded till a charge of grape-shot from the Frenchmen killed him. On the bronze peace memorial are two graceful figures of kneeling angels in memory of men who left their quiet homes in this beautiful town to die 100 years later side by side with Frenchmen. In the churchyard is part of a medieval cross, and an ancient stone coffin in which there may have been laid to rest a prior of Wenlock in the days when solemn chantings were heard where now the birds sing in these ruins.

Wenlock is rich with fine old inns and houses. There is a timbered Elizabethan manor house with a massive oak entrance, an odd-looking black and white house in the Bull Ring, an inn which was once the Almoner's House, and an inn with the iron sign of a raven beautifully wrought centuries ago. By St Owen's Well is a 15th century house with a remarkable archway made of great boughs of oak with their natural curves meeting to form arches, the timbers having been roughly squared with an adze. We have come upon single arches like this at church doorways, but this house is unique in our experience for it has three pairs of these natural arches set parallel at about 16 feet apart, a horizontal beam joining them and forming the ridge of the roof; the space between was filled in with small timber and finally with wattle and daub; all this done in the 15th century to make a house for the priest. One of the most charming old houses in the town is the three-gabled Raynald's Mansion, now a shop that we may see. It has two square bays and a little balcony between, and the timbers are quaintly carved, having on them the gilded names of John and Mary Raynald with the date 1682. Ashfield Hall, in the High Street, is half stone and half timber, and was probably a leper hospital 500 years ago, when the timbered frame was added. It still has its Elizabethan chimney stack, and in the 17th century it was an inn at which Charles Stuart stayed on his way from Shrewsbury to Bridgnorth.

In his poems of A Shropshire Lad, A. E. Housman pictures a Roman and an English yeoman looking up at the great mass of Wenlock Edge, and was moved to reflect that all our troubles pass like Uriconium, while this remains:

> The tree of man was never quiet:
> Then twas the Roman, now tis I.
> The gale, it plies the saplings double,
> It blows so hard twill soon be gone:
> Today the Roman and his trouble
> Are ashes under Uricon.

A Brick From the Great Wall of China

MUNSLOW. Its busy highway climbs among the little orchards and drops gently down to the church nestling in the hollow. The black and white Crown Inn was once the Hundred House at which the ancient courts were held, and the gabled stone house near the peace memorial was the birthplace of a very prominent but inconsistent judge of Charles Stuart's day, Edward Littleton. Two magnificent Scotch firs stand sentinel at the gate of the churchyard, and roses and ivy climb up the old lychgate to make a lovely canopy over the grave of an 18th century rector. The rectory has a fine lawn and a little lake to add beauty to the scene.

The church has the dignity and the charm of old age. The Norman work remains in the lower part of the tower, but the upper part is medieval. The splendid north porch, with eight open bays and seats of gnarled oak, has timbers which were felled soon after Agincourt, and the ancient door is still on its hinges. But here is something compared with which our medieval days are young, for the doorstep of this church has a history which may make it unique among all the stones in our English churches. It was part of a great monument set up on the earth before the Roman Empire, for it is nothing less thrilling than a brick from the Great Wall of China, which was built before Julius Caesar came to Britain, 20 feet high and 1400 miles long.

The old door opens into a pleasant interior with walls of rose and grey lit by deeply splayed windows rich with old glass. The nave and chancel are 700 years old, but the arcade was added in the 14th and 15th centuries. The wide tower arch is Norman and is carved with heads and lilies. There are more flowers carved on the 15th century font, and roses on a 14th century chest. From the 17th century come two carved chairs, and there are ten fine old pews. On a windowsill is a coffin stone with a cross, and a 17th century slate tablet has on it a skull, an hourglass, and the shrouded figure of William Churchman, whose daughter appears as a shrouded figure in wood. The portrait of John Lloyd, a 16th century rector, is engraved in alabaster, showing him at prayer, and he appears again in fine old glass kneeling before Our Lord. One nave window has a medley of fragments of glass 600 years old with two crowned Madonnas and several figures kneeling, and there is 16th century glass with a Crucifixion scene and a crowned Madonna attended by St Thomas and St Anthony. In another window St John with his chalice and St Anthony with his staff, bell, and book appear in old glass, St Anthony having his dog with him, with a bell hanging from its collar. Above them are little figures in golden roundels.

Edward Littleton, born here in 1589, was educated at Oxford, distinguished himself as a lawyer, and at 32 succeeded his father as Chief Justice for North Wales. Entering Parliament, he opposed Buckingham, was chairman of the Committee of Grievances on whose report was founded the Petition of Right, and stoutly vindicated the authority of Parliament against arbitrary action by the Crown.

Charles attached him to his side by making him Solicitor-General, and, changing front, Littleton supported Charles on Ship Money and spoke for three days against John Hampden at the trial of that patriot. In 1640 he was appointed Chief Justice of England, and then Keeper of the Great Seal, being created a peer. Wavering afresh, he returned to his opposition to Court tyranny, refusing to seal the proclamation for the arrest of the Five Members, and voting with Parliament concerning the Militia.

Charles was furious with him, but Littleton appeased his wrath by declaring that he was only playing a part in order to allay the suspicions of Parliament lest he should be deprived of the Seal. The Seal being necessary to make an Act of Parliament valid, he secretly sent it away to Charles, and himself followed it to York, Parliament having to order a new one to replace the old. He died at Oxford in 1645, after being forgiven by the king. He could not be relied upon, lacking moral backbone and failing in decision and consistency in every crisis.

Five Pounds a Yard

MYDDLE. It comes into the Conqueror's Domesday Book, but has nothing older to see than the ruin of a 13th century castle on the edge of the village which clusters in a hollow of a rocky hillside. All that is left of the castle is the moat and the staircase turret; it was allowed to fall into ruin by the wild Humphrey Kynaston, who was outlawed in the 16th century. We come upon him at Nesscliffe.

It would seem that the tower of the church fell into ruin about the same time, for we read of another Kynaston (rector here and chaplain to James the First) offering to rebuild the tower as far as his own height if the village would do the rest. It actually was rebuilt by one John Dod, who had £5 for every yard from the foundations to the battlements.

The church has a medieval brass with the portrait of Arthur Chambre, wearing a rich gown with the Tudor ruff, his wife in an embroidered gown and veiled headdress and their son and daughter with them. On the chancel wall is a brass cross in memory of a rector for 58 years (G. H. Egerton). He lived into our own century and carved the font cover in olive wood brought from the Holy Land. The finely timbered lychgate, with figures of Christ and Peter in the gable ends, is the memorial of his jubilee here.

Panorama

MYNDTOWN. We come to it by narrow winding lanes, a lonely hamlet looking out on a magnificent panorama of hills.

Its little church, rectory, and farmhouse shelter under the bare ridge of the Longmynd, the church with a fine old yew for company, and a big wooden fish aloft on the bell turret. An ancient timber porch, carved at the entrance with trailing foliage, brings us to a dim interior with a few old windows. One in the nave is 14th century, and another, deep in the chancel wall, has a seat in the frame and shines with a picture of the baptism of Our Lord. The font has a plain bowl unusually mounted, and may be as old as the 12th century. A very odd chancel screen is fashioned like a great pointed window of three lights; and a second screen at the west of the nave was once part of the pew of a Jacobean squire. The altar table is Jacobean too and so are the altar rails with their elaborately carved posts.

A Veteran

NASH. It is just, and only just, accessible by car, though its delightful wooden spire, in a lovely sylvan setting, is seen from afar. The chancel, the nave, and the splendid tower of the church have stood 600 years, and outside, under a gable, is a quaint carved head of stone which has been looking down on the churchyard all those years. The finest possession of the church is the modern oak screen from Louvain, adorned with a wealth of leaves and floral work; in the middle it has a figure of Christ giving benediction to all who come here, and below are four more sacred figures. A 19th century window, showing Christ with two angels holding the hem of His garment, is to Admiral Lowe, who lived at the 17th century house known as Court of Hill, a mile or two out of the village. The most impressive sight Nash has to show is the marvellous old oak at the junction of the road to Coreley, so huge that it dwarfs the old cottages near it. Its gnarled trunk is 40 feet round at the ground; about 60 feet high, it has a spread of about 90 feet. Although its main stem is decayed, it is a grand veteran, which may have been planted here before the Conquest.

Walls Five Feet Thick

NEEN SAVAGE. It has the little River Rea keeping company with its highway, and a ford where the stream broadens into merry shallows in the shade of lofty trees. It is also memorable for the treasures in its Norman church. Chief among these is the oak screen, with its lovely borders of vine and its 15th century canopy,

with ribs of vaulting ending in tiny flowers; two of its elegant
traceried panels are old, and the other are copies. The screen was
damaged by fire in 1825, and a brass inscription records that it was
saved from total destruction by Thomas Lambert Hall, who sleeps
near it with his wife. It is fitting that it should have been so finely
restored in his memory.

The nave and chancel are beneath one roof, the 15th century
timbers adorned with roses. The tower has three Norman windows
cut through walls about five feet thick, and a Norman arch; the tall,
deeply splayed lights of the east window are possibly 13th century.
There is also a Norman doorway walled up in the nave, and the
south doorway, perhaps 700 years old, is sheltered by a grand
timbered porch of Tudor days.

The peace memorial cross in the churchyard has the lines:

> *Do thou for England live:*
> *We for England died.*

The Pen and the Sword

NEEN SOLLARS. It hides among the pine-clad hills by the
River Rea, and has a few timbered cottages, a tiny old timbered
inn, and a 14th century church with a wooden spire peeping out
among the cherry orchards. The nave still has its 14th century roof,
and the four pointed arches of the central tower, the deep windows of
the nave, and the crude masonry of the walls, are all impressive.
There is an old round font with a modern base, and under an
imposing canopied arch reclines the figure of Humphrey Conyngsby,
lord of the manor in Shakespeare's time—"a perfect scholar by
education and a great traveller by his own affections." A man of the
pen and the sword he appears to have been, for he is in armour,
resting his head on one hand and grasping a sword with the other, a
deeply carved figure of Father Time on each side of him, one with
an hourglass, the other with a sickle, and two women and a painted
coat-of-arms above.

There is a brass inscription to Lieutenant Arthur Gordon, a
rector's son who was killed in Mesopotamia. The oak reredos has
nine panels with paintings of the Assumption, the Nativity, and
other incidents in the life of Christ, and the modern window above
has Crucifixion scenes.

The Prior's House

The Impressive Ruined Walls

MUCH WENLOCK'S ANCIENT PRIORY

Much Wenlock   **Panel at the Priory**

NEENTON. It is a tiny place by the River Rea, with a church rebuilt last century by Sir Arthur Blomfield. It has a carved 15th century chest and a plain Norman font with the marks of the staple from the days when it was locked against witches. The modern oak pulpit, neatly carved with quatrefoils and tracery, was made by craftsmen of the village.

A Shropshire Robin Hood

NESSCLIFFE. Here stands a little wayside school, founded in the 18th century, with two happy lines set up for all to read:

> God prosper and prolong this public good,
> A school erected where a chapel stood.

It is below Nesscliffe Hill, which rises abruptly from the plain and wears a fine mantle of firs outlined against the sky. On the top are the remains of an ancient camp; but far more intriguing is Kynaston's Cave which we come to by a footpath up the hill. Here it was that Humphrey Kynaston came to live in the first years of the Tudor Age, a merry robber who reminds us of Robin Hood. The stories of him tell how he robbed the rich to help the poor, how he had a fine horse shod backwards to cover its tracks, and how he leaped the Severn on horseback when the sheriff's officers thought to trap him by removing planks from Montford Bridge. His cave is divided into two parts, and one, we are told, was a stall for the famous horse.

Offa's Dyke and Folly Brook

NEWCASTLE. Its charm is in its lovely situation among the towering hills where the Folly Brook comes hurrying down to the little stone bridge to meet the River Clun. Away from the village on a high bank looking over the valley is the bellcot church, hardly yet a centenarian, with nothing to draw the traveller but a black and white hammerbeam roof.

A fine piece of Offa's Dyke runs along the hillside east of the church, and on a ridge which gives us a splendid view of the valley is the ancient Fron Camp. A little way off, at Whitcot Keyset, a stone eight feet high is said to mark the grave of a prehistoric hero.

Tom Brown's Schooldays

NEWPORT. One of the old market towns, it has in its wide street a medieval cross and a big church. The bold tower is

14th century, and in a niche near the top is a figure holding a sword and a shield.

Within the church a gilded 15th century roof looks down on tall arcades, over one of the pillars being a medieval relief of St Andrew, shown with hands and feet bound on a cross. There is a collection of more than 50 small brass tablets dating from the 15th century to the 19th, among the oldest being an inscription to John Salter with these beautiful words:

> *To him his own wife Isabella joined herself. To these*
> *may the founder of all things give solace. Amen.*

On a splendid altar tomb lie an unknown Tudor and his wife, with quaint children and angels in the panels. A marble of 1828 is carved with a seated angel, and a fine modern window shows St Nicholas with his anchor and three golden apples. There is a font from the year of the Restoration, a coffin lid elaborately carved 700 years ago, and a list of rectors going back to the Normans.

Near the church is the grammar school founded in Cromwell's time by William Adam, a charming building with a cupola and its original clock.

It has sent two famous men into the world, a satirical poet of Shakespeare's day and a far wiser man of ours. The poet is Thomas Brown, the wise man Sir Oliver Lodge. Brown, son of a Shropshire farmer, was a turbulent spirit responsible for a great deal of satire and humorous verse in the last quarter of the 17th century and it was written of him after his death that:

> *Each merry wag throughout the town*
> *Will toast the memory of Brown*
> *Who laughed a race of rascals down.*

Four lines from the prolific outpouring of his wit have become immortal, and most of us know them.

> *I do not love thee, Dr Fell*
> *The reason why I cannot tell,*
> *But this I know, and know full well,*
> *I do not love thee, Dr Fell.*

Sir Oliver Lodge, the most famous boy of Newport School, was a potter's son who narrowly escaped being a potter by having his interest turned to science through reading penny encyclopedias. He was one of the first experimenters in wireless and sent wireless telegrams long before Marconi. Hertz discovered wireless waves; Lodge harnessed them. A man of boundless imagination, he has tried to conquer fog, and has interested himself particularly in the mysterious problems of telepathy.

Dedicated to King Charles

NEWTOWN. A small village near Wem, it has one of only four English churches dedicated to the unhappy Charles Stuart. The church as we see it was refashioned last century. Framed on its walls are pictures of Charles's execution and burial. The reredos is a copy in stone of Leonardo's Last Supper, and there are two windows in memory of men who died in the Boer War, one a Nativity scene and one a figure of a warrior kneeling before an angel.

The Living Giant

NORBURY. Its church is almost all new, but the 14th century tower was spared by the rebuilders, who gave it a shingled spire and a new arch into the nave. The chancel is built of old stones, and at the end of the sanctuary step is a rough stone like a boulder, said to have been once used as a penance seat. There is an old chest with three locks, a studded door with ironwork perhaps 300 years old, and an attractive east window of Christ with the Children. Another window shows Our Lord holding a chalice, and is in memory of a vicar who served at this altar for 44 years. The big font is 14th century. It is probable that the great yew in the churchyard is as old as the church; it is a vigorous and shapely monster with a trunk about 30 feet round, though its chief branches have gone.

The Bumping Stone

NORTON-IN-HALES. Its curiosity is a big stone in the middle of the green, the Bradling Stone on which they bumped anyone found working after mid-day on Shrove Tuesday. The church, close by, has a chancel of the 13th century, a tower of the 15th, and an unusual octagonal baptistry. Filling one wall of the tower is a rich monument with carved columns, coloured ornament, and figures of Sir Rowland Cotton and his wife. He is in ornamental armour of Shakespeare's time, and she is holding the babe whose birth brought death to mother and child. Angels are about them, carved on the sides and corners of the tomb. There is excellent woodwork in the chancel, much of it Jacobean. Figures with folded arms are the pilasters of two rich arches, and 14 heads form the arm-rests of seats in the choir. Other fine carving is on the seats in front of the organ, and more heads appear on modern pews in the nave and transept. In the churchyard is a plain font about 700 years old.

The Faith That Moves Mountains

OAKENGATES. It is a crowded mining area, a creation of last century, with a church of that time and rows of little houses, and nothing to attract visitors to it; yet the visitors came. They came from countries all over the world, young enthusiasts of the International Voluntary Service for Peace, which tackles anything anywhere that is too big for ordinary men and ordinary enthusiasms, from helping to clear up the ruin of an earthquake in India, a landslide in France, or floods in some other country. They came to Oakengates because here was a giant man-made mound left from the days before history, which was in the way of everything, but seemed too big for the municipal authorities to tackle. There were 30,000 tons to be shifted, and when we called they had shifted half of it, one set of young people following after another, sleeping on paliasses at night, putting aside an evening now and then to discuss in their various languages all the world's problems, and to seal with their voluntary work a new pact of international friendship and peace.

A Lady of Mercia

OLDBURY. In Domesday time Oldbury was an important town, and Ethelfleda, Lady of Mercia, had a castle here the mound of which can still be traced on the quaintly-named Panpudding Hill. Today it is chiefly memorable for the wealth of lovely woodwork in its church, carved at evening classes by young men of the village. The pews by the organ, the panelling round the nave and chancel, and the priest's door are all richly carved in Elizabethan and Jacobean style, and the panels by the altar, with borders of roses and floral centres, are gilded. The finely carved pulpit, reading desks, stalls, and lectern are all in memory of John Purton, rector here for 49 years of last century; the east window of Christ and the Marys is also a memorial to him. There is a Jacobean chest.

A Flower from Ancient Rome

ONIBURY. It is nearly unique among the ten thousand villages we have seen, not for its setting among the hills, or its great house, or its ancient church, or its mill wheel turning above the bridge, but for a humble flower growing wild. It grows in Stoke Wood across the river, and was brought to our shores by the Romans. We know its name, but withhold it for its own sake, for there is perhaps only one other patch in England. Onibury keeps its whereabouts a secret, but some plants of it are in these cottage gardens.

The great house is Stokesay Court, a fine 19th century house in Elizabethan style, with beautiful gardens sometimes thrown open to all. Oak from its estate was used to make the lychgate, which is in memory of one of the Allcrofts who did much for the restoration of Stokesay Castle higher up the valley. Growing beside the lychgate is a very beautiful cedar brought from Lebanon.

A 14th century porch brings us to the church, which has a medieval tower and a fine little chancel arch, so tall that it has been thought to be Saxon. The interior is very quaint, with two rows of old-fashioned lamp-posts at the ends of the pews, a roof with five ancient beams, and a Jacobean pulpit with three panels of linenfold which are perhaps 15th century. Other old possessions are the font and the piscina, and some panelled pews at the west end.

A tablet tells of good John Hodges, who was here 62 years, curate 13 years and rector 49. An oak chair, given in memory of a child's return to health, is carved with the scene of Hannah bringing little Samuel to Eli in the Temple; and a fine east window shows the King of Glory with the Madonna and St George and St John, in memory of John Allcroft and his wife, to whom there is the loveliest of all inscriptions to two people:

They were lovely and pleasant in their lives,
and in death were not divided.

A Pretie Towne Full Fine

OSWESTRY. A very old town on the Welsh border, it is named after St Oswald whose body was nailed to a tree. He was the Christian King of Northumbria 1300 years ago, slain here in battle by the Mercian King Penda. Tradition points to a field across the road from the grammar school as the scene of battle; and close to the school, in a dingle, is St Oswald's Well, the old legend telling how its waters gushed from the spot where part of the saint's body fell as an eagle was carrying it off.

Five centuries afterwards the Normans were fortifying the town with a castle, used by Henry the Second and King John for their attacks on Wales, and by Richard the Second to hold a Parliament in 1398. Its great days have gone, and only fragments of its walls are left on the high ground where Oswestry people come for recreation and the view. They look out at a fine old town of which Thomas Churchyard, the Shropshire poet, wrote 350 years ago:

> As Ozwestry, a pretie towne full fine,
> Which may be lov'd, be likte and praysèd both.
> It stands so trim, and is maintayned so cleane
> And peopled is with folk that well doe meane:
> That it deserves to be enrolled and shryned
> In each good breast, and every manly mynde.

Many struggles has the town seen, and three times in the Middle Ages was it destroyed by fire, so that we do not look here for the ancient possessions found in many a peaceful village. Preserved in the municipal buildings are copies of old charters, a silver cup given by Hugh Myddleton (a burgess of the town), and two 17th century maces; and on the mayor's chain is a Tudor badge with a figure of St Oswald holding a sword. The best of the old houses is the Lloyd Mansion in the heart of the town, a black and white house with fine window tracery and the crest of the Lloyds of Trenwydd. At the entrance to its park are fine iron gates in memory of those who died for peace, their names on the columns at the sides. The grammar school was founded a few years before Agincourt, and though its present buildings are not medieval there stands near the church an old gabled house said to have been the original school, now bought as a memorial to the old boys killed in the war.

Coming to the church we pass under the Griddle, a kind of lych-gate roof built about 300 years ago. The churchyard has very good 18th century gates, and prominent in it is an enormous 20th century cross in memory of a vicar, carved in typically Celtic style with designs of serpents and knotwork, animals and men, and the Holy Family.

The church is of ancient foundation, but mostly 17th century as we see it, though the lower part of the massive tower is 700 years old and stands partly within the building. On the splendid modern porch are figures of Christ, St Mary, and St Oswald; and within is a beautiful doorway in 13th century style, with flower hinges decorating a fine oak door.

Very striking in the spacious interior is its great number of arches, more than 30 in all, with a few of the original windows. The centrepiece is a good alabaster reredos by George Edmund Street, with lifesize figures of Peter and Paul under rich canopies, and smaller figures of the Four Evangelists, Christ and Mary, and John the Baptist. But finer carving is in the oak reredos of the lady chapel, with the Annunciation and figures of four Welsh saints. There is an old chest in the chancel, and another forms the altar in the south chapel, above it being an alabaster peace panel carved with St George and all the paraphernalia of modern warfare. The vestry has a fine Jacobean cupboard enriched with dragons and serpents, grotesques, and human heads.

There is a good eagle lectern with three lions at its foot, a handsome modern pulpit, and an attractive oil painting of John the Baptist. A new font has the signs of the Evangelists, and an old one of the Restoration period is carved with shields, an eagle, and other ornament, its quaint pyramid cover a mass of fluting. On the wall near by is a collection of memorial brasses from the 18th century.

A canopied monument has rather ungainly kneeling figures of two people alive with Shakespeare, Hugh Yale in a cape bordered with fur, and his wife in a great headdress which nearly covers her. They are interesting because Hugh was a kinsman of the founder of Yale University.

At Holy Trinity church, built at the beginning of the Victorian Era is one of the biggest lancets we have seen, with a glass portrait of the Queen as a young woman receiving a heavenly crown. At the Congregational Chapel is kept a pulpit believed to have been used by John Howe, Cromwell's chaplain and Milton's friend.

Three miles away, in the grounds of Aston Hall, stands a private Elizabethan chapel rebuilt two centuries ago. It has a chair probably carved by Elizabethan craftsmen, and a brass memorial of 1742 engraved with an hourglass and the emblems of death.

Two sons of Oswestry have become famous in our own century, a musician and a poet. Here was born Sir Walford Davies, honoured as a Freeman of the town. His music is played and sung everywhere, and his voice has carried the message of music to thousands of schoolchildren and millions of grown-ups all the world over. Here also was born Wilfred Owen, great enough to have been called the modern Keats, who gave his life in France a week before the Armistice and left his country poorer for his loss, but richer for his courage and his genius.

The Young Poet Lost

WILFRED OWEN, born at Oswestry in 1893, had been educated at Liverpool, had travelled a little in France, matriculated at London University, and had started writing poems when the Great War took him into its maelstrom at 21. He was in France at the time, learning French and teaching English, and he came back to join the Artists Rifles, returning to France with them at the beginning of 1917. One of his letters tells how, at Folkestone, he found the hotel a place of luxury, with pages and golden flunkeys, and how in France they were let down gently into the real thing, Mud. He reached a dugout in the middle of No Man's Land, marching three miles over a shelled road and three more over a flooded trench, over ground that was not mud, not sloppy mud, but an octopus of sucking clay five feet deep, relieved only by craters full of water in which men had been drowned. High explosives were dropping all round, and every man was three-quarters dead.

There are few letters written from the front which describe these things more vividly than his, and one of his poems begins:

> *Red lips are not so red*
> *As the stained stones kissed by the English dead.*

He came home wounded and went back again, and on his last day with his mother continually quoted the saying of Rabindranath Tagore: "When I go from hence, let this be my parting word, that what I have seen is unsurpassable." He wrote to a poet friend that a serenity Shelley never dreamed of crowned him as he went back; would it last, he wondered, when he had gone into caverns and abysmals such as Shelley never reserved for his worst demons? It is almost impossible to realise the calm courage of this man who loathed the beastliness of war and yet must do it. He was in a village in which five healthy girls died of fright one night, and yet he was so sensitive that a companion with him in the hospital days wrote that "he was one of those to whom the miseries of the world are misery, and will not let them rest." He was at the head of his company all through 1918 till the week before the Armistice, when he was getting his company across a canal and they were suddenly overwhelmed by heavy fire. He patted his men on the back with a "Well done" here and a "Well done " there, and then he was hit and killed.

He had begun writing poetry when he was 17, and was filled with the spirit of it. Those who knew him best have called him our modern Keats, and the British Museum has received his manuscripts to keep for posterity. They have been presented to the museum by the Friends of the National Libraries, and are the first manuscripts of a modern author bought by the Friends. This is one of his verses on one of the Fallen:

> *Move him into the sun:*
> *Gently its touch awoke him once,*
> *At home, whispering of fields unsown.*
> *Always it woke him, even in France,*
> *Until this morning and this snow.*
> *If anything might rouse him now*
> *The kind old sun will know.*

The Rich Windows

PETTON. Solitary in a field by the park and its great school, the little church is so rich a storehouse of glass, mosaic, and woodwork as to reward us for a long, long walk for the key. The church is of the last two centuries.

Of chief interest among much admirable woodwork is the splendid Jacobean pulpit, towering above the pews with its wealth of fine carving. The oak reredos, with six cherubs spreading their wings to form the five canopies, is also beautiful work. On the chancel wall are two delightful old Dutch carvings, one of St Martin on his horse dividing his cloak for the beggar at his feet, the other showing the startled Roman soldiers at the Resurrection. Perhaps by the same hand is the carving of the Baptism on the oak cover of the font. Richly carved oak pillars support the narrow balcony, with its splendid linenfold, and the walls (even the window splays) are all finely panelled.

Delightful modern glass fills the seven windows. One light, in memory of a lady of the manor, shows her as a beautiful woman in a blue cloak and ermine gown, with a girl in white and gold; another is in memory of one of her sons who fell in the war, showing him as St George in silver armour under a red cloak. In the splay of the window is his bronze plaque from the War Office.

The sanctuary window has Christ as the Light of the World in red and gold. Another window has a red-winged angel under a canopy, with a background of blue sky; and there is a copy of Sir Joshua Reynolds's famous cherubs. There is a charming St Elizabeth with fruit in her lap, a pretty scene above it with two children; and finally there is a delightful St Francis holding a rabbit, a lamb at his feet, birds hovering, and a grasshopper making its way towards him.

Fine mosaics add charm to the scene. The centre panel of an alabaster wall monument has a mosaic figure in armour of Ellis Brook Cunliffe, who fell for his country in 1915. A second beautiful alabaster wall monument, inscribed "Write me as one who loved his fellow men," has a mosaic of St George, wearing a jewel-clasped robe as he slays the dragon, and is in memory of John Brook Cunliffe.

Under the balcony is a tablet to a faithful servant for 40 years; we liked to read these lines from our great Englishman on his stone:

> Fear no more the heat of the sun,
> Nor the furious winter's rages;
> Thou thy worldly task hast done,
> Home art gone and ta'en thy wages.

A relic strangely redeemed is the ancient stoup under the balcony, found last century in the moat of an old house in the village.

The Giant in His Wooden Tomb

PITCHFORD. Who could forget the sight of its hall, a glorious heritage from Elizabethan England, with all the charm that time can bring, and in a perfect setting of lawns and trees? It is a picture in black and white, half-timbered from ground to gables, and forming three sides of a square. Its builder was one of the Ottleys, whose family held the manor for over 300 years, and many of whom lie in the church. Here lived Sir Francis Ottley, who was Governor of Shrewsbury in the Civil War; and here came the princess who was to be Queen Victoria, to stay with the Earl of Liverpool.

The house has a clever hiding-place behind panelling which will swing out to a show a door, leading first to a small room and then by a trap-door to a second cavity 15 feet deep. In such places as this did Roman Catholic priests hide when an Englishman could not worship as he pleased.

A huge lime tree in the grounds has in its branches a timbered summer-house of the 17th century.

We may admire this wonderful hall from its lodge gates, or may have a more intimate view of its lovely walls from the churchyard at the end of a fine avenue through the park. Splendid trees shelter the little church, which was 300 years old when the hall was new. In its walls is herringbone masonry older still, with a filled-up Norman window, and medieval windows in which one has kept a little of its old glass, showing the head of Christ; another has fine modern glass of St Hubert with his spear and horn, and St German with his bow and arrows, below being scenes in which the two saints appear.

There are old tiles in the sanctuary floor, a quaint bearded head over the vestry door, and a tapering font bowl perhaps 700 years old. Much woodwork is from the 17th century, the box-pews with bobbin-tops, and the high-perched pulpit with carved panels and a sounding board.

Four memorial stones to the Ottleys are engraved with portraits making a remarkable family album of the 16th century. We see four fathers, four mothers, and no less than 50 children, 48 belonging to three sets of parents. William of 1529 and his wife are under fine canopies, he with wide eyes and a youthful ace, she in a pointed headdress and a gown with graceful folds; and with them are two jolly groups of children, the eldest son and daughter honoured with special dress, and the 12 daughters peeping over one another's shoulders. Thomas of 1534 and his wife are also under canopies, she with a purse and a little case hanging from her belt; Adam of 1578 is in richly chased armour, his 13 children kneeling; and on the fourth stone, more decorated and less artistic, we see Richard Ottley in Elizabethan armour, with his wife and 15 children.

But the great treasure of the church is something three centuries older than these fascinating engravings. It is a splendid tomb, not of stone or alabaster, but of oak, with clustered pillars, trefoil arcading, and heraldic shields. On it lies a cross-legged giant more than seven feet long, cut, with the slab on which he rests, from a single block of oak. Believed to be Sir John de Pitchford of the 13th century, he is finely carved in chain mail and surcoat, drawing his great sword for the defence of the faith, and resting his feet on a grotesque lion which is gnawing the end of his scabbard. He is one of only a hundred oak figures lying in our churches. On the tomb is a fragment of tracery thought to be from the 15th century chancel screen. Other parts of the screen are worked into the reredos, which also has linenfold panelling.

The Home of Mary Webb

PONTESBURY. A village of winding ways at the foot of the hills, it came into history 13 centuries ago as the scene of a battle between a King of Mercia and a King of the West Saxons. Fine views it has over the Rea valley, and a magnificent panorama from Pontesford Hill near by, a striking landmark with two humps like a camel's back. On this hilltop, and on Pontesbury Hill nearer at hand, are the banks and ditches of prehistoric camps.

Looking proudly over the housetops is the fine tower of the church, a spacious building refashioned last century except for its 13th century chancel, which has kept its original roof of trussed beams. The walls are lined with Jacobean panelling, and the modern altar has excellent painted panels of Peter and Paul and the Madonna. The screen is richly traceried.

There are three chairs and a table from Cromwell's century; a Norman font with a fluted bowl; six ancient tiles with designs of birds, a man, and a shield; an oak chest of 1700; and a still finer old chest with latticed iron bands, painted very quaintly with flowers and leaves and little scenes.

All the ancient chancel windows are shining with colour, among the pictures being a very good Baptism of Jesus. In the east window we read of the consecration of the chancel by Bishop Cantelupe in 1280, and we see him as St Thomas of Hereford with other figures including Bishop Percival who rededicated the chancel in 1904. Two aisle windows were given by the fellow-passengers of a nurse who died at sea.

There is a brass to William Harrison who was rector 54 years, and a monument to Thomas Davies who plied his trade in Tudor London and left money to Christ's Hospital. It shows a woman with an anchor, another woman with two children, and a ship blown along by the Spirit of the Wind.

One of Pontesbury's houses, Roseville, will touch the imagination of many pilgrims, for it was the home of Mary Webb. Here she lived with her husband (also a writer of books, under the name of John Clayton) for two years after her marriage, and here she wrote one of her best-known books, The Golden Arrow. From here the Webbs went to Lyth Hill, where they built a cottage ; it is a beauty spot not far from her old home at Meole Brace, and there she was where she loved to be, within sight of the Wrekin and the smoke of Shrewsbury's chimneys.

In a circle of trees at Lea Cross stands a modern church with the beautiful alabaster tomb of Ann Hawkes in whose memory it was built. A portrait of her rector son is seen on a plaque on the wall. Seven windows in the west bay make an attractive little gallery of Gospel scenes, and in the east is a pleasing window of the Ascension.

The Praying Warrior

PREES. Its houses are on the highroad, but its church is on a hill with fine views. Mostly 600 years old, it has a fine 18th century tower, a rebuilt chancel, and a porch 500 years old. Among the old beams of the roof is one dated 1610. Many treasures are in a side chapel said to have been built for Richard Sandford, who died at the Battle of Shrewsbury in 1403. In the window we see a portrait of him at a prayer desk, on each side being a medley of 15th century glass from the church at Battlefield. In it can be seen parts of armoured figures, crowned heads, and scenes of John the Baptist. A modern window to Sarah Sandford has pictures of St Elizabeth of Hungary, one showing her giving a mantle to a beggar, and another a dish of food miraculously changing into red roses. On the west wall of the church are coloured tiles of Our Lord and the little children, a tribute to Lord Sandford, who died in 1893.

There are Jacobean seats and an altar table, and a reredos with a big painting of the Resurrection. An old frieze in the sanctuary is carved with birds; but the best carving is an Elizabethan figure of Charity with two babes in her arms. Among many memorials to the Hills is a relief showing the funeral of Sir John Hill in 1824. His son, born here at the Hall, was Wellington's right hand man, General Rowland Hill, whose story we may read at Hadnall.

Martin Luther Dies for Us

PRESTON GUBBALS. A pretty village just off the highroad, its odd name keeps alive the memory of a Norman priest, one Godbold. We imagine he was shepherd of this flock; and still standing here are chancel walls he must have known, with a doorway through which he would go.

Old gargoyles look out from the tower, and in the churchyard a 300-year-old sundial stands on the base of a medieval cross. The nave was built anew last century. There is a huge 17th century font, a massive coffin lid, and a stone with a medallion of a priest holding a cross against his chest. The pulpit and some of the other woodwork was made by a faithful vicar of our own century, E. D. Poole; and an attractive window is in memory of three friends, one a Welsh Guardsman who fell in the war.

On a hill to the north stands a gabled Tudor house with splendid views, Lea Hall. It has a perfect dovecot with as many as 460 nesting holes, inside being the revolving apparatus by which each nest was reached.

From this corner of Shropshire 13 men went out to give their lives for peace. Their names are on a memorial cross; one was Martin Luther.

Lost and Found in the Alps

PRESTON-ON-THE-WEALD MOORS. It will always remember the story of a lady of Queen Anne's time, Lady Catherine Herbert, who was lost in the Alps and rescued by one of the famous St Bernard dogs. Here, on her own lands, she founded as a thank-offering a big institution for women and children, and the children still wearing the kerchief and crimped cap of her day. The original furniture and pewter of her gift are still in use, and in the hall is a portrait of her brother Lord Torrington, who gave £1000 toward the building. The church has a 19th century chancel, but the rest of it is about 200 years old, with fine panelling inside and a pulpit carved with sacred emblems.

The Strange Miller's Son

QUATFORD. A deep road runs through it, rough-hewn in the sandstone cliffs where the Danes camped and the Normans built the church. Below it flows the Severn, past an earthwork still known as Danish Camp, and above it rise the wooded slopes which were the hunting grounds of Roger de Montgomery, the powerful Norman who became Earl of Shrewsbury, and owner of nearly all Shropshire for his valiant share in the Conquest. It was at Quatford that Roger met his second wife, the Countess Adelisa, after her journey from France, and wild imagination here will still point out the tree under which he greeted her. Roger de Montgomery, who founded the abbey at Shrewsbury, where he lies, had a house here and built the village church in fulfilment of a vow his wife made during a storm at sea—that if she reached home safely a church should be raised on the spot where she met her betrothed.

This church, approached by a steep flight of steps cut in the rock, has been altered through the centuries, but still has much Norman work to show in the north wall of the nave and the tower arch and chancel arch. The church has a Norman font carved with flowers in the 14th century, a fine array of medieval tiles, some fragments of a 15th century screen, and many ancient carved stones. The registers here were kept for the long period of 69 years by a vicar who served all that time and brought up a big family on £15 a year. He was John Higgs, the son of a local miller. He wrote a beautiful hand and kept the registers carefully from 1694 till 1763. This is what Bishop Percy wrote of him soon after he passed away.

He led the life of an anchorite, labouring his little plots of land with his own hands and making his children work harder and fare more hardily and go worse clad than the meanest labourer in the country. His own food and raiment were of the simplest and meanest kinds. He and all his children have been found after a hard day's work sitting contentedly round a bowl of turnips without any addition but salt and bread. He had a considerable share of learning; was a very good theologian and particularly read in school divinity and ecclesiastical history; he was also conversant in English antiquities. He was upon the whole the most extraordinary character I ever knew.

Lords of the Manor

QUATT. The road runs between beautiful stretches of woodland, passes a Queen Anne house in a park with five lakes, and brings us to a church on a hill. It has much fine woodwork, and the chancel has a 13th century priest's doorway with an oak door which may have been here through all these years. There are finely carved oak bosses on the 15th century roof, and Tudor flowers in the elaborate reredos. The pulpit, reading desk, and book-stand are all 17th century. In the north chapel (600 years old) is an oak screen with 15th century carving. The font, which has apparently been locked against witches, is Norman. Many memorials recall old lords of the manor, chiefly 17th century. Francis Wolryche is an imposing figure in armour with his wife, three sons, and five daughters, and a shrouded infant below; they are all finely carved, though all save one have lost their heads, probably in the Civil War. Another marble figure is of Mary Wolryche of the same century, and of a later Thomas Wolryche we are told that though he died at 29 his wife lived to be 93 years old.

The Great Camp

RATLINGHOPE. We come to it by narrow winding ways, to find it hid in a deep fold of the hills, with a track often impassable in winter. Proofs of prehistoric activities abound; the hills are dotted with earthworks, among them the great oval camp on Ratlinghope Hill described by Mary Webb in her Golden Arrow. The little church is hard to find, set among yews in and out of the churchyard. It has a bellcot with gabled roof, and a sturdy oak door with the date 1625 and the names of the churchwardens then. The windows are pleasing, with Christ as a boy in the Temple, Mary and Joseph anxiously watching Him from without, the Madonna in gold and white, and the Good Shepherd in a red robe. An oak tablet tells of 29 men who went to the war, all but one coming home.

Roman, Saxon, and Norman

RUSHBURY. Three great eras are reflected in this small place. Here was a Roman station, and here in the church is Saxon and Norman work.

Near the church in Bury Field, facing a charming old black and white manor house, is an ancient mound, 140 feet across, surrounded by a fosse ten feet deep. The hill above the village is still known as Roman Bank. An old packhorse bridge spans Eaton Brook, from which the legionaries drew their water supply.

Even in the Norman church the Roman signature is clearly written, for the leaning walls, with Saxon and Norman herringbone,

Pitchford   **The Elizabethan Hall**

Whitchurch   18th Century Church   **Wellington**   All Saints Church

Stanton Lacy
Saxon Doorway and Cross

Worfield
Medieval doors

Condover

Medieval Church Chest

Wroxeter

13th Century Chest

THE ENDURING WORK OF ANCIENT CRAFTSMEN

have Roman masonry and Roman cement, taken from some building standing here when Britain was a colony of the mistress of the world. We come into the church by one of two doorways made by the Normans, one with a plain tympanum over it, the other sheltered by the medieval timbered porch and having slender shafts and foliage capitals. The fine old studded door in this doorway still swings on its ancient hinges.

There is Norman work in the sturdy tower and in the chancel. They made the wide chancel arch and the neat and narrow priest's doorway, adorned the chancel walls with a continuous line of moulding, and crowned its charm with 11 dainty windows. The chancel walls have rich Jacobean panelling, the old font has an elaborate old cover, and there are fine black and white roofs, the chancel roof having hammerbeams.

The Town Becomes a Village

RUYTON-OF-THE-ELEVEN-TOWNS. It was one of eleven townships making up the manor, and its vicar cherishes a relic of its ancient dignity as a chartered borough, having in his keeping a fine old mace with silver bands engraved 300 years ago.

The town has become a village, with a very interesting church, a few fragments of an ancient castle, and a unique peace memorial cut as an alcove out of the rocky hillside. The castle fragments are in the churchyard, where a propped-up yew looks old enough to have seen them built perhaps 800 years ago. The sundial of 1725 is a youngster in such company.

Something from each of our great building centuries is left in this shrine high above the village. There are lovely little windows, a simple doorway, and an aumbry, all seen by men whose fathers fought at Hastings. There are arches and pillars of the 13th and 14th centuries, a massive tower of the 15th, and roof timbers as old. At one end of the chancel is a 14th century window, and at the other a 19th century arch. A small opening in the north wall may have belonged to an anchorite's cell, and all about the church we come upon quaint heads in stone and wood, old and new, many of them corbels under the roofs.

A lovely Elizabethan chalice is used at the altar, which has a very fine frontal embroidered by two disabled soldiers whose names are on it at one corner. It is in many colours, with flowers and fruit on a background of green; and its companion here is a small pulpit frontal similarly made. The reredos is richly carved, with canopied figures of John baptising Our Lord, St Chad with Lichfield Cathedral, St Andrew, and St George. Part of a floriated cross stands in the aisle, oddly engraved with a footprint beside the stem. One of the windows is aglow with two saintly figures, and another has unusual glass from Munich, showing Christ with a babe and three little ones, a picture all Ruyton children must love.

A brass tells of a vicar's son who died by a tragic accident; and a big dormer window is in memory of a colonel who won the DSO. But nothing moves us more than the simple wooden cross from the grave of a youth who, losing his health in the Navy, became a soldier and fell. He lies at Etaples, facing the sea and Old England.

RYTON. Though it has no rare treasures of art it is a delightful little place near the River Worfe, with neat and attractive old houses. Guarding the porch of the church are two worn old heads, one of a woman wearing a crown. There is a 14th century font, and two ancient corbels which probably supported a gallery, and the east and south walls may be 800 years old.

A Just Judge but Corruptible

ST MARTIN'S. It lies on the main road with a medieval church standing proudly above a neat row of almshouses. The massive low tower is of Charles Stuart's day, but the church is of our three medieval centuries, the walls mainly 13th, the doorway 14th, and the roofs 15th. The nave's roof is black and white with seven arched beams, the chancel's is wagon-shaped with carved beams.

There is a patchwork of Jacobean panelling on all the walls, and among its carving we noticed a panel with sea-serpents and a quaint little man wearing a spotted skirt. Set in the panelling is a metal relief from Italy of the Last Supper. The oak pulpit is a Jacobean three-decker, standing very high above its flight of steps. There is a Jacobean chair and two chairs with 15th century panels like bench-ends. The west door has its old hinges and its wooden bolt, and there is an ancient chest with 11 broad iron bands only an inch apart. In the porch is an old almsbox with fine ironwork, and by the porch is an 18th century sundial.

A strange little brass portrait shows the wife of Thomas Cupper, who died in 1695, when Judge Trevor was a landowner here and a power in the land. Only her head and shoulders are shown, and above is a cloud from which reaches a hand to touch her head with the fingers while the thumb rests on a skull. By the skull is the scythe of Time with a severed leaf lying across the blade, and at her side is an hourglass with the sands run down.

There is a tablet on the wall to Sir John Trevor, a just judge but a corrupt politician, who, as Speaker of the House of Commons, was made to read his own condemnation for accepting a bribe of a thousand guineas for furthering a Bill for the care of orphans. Degraded from his high office, he was yet allowed to remain Master of the Rolls till his death in 1717, when he was buried in London. His daughter Anne married Michael Hill, and their son became Viscount Dungannon, whose granddaughter Anne was the mother of the Duke of Wellington.

The Wonderful Roof

SELATTYN. Its tower on the hilltop is seen for miles and was set up last century to keep alive the memory of a warrior killed hereabouts in the very long ago. His name was Gwen, and his death in a battle between the Saxons and the Britons is told in one of the poems of his father, the poet-prince Llywarchhen, who is thought to have spent some of his time at the Court of Arthur. We should climb up to see this tower and its inscription on a fine day, for the panorama is a magnificent one over Shropshire and the Welsh hills.

The village has a pretty church with a quaint tower of Queen Anne's time, a few medieval windows, and a doorway from the 13th century when the bowl of the font was made. The interior is spacious, with a handsome modern arcade, attractive glass of the Wise Men and the Crucifixion, and 18th century woodwork including wall-panelling, the pulpit, and the altar rails. An interesting old chair is carved with six little men and two heads, and has two panels one above the other, the first showing an angel with two figures, and the second Mary with the figure of Christ. Finest of all, however, are the splendid Tudor roofs, the nave with six arched beams, and the chancel a wonderful wagon roof with 220 traceried panels, its beams and bosses all enriched with carving and its borders pierced with quatrefoils. It is the pride of Selattyn, and can have few parallels.

Four Angels Look Down

SHAWBURY. An ancient place by the River Roden, it has a mound with a moat through which water still flows from the river; but the chief of its old possessions is a church mostly built by the Normans, standing in the middle of the village, where, it is said, a Saxon church was standing when the Conqueror came.

The tower has medieval pinnacles, the north aisle is 15th century, and the chancel has a fine 13th century arch; but older than any of these are the nave columns with carved capitals, the two doorways adorned with patterns and leaves, and the big font with five rows of bold moulding, all the work of artists and masons 800 years ago. One of the Norman doorways was moved by the 15th century builders and has kept the door they made for it. Also from their time are fragments of glass showing the Madonna and a priest, and a poor-box on a very low pedestal.

Four angels have looked down from the chancel roof for about 300 years, watching the parson in his Jacobean seat, and seeing him step to the pulpit with its rich Jacobean carving. The modern reredos, carved in wood and painted, is the work of a lady of the Corbet family, so well known in Shropshire. Its carvings are the Nativity, the Last Supper, and the Descent from the Cross; and with these scenes are many figures of saints and angels.

Unknown Lady of Long Ago

SHEINTON. It lies on a wooded slope below lovely Wenlock Edge, with a quaint weathercock looking down from its turret. The west door of the church is a sturdy veteran of oak brought from Buildwas Abbey untold years ago, and another rare old treasure is a stone figure of an unknown woman not quite two feet high standing near the chancel steps with a book under her arm. After remaining unseen for hundreds of years, she was found during the restoration of the 14th century chancel and is here again for all to see, a quaint figure in simple medieval dress and one of the oldest sculptures in Shropshire. The chancel has some 14th century timbers in its roof and a cornice of queer faces and devices carved in stone. Two carved chairs, the choir-stalls adorned in foliage, and the canopied pulpit, are all the work of Jacobean craftsmen.

In the Tumult of the Hills

SHELVE. It is nothing but a church and a farm, a few cottages, and sheltering trees, but its glory is its place among tumultuous hills, looking out from a dip in an airy upland to a skyline where Stiperstones stand out in bold masses. The little church is 1100 feet above the sea, rebuilt in the first half of last century and made new in the second, but it has a font which may be eight centuries old, a pulpit and an altar table and a reading desk all Jacobean, and two black and gold roundels of ancient glass.

The Little University

SHERIFFHALES. Its black and white manor house has a most interesting chapter in its history, taking us back to the years of religious strife and intolerance after the Restoration of the Stuarts. Laws were passed against both Roman Catholics and Nonconformists, and in this remote country house the Revd John Woodhouse conducted an Academy, a kind of little provincial university, to which came some of the young men whom these Test Acts barred from the great Universities. It was an idea which the great Richard Baxter had put forward, and among those who came to Sheriffhales in that last quarter of the 17th century were two young men who were to be famous as statesmen in Queen Anne's reign, Henry St John and Robert Harley, prominent in every history book as Lord Bolingbroke and Lord Oxford.

They would know well this church encircled by evergreens, and its nave would be new in their day, built with pillars and arches from the ruins of Lilleshall Abbey not far away. The tower was refashioned in 1721, and what is now the north aisle was the whole of the church in medieval days.

The nave has its old carved ceiling, and there is glass of the 14th and 15th centuries in the tracery of the windows. The oak reredos, with two angels holding a crown, is in memory of a vicar of our own day; and the attractive screen is a tribute to old village families and to those who died in the war. We heard here of a cobbler and parish clerk with a proud record, 50 years as clerk, 60 as bellringer, and 70 as chorister; he was John Lovekin.

Something is left here of two medieval crosses, one in the churchyard restored as a peace memorial, the other by the wayside on

Heath Hill a mile away. Far older, however, is something at the hamlet fittingly called Chadwell, which has a well said to have been consecrated 13 centuries ago by St Chad.

The Discoverer of Humphry Davy

SHIFNAL. It sets us thinking of Dickens and the Old Curiosity Shop. We may fancy ourselves walking with him through these narrow streets, under these timbered eaves and gables burdened with age. A little house near the marketplace has old beams with quaint faces looking down on the pavement, and across the way is a black and white house with nine gables. Close by is a fine house where Bishop Percy, when he was a boy, found the old manuscript which made the groundwork of his famous Reliques of Ancient English Poetry. Old Idsall House perpetuates the ancient name of the town, and its brick and timber front is an enchanting sight to see from the churchyard. The Nag's Head, which has been an inn since the 14th century, has original beams in the walls and a tiny window (now filled up) where the lantern used to hang in the days of the stage coach. One of the rooms has a queer old candlestick made of iron links so that it can be bent over in any way; it may have guided the weary footsteps of travellers in the Middle Ages. Just outside the town is old Shifnal Manor, which has been made new but is still on its old foundations, with part of a moat and a barn which was part of a chapel before the Reformation.

In a quiet corner of the town rises the 700-year-old tower of Shifnal's noble church. The two-storeyed porch, with its graceful trefoiled arch and vaulted roof, is 13th century. The south transept has beautiful Norman capitals from the older church, and under a canopied arch in the chancel is a lovely stone figure of a 14th century priest.

The interior has a bewildering variety of styles, and the east end is remarkable for having two chancels, for when the lofty 14th century chancel was built the Norman chancel was left intact, and they stand one behind the other. The round arch has a carving of a face with flowers coming from the mouth. There are two Norman windows, and a 14th century east window with noble tracery. The north transept also has remains of a Norman arch and a 600-year-old doorway now made up. Under a canopy lies a stone figure of Thomas Forster, a 16th century vicar in a long robe with his feet on a dog. On an Elizabethan altar tomb is a fine marble figure of Oliver Briggs, and on a Jacobean tomb lie Humphrey Briggs with his wife, both elegantly dressed, with two children kneeling looking at their mother. There are many windows suggestive of the tragic toll of war. One shows Our Lord offering a crown to a soldier in memory of George Brooke, who fell near Ypres, and another window with St George and St Andrew and the Crucifixion is to his brother William John Brooke, who also fell in France. The peace memorial is a series of windows showing the ritual of chivalry, a young knight receiving instructions, spending a night of vigil, and arming himself with faith and charity; we see him again defending the weak, fighting sin, attending the wounded, and receiving the Crown of Life. A window with St Chad, St Augustine, and St Alban is in memory of a vicar, William Cunliffe, and another, showing Our Lord surrounded by an admiring host, is in memory of a last-century Bishop of Lichfield. The altar table and the chest are 17th century, and there is a fine oak pulpit with gilded saints and cherubim.

A curious stone in the nave asks us to believe the story of two remarkable townsfolk whose ages totalled 251 years. William Wakeley is said to have died in 1714 at 124, and Mary Yates to have died later in the century at 127. William, we are told, was baptised here in 1590 and lived through eight reigns; Mary walked to London after the Great Fire in 1666 when she was in her teens, and married her third husband in her nineties.

There are three interesting possessions in Shifnal's Roman Catholic Church, a little marble font picked up on the battlefields in France and now at home in the porch; an Italian painting of the Madonna and Child; and a Tudor chalice of beaten silver which disappeared from Shifnal after the Reformation and was lost for centuries. It found its way into a curio shop in Yorkshire and as it has the words engraved round it "Return Mee to Sheafnall in Shropshire," somebody sent it home again. It is one of the happy returns we like to hear of.

Shifnal comes into our annals of fame for two of its discoveries, the discovery of Humphry Davy and the discovery of a manuscript which inspired Bishop Percy to his famous collection of Ancient Poetry. It was Thomas Beddoes, born here in 1760, who launched our immortal scientist on his career.

Sir Humphry Davy used to say that his greatest discovery was Michael Faraday; this son of Shifnal might have said that his greatest discovery was Humphry Davy. Educated at Oxford, where he distinguished himself in languages and science, Thomas Beddoes was afterwards at Edinburgh and in Paris, where he was friendly with Lavoisier and other chemists. Oxford appointed him its reader in chemistry, but found his liberal opinions intolerable, so off he went to Bristol to establish a hospital which, because he favoured gases for respiratory complaints, he called the Pneumatic Institute. The chief of his chemical laboratory was a lad of 20, no other than Humphry Davy himself, who there began his career of discovery.

Beddoes was a close and keen observer and, having struck a blow for temperance with a book which made a great impression in its day, he enriched the literature of medicine with works fruitful in teaching and suggestion. He died at 47, leaving his four-year-old son, Thomas Lovell Beddoes, heir to the family property and to his father's taste for research, and for languages. Educated at Charterhouse and Oxford University, the son grew up a writer of verse at 13 and a year later wrote a drama echoing the plays of Tudor and Stuart days. On leaving Oxford he took up anatomy, persuaded that by study of the body he would secure a more intimate knowledge of the soul. Before he was 25 he began his most famous poem, Death's Jest Book, and, taking it abroad with him, worked at it for twenty years. A melancholy spirit, he moved from place to place and at last ended his life tragically by his own hand.

As for Bishop Percy, it was here that he received the inspiration which has kept his name alive in English literature. A Shropshire man born at Bridgnorth in 1729, he was one day at the home of his friend Humphrey Pitt (at Prior's Lee, Shifnal) when he found on the floor a dirty old manuscript volume which a maid had been tearing up to light her fires. Two pages were missing, 54 leaves had been torn in two, but there remained, written in a Jacobean hand, 195 sonnets, ballads, historical songs, and metrical romances dating from before Chaucer to the middle of the 17th century. Percy begged the book from his friend, worked on it during the next four years, and searched for forgotten collections throughout the kingdom; and in 1765 he published his immortal Reliques of Ancient Poetry. It was an epoch-making work, simple as it seems to us, for in an age weary of formal verse he opened a door into the magic of the past, and revealed a field of literature unknown to his generation.

Below Wenlock Edge

SHIPTON. It has a delightful situation by the River Corve and under Wenlock Edge, and a charming Elizabethan great house by the wayside. A fine old English home is Shipton Hall, with its grey walls and mullioned windows, its tower and mellow chimneys, its beautiful ceilings and handsome woodwork. In the grounds are a stone dovecot and an old bowling green; and not far away in a roadside hollow is the arched entrance to a mysterious tunnel. Above the hall stands a tiny church with an old tower, a Norman nave refashioned, and a chancel rebuilt just after the Great Armada. The chancel is on its old foundations, and is an unusual example of Elizabethan builders imitating the style of the 14th century men. The font may be Norman; certainly the chancel arch is, simply designed with a rounded opening on each side. There is a fine 14th century window, a long oak chest not quite so old, a pulpit thought to be Elizabethan, and an east window with fragments of old glass. One of the memorials is a painted board with ironwork pinnacles, telling of Mary Mytton 300 years ago. Her family lived at the hall.

Bird Sanctuary

SHRAWARDINE. It has the Severn running by and the still beauty of a shining mere of 40 acres, a sanctuary of rare birds. Among the thatched and timbered cottages the old Court House stands halfway up the hill. Fortified for the king in the Civil War, the Norman castle surrendered after a five days' siege in 1645 and was afterwards dismantled, its stone used for repairing Shrewsbury Castle. Today there remains but little of its walls, and on its hilltop site the village cricket matches are played. The church, largely rebuilt under Cromwell, has still the bowl of its Norman font, part of an ancient wall, and in its wooden turret are two bells of Chaucer's time. Following the line of the hill and sloping up to the altar, the neat little building has a brightly contrasted interior, with the red splays of its windows set in cream walls. Most of the woodwork is Jacobean, and there is a small 18th century brass with arms and cherubs to Martha Botevyle.

The Old Town Moated by the Severn

SHREWSBURY. In its matchless journey through a hundred villages, a score of towns, and four cathedral cities, the second longest river in the land makes a wondrous loop, and Shrewsbury lies within it. Almost it is an island, except that its castle stands in the narrow strait, an island about half a mile each way with half a dozen bridges crossing to its overflow, and with its high town and low town pierced by narrow ways and winding streets crammed with the legacy of the centuries, old walls, doorways, windows, churches, houses, archways, towers, spires, lovely vistas and surprising peeps such as we shall not find crowded in so small a spot in many other towns.

On one hill Darwin sits in front of his old school; on another hill the old school carries on in a new home of natural splendour remembering that one of its boys was Sir Philip Sidney. Something of the old abbey remains across the river, and something of the castle on the hill. Everywhere the marvellous fronts of old houses look out in black and white across the streets, some overhanging with their lovely oriels, some raised on posts, some with their rooms still filled with carving of medieval days. It is as A. E. Housman wrote in his Shropshire Lad:

> High the vanes of Shrewsbury gleam
> Islanded in Severn stream;
> The bridges from the steepled crest
> Cross the water east and west.

We may begin our walk round the town inside the river loop. Even if we do not go indoors there is as pleasant an hour for us as we shall find in any town, merely looking at these streets. Combining extreme old age with a stimulating liveliness, the town finds a new use for all its ancient buildings. Shops hang their wares round the timbered entrances of medieval mansions (we found Mr Mudd the fishmonger selling salmon in the house where Henry Richmond stayed on his way to Bosworth Field). To cash a cheque we entered a grand three-storeyed magpie house with bay windows, the town mansion of the Irelands 400 years ago. We bought something from a shop at the top of Mardol and found a handsome plaster ceiling with the arms of Queen Elizabeth. Cottagers use as an outhouse a 13th century room which was once a Mint, reached by ten steps. The house built for Shrewsbury's Royalist MP in the Short and Long

Parliaments is now the Guildhall with civic treasures in its strong room—a Tudor and a Stuart mace and a 15th century seal of medieval Shrewsbury. The magistrates hold court in the market hall of 1595. Admiral Benbow's birthplace is a garage. The 300-year-old buildings outgrown by Shrewsbury's famous school serve as a library and museum. We can motor along a sturdy stretch of the town walls and find someone at home in the last surviving of its 20 towers, a 14th century relic handed over to the National Trust.

Here are whole streets with a look of 300 years ago, sometimes charming, sometimes sordid, absurdly narrow, with names as old and as delightful as their timbers—Grope Lane, Shoplatch, Dogpole, Wyle Cop, Pride Hill. The very narrow passages are locally known as "shuts." We come upon an open space sloping to the Severn, as lovely a park as any town has, crossed and flanked with avenues, one following the curve of the river for a quarter of a mile, others marching up the hill to the extraordinary round church of St Chad. Some trees were planted 200 years ago, and with the young ones taking the places of the fallen they must number at least 500. Hercules rests from his labours at the bottom of the central avenue and an angel spreads great wings in the little temple at the top. Hercules is a leaden copy of the Farnese sculpture in Rome; the temple is the peace memorial of the Great War, a lovely open structure with a small dome set on six Ionic columns, and inside the lifesize figure of the Archangel Michael, with a lance in his left hand and his right hand raised in blessing. The figure is floodlit at night from a hidden source in the dome, and round the dome inside are the arms or seals of six Shropshire towns. A little way off is another memorial to our heroes, in memory of those who fell in the South African War; it has a soldier in khaki resting his hands on his rifle.

The lovely park in which these memorials stand is called the Quarry, for in its centre is the deep hollow from which came much of the town's red stone though now the once-scarred sides are planted with brilliant beds, flowering shrubs, and rockeries. The Quarry itself is one of the best examples we have seen of what can be done with the ugly gashes our quarrymen are allowed to make in the face of England. It has long been thought that these scars on our countryside should be filled up or made into gardens, and Shrewsbury has shown the way, for this old quarry is one of the most delightful spectacles in Shropshire. It has become the Dingle, a sun-trap garden with a lake at the bottom paddled by water birds with plumage as varied as the flowers. We were there when the wall-flowers and polyanthus, tulips and rhododendrons were ablaze, and we remember it still like a colour print in the mind. There is no lovelier little dell. To the grotto has come the quaint little Arbour of the Shoemakers Company from the old show ground at Kingsland, where the pageants of the trades were held before the School crossed the river and occupied the site. This Arbour was part of the pageantry, with its 17th century figures of Crispin and Crispinianus, patron saints of the shoemakers, unfortunately damaged centuries ago in spite of their pathetic appeal:

> We are but images of stone;
> Do us no harm; we can do none.

Here also is a figure of Sabrina, the goddess of the Severn, pouring water from a jar among the plants.

On one side of the park are the playgrounds, on the other the grass slopes down to make a natural grand stand for Shrewsbury's shows, the most important being the annual flower show, the biggest in the country, and one of the wonders of the Shropshire countryside. Out of its profits the Shropshire Horticultural Society has presented the town with gifts unimaginable—buildings and statues and the very castle itself. So the old quarry has yielded more than stone; it has given the town beauty and a little gold mine as well. Shrewsbury deserves it all, for it has made a little paradise from what was once waste ground and a patch of ugliness.

Back to the height of the town, at what we may call the Castle Isthmus of the Severn, the old Castle and the old School stand face to face. The school the Shrewsbury boys left behind when they moved over the river to Kingsland has a stately front, with a pinnacled tower looking across the square in which Charles Darwin sits on the spot he used to cross as a Shrewsbury scholar. He sits in bronze, with his birthplace a little way behind him, across the river over the Welsh Bridge. The house remains near the 18th century almshouses in the suburb known as Frankwell, which fills the next loop of the winding Severn; Darwin would see his home looking across from the school windows.

Over the doorways of the school are two stone figures, an Elizabethan schoolboy and an undergraduate; they have been copied for the new school buildings, and are a Tudor anticipation of the idea so familiar in the Victorian Era, the Boy and what he will become, for the clumsy schoolboy is urged in the Latin inscription to realise that he too, by learning, may become learned. Above the figures are the arms of Charles the First, for though the school was founded in the 16th century its grey-crested old home was mainly 17th.

This fine old school (which still serves the town educationally, having become the library, museum, and reading room), was built in the ten years following the death of Shakespeare, when the school itself had existed for two generations. A timbered gable in School Lane is believed to be part of the original school buildings to which Fulke Greville and Philip Sidney went. The rooms of the old school are now of greater interest to the visitor than they have ever been, for in them are fine collections of natural history and Roman Shropshire, while the shell of the old chapel (now the town's reading room) has on its walls portraits of local worthies. One of these is Admiral Benbow, painted by his sister. He was the son of a Shrewsbury tanner, and it was from here that the young apprentice ran away to sea to become an admiral of the blue after a swift upward career dimmed only by his last engagement with a French squadron off Jamaica, when five British commanders refused to go into action with him. They were courtmartialled and two were shot. On Coton Hill is the house where the Admiral was born in 1653, drawn into the whirlpool of a garage and screened from the road by a new front.

In the Natural History Gallery, Darwin's father, a Shrewsbury doctor, appears among the portraits, with Zoffany's painting of John Gwynn, architect of the town's English Bridge, and Charles Clive's portrait of Lord Clive, who was MP for Shrewsbury (as Disraeli was). Elected in 1760 on his triumphant return from his first Government of Bengal, he was still the town's MP when his career came to its tragic end. Under Clive's portrait is a bomb found unexploded beneath the city walls, and here, in this remarkable collection of things, are the skeletons of two boats which skimmed the Severn a thousand years before the canoes which now swarm over it like summer flies. In a frame is a bit of cloth from Charles Stuart's scaffold. We noticed on the stairs a delightful print of a once familiar figure in the town, the dwarf clerk of St Chad's, 3 feet 4 inches high, with a book almost as big as himself tucked under his arm. On the wall hangs the old coiled wind instrument called the serpent, which was part of the church orchestra in the time of this miniature clerk.

In rooms lined with lockers and woodwork scrolled with the initials of generations of schoolboys is a grand collection from Wroxeter, the Roman Uriconium. Here are scores of pots and dishes used on Roman tables, a vivid blue vase, fragments of columns carved with figures (Bacchus among them), patterned pavements, tiles with the footprints of straying animals of 1800 years ago, a Roman chemist's label for eye lotion, tombstones of legionaries and one to a lady (Placida), and the bronze fragment of a Roman soldier's certificate of citizenship when he left the army and settled down at Uriconium in April AD 135. Today the road from Uriconium to Verulamium at St Albans, once picturesque with Roman chariots, is a motorist's delight, perhaps the longest straight run in England.

Farther down the street is the 16th century school tuckshop where we may still find the Shrewsbury cakes immortalised in the Ingoldsby Legends, from which the shop front still quotes:

> *Oh, Pailin, Prince of Cake Compounders,*
> *The mouth liquifies at the very sound of thy name.*

Close by is something else which might have come out of Ingoldsby, a black raven, the sign of the hotel whose proprietor ran the first mail coaches between London and Holyhead. The Crown Hotel opposite has for its sign a fantastic model dragon, and displays two plaques to tell us that it is a historic spot, where the High Cross stood.

It is historic because here in 1282 David, the rebel prince of Wales, was hung, drawn, and quartered after being sentenced by a Parliament hastily summoned at Shrewsbury by Edward the First. Then his head was sent to the Tower of London to join his brother Llewellyn's, already there derisively crowned with ivy. Here just over a century later the dead body of Hotspur was put on show to kill the rumour that he was still alive. In rebellion against Henry the Fourth, Hotspur had come here from Chester on his way to join Owen Glendower, but the king greeted him with the royal standard flying over Shrewsbury Castle, and the two armies met at Battlefield, within three miles of the town walls. Hotspur and Douglas beat down the royal standard and thought they had slain the king, but it was Shakespeare's "hare-brained Hotspur," who met his doom. His body was taken to Whitchurch, but as rumour persisted that he was still alive it was brought back here and propped up on this very spot between two millstones. The Civil War is recalled by the Water Gate at the foot of the castle, sometimes called Traitor's Gate because it is said that through this archway someone in 1645 let in the Cromwellians to capture the town. Close by is the site of the Dominican Friary where two sons of Edward the Fourth were born, one dying in infancy and the other with his king brother, smothered in the Tower of London.

Only the Norman gateway is now left of the castle built by Roger de Montgomery, the Conqueror's kinsman and adviser, who supplied part of the fleet which brought the Normans to England and was given Shrewsbury and most of Shropshire as his reward. He also founded the abbey outside the city walls, where he lies in an unknown grave beneath the noble church. Inside the castle wall is a pretty green close, but the place disappoints those who seek antiquity, for, though one side and two corner towers remain of the 13th century, little of the atmosphere of a castle was left when Sir William Pulteney claimed the castle as a house and Thomas Telford transformed it for him.

On the hillock of the old keep Telford raised a tower for Sir William's wife, a look-out for the wonderful view of the town, with its spires and its towers, its round church, and its amazing statue to Lord Hill, which puts this Shropshire General on a pedestal only 13 feet shorter than Nelson's in Trafalgar Square. On the horizon are the enticing hills of Shropshire and Wales, with the delights of Stokesay and Church Stretton, the impressive dignity of Ludlow Castle, and the far remoteness of Clun. We have another good view from the oldest-looking room in the castle, the octagonal chamber of one of the towers. There are dungeons below the two towers, and the space between them is filled with a great hall where the town council meets under a roof of massive beams, behind a solid timber and plaster screen, both 17th century.

If too little is left of the grim old castle, there is no disappointment in Shrewsbury's old houses. They are here in dozens, mostly black and white beauties from the 15th, 16th, and 17th centuries. One close to the castle has gabled rooms rising like turrets, an armed figure mounting guard on the top and four mermaids curvetting on the beams below. It is the charming Jacobean gateway of the Council House, where in Tudor days the Lords of the Marches who governed Wales would sometimes meet, and where Charles Stuart held his court for three weeks while rallying Shropshire to his side. The house was originally within the castle walls, and here Henry the Seventh came with Prince Arthur (whose heart still rests in Shropshire), here Mary Tudor came, and here Charles Stuart slept on a bedstead still in the room. The house is private and not shown; it has the richest interior in the town. Its gateway all may see, and it is a captivating entrance to a lovely home.

The Elizabethan houses of the rich Shropshire families still carry on their names, Ireland's Mansion faces Owen's Mansion in the High Street, both in their black and white magnificence. Ireland's is one of the enchanting fronts of Tudor England, a four-gabled mass with delightful oriels and timbers which show what a marvellous variety of effect can be had with straight lines. Lloyd's House close by has the mark of the merchants of Calais on its gable. In the old house between the Drapers Almshouses and the Drapers Guildhall (a delightful place in St Mary's Square) Prince Rupert is said to have slept, and there is a black and white inn near the English Bridge where Henry the Seventh is said to have stayed on his way to Bosworth Field. Mary Tudor stayed at another house in Dogpole, the home of her mother's steward, John Rocke. The Golden Cross Inn (with a sacristy over its arch) has a note of the money spent on wine for "King Henry's gentlemen." The Old Post Office Inn was the Elizabethan home of the Proud family. The Unicorn Inn in Wyle Cop has one of the best timbered overhanging fronts of the 16th century houses, contrasting with the solid brick front of the Lion Hotel, where Charles Dickens stayed and Disraeli addressed the electors from the balcony. Dr Johnson stayed in what we found as a warehouse but was then Rowley's Mansion, the brick and timber home of a Jacobean brewer, whose malthouses have disappeared in Shrewsbury's clearance of the slums.

Many of the old houses have modern shop windows, but in the lovely Butcher Row, a street scene not to be forgotten, is a line of actual 16th century shops, their windows framed in rare wooden arches. They form the ground floor of the house of the Abbot of

Shrewsbury   Ireland's Mansion

Owen's Mansion, built in 1592

The Old Market Hall of 1595

ELIZABETHAN SHREWSBURY

Lilleshall still here after 500 years though the abbey itself is a ruin. The abbot's arms of three fishes gave the next lane its name of Fish Street, and leading out from it is Grope Lane, where we may fancy ourselves back in the abbot's day.

In the market square, behind the statue of Lord Clive (a determined figure by Baron Marochetti), stands the market hall of 1595, with open arcades and an upper floor where the magistrates sit in a room in which cloth was sold in Elizabethan days. Over one entrance is a comically apologetic figure of Edward the Fourth's father, Richard of York, brought here from the old Welsh Bridge. On the opposite side is a sundial and an angel holding the arms of France and England, brought from the castle's town gate. In the new market is felt the pulse of the country for miles round, the giant hall covering a miniature Smithfield and Covent Garden in one, with the Corn Exchange on the floor above, all indicative of Shrewsbury's importance as the thriving capital of agricultural Shropshire.

It was to this market that Mary Webb came with her husband to sell the produce of their garden. The Shropshire storyteller, whose imaginative novels Lord Baldwin made popular by a single reference in one of his speeches as Prime Minister, was only for two years of her life out of this county, and she lived for ten years with her parents at Meole Brace, within a mile of her grave in Shrewsbury cemetery.

Shrewsbury has fragments still left of its three friaries; the Austin Friars by the Welsh Bridge, the Black Friars by the Water Gate, and the Grey Friars by the Coleham Bridge, where people still go in and out of their home through a doorway cut in the tracery of a Gothic window of the old friary. Of the five Saxon churches, three have been made new and have lost all Saxon interest, but St Mary's is all glorious within and the Abbey Church of the Holy Cross, which the Conqueror's kinsmen set up in place of a wooden shrine, is a noble spectacle, and has given sanctuary to treasures from the other churches.

St Chad's Church was rebuilt in 1790 on a new site above the Quarry and the lovely Dingle, which is not surprising, for the townsfolk woke on a rainy morning in 1788 to find the church a dismal heap of debris. Two chimneysweeps and a man walking early by the river saw this terrible thing happen—an unexpected jingling of chimes, and the tower suddenly opened, hung suspended for a moment, and crashed, bringing most of the nave with it. It was all because of a Norman jerrybuilder. Norman piers were often made hollow, the casing of stone filled with rubble and chips bound together as strong as concrete by the pouring-in of hot lime; but the builder of St Chad's omitted the strengthening lime, and the tower pillar which caused the damage was found to be a hollow shell. Even so, if Telford's advice had been taken and the pillar strengthened in time, Shrewsbury might still have its grand collegiate church, whose great size may be guessed from the only part left standing, the lady chapel where services are still sometimes held. It has wide Norman arches to the vanished transept and the chancel, and a curious head with a twig in its mouth has been added to the now blocked north arch. Outside, against what was the chancel wall, are three sedilia with their seats gone and their 15th century vaulting. Let into the back of these old priests' seats are two 17th century tablets to Rowland Lee, Bishop of Lichfield, and John Bryan, the Nonconformist rector ejected in 1662.

We enter what is left of old St Chad's by a door hung in 1663 between two broken piers, one belonging to the fallen tower, the other having in it the stairway to the bell-loft. The massive beams of the roof are 300 years old, and there are painted shields round the panelled walls. The 18th century pulpit, carved with an open book, is poor compared with the twisted altar rails and the curious 18th century font at which Bishop Heber was baptised, a basin let into a solid wooden pillar with a domed cover. On a wall monument kneel two figures from Stuart England, Thomas Edwardes and his wife, both wearing ruffs, two of their children kneeling above them. In the nave are three museum cases with a collection of old church books, medieval tiles showing countrymen in the costume of 700 years ago, and a model of Buildwas Abbey cut in cork by a Shrewsbury man.

Whether we like the new St Chad's Church or not, it is the best of our few classical round churches, and has a cupola tower rising 154 feet with a fine peal of bells. Doric columns hold up the portico, Ionic columns support the round gallery, and Corinthian columns rise from the gallery to the roof. The east window is a copy of the Rubens Descent from the Cross in Antwerp Cathedral, and another window has a vivid illustration of the text Render unto Caesar. The great carved reredos (the peace memorial) symbolises self-sacrifice, with a central scene of the Crucifixion, and in niches on each side figures of King Oswald and King Edmund, St Martin and St Chad. Perhaps the finest things here are the two busts by Chantrey of William Hazledine, the Shrewsbury ironmaster who built the Menai Bridge for Telford, and John Simpson, who superintended the building of this unusual church. Tattered banners and memorials of the Shropshire regiment hang from the walls and a white soldier stands outside with reversed arms in memory of the Fallen.

In the old churchyard are stone figures of a bishop and a king, and also outside is a great bowl of a Norman font which was once locked against witches; another font bowl keeping it company has animal heads linked round it in festoons. A new stone has been cut for the grave of Captain John Benbow, the admiral's uncle, who fell in the Civil War. Before we leave the neighbourhood of St Chad's there is Belmont to see, with a row of charming Queen Anne houses, and hereabouts are doorways and fanlights as graceful as anything designed by the Adam brothers. Shrewsbury can boast also of its lovely ironwork, in window balconies and in the magnificent gates of a house facing the Abbey Church.

A group of cathedral-like towers draws us to them; they are the pride of St Julian's, St Alkmund's, and St Mary's. St Julian's has a 13th century tower with a niched figure of a saint, and joined to it is an 18th century pillared nave with 500-year-old bosses in its roof. The east window has a copy of Raphael's Transfiguration darkening the chancel, and another chancel window has St James in 15th century glass brought from Rouen during the French Revolution, the head being new. There are two old chests and some Queen Anne chairs in the vestry. In the tower is a stone inscribed in Norman French 700 years ago, and a brass tablet recalls a Shrewsbury surgeon and his wife who died within a day of each other in 1692:

> We man and wife conjoyned for life,
> Fetched our last breath so near that Death
> Who part us would yet hardly could.
> Wedded again in bed of dust
> Here we remain till rise we must.

St Alkmund's has kept its beautiful 15th century spire rising 184 feet, although the church was refashioned at the end of the 18th century, when all its brasses were sold as scrap metal. A few wall monuments were saved, including those to many generations of Thomas Joneses, from the first mayor of Shrewsbury who died in 1642 and the Thomas Jones who was Charles the Second's Lord Chief Justice. The east window is an 18th century sepia copy of Guido Reni's Assumption at Munich; the west window has fragments of Tudor heraldic glass.

It is a joy to come from these two spoiled churches to old St Mary's, so patched outside, so beautiful within. If Shrewsbury should need a cathedral, here is a small one ready-made, representing all the centuries from the 12th to the 17th, for the north aisle was built during the Commonwealth. The spire rises 220 feet on a Norman tower, and there are several Norman-looking doorways, an elegant one to the north carved with giant leaves, a narrow one opening by an old studded door into a transept, and two grand zigzagged ones to the south porch, which has original windows under double arches on carved capitals, and two of the strangest creatures in medieval glass—an elephant and a spidery crab from the Zodiac, and some old Flemish roundels, a promise of the amazing show of medieval glass awaiting us within. Over the vaulted porch roof is a 15th century room. The modern porch has in its vaulting a beautiful boss of the Crucifixion copied from the monk's pulpit standing looking out on the street near the ancient Abbey Church.

The nave and transepts of St Mary's are Norman, but the stately arcades, finished in the 13th century when the aisles were added, have a grace rare in rounded arches, and the capitals to the north are specially elaborate with the heads of a king and a bishop among curling fern fronds. A 14th century clerestory of double windows stretching from one end of the church to the other lights up a splendid nave roof 84 deeply cut panels, with twin angels on the tiebeams, and eight oak angels to support them. A group of little windows over the chancel arch belonged to a central Norman tower which has now disappeared; the group of pointed arches between the nave and chancel supported that tower. A little chevron arch on miniature pillars with scalloped capitals shows where the Norman chancel ended before it was lengthened; this lovely arch now forms a priest's seat, with an aumbry beside it. Great round arches with carved capitals open from the aisles into the transepts and from the north transept into the chapel beyond, where the hood-mould curves round into a weird beaked head. Here is a modern memorial to Admiral Benbow, the boast of the British navy in his day; his curly-wigged bust is over a relief of his three-masted ship. Beside it are the 15th century portraits of Nicholas Stafford and his wife, outlined on an alabaster slab with all the detail of a brass portrait.

The altar in the north transept is under a Norman arch with a charming medieval window over it. The south transept looks into the aisle through unglazed lancets, and opens one window on the beauties of the 14th century Trinity Chapel which has four big windows, one filled with excellent modern glass, including a copy of Murillo's Adoration of the Wise Men. Three canopied priests' seats are inset at the back with curious stone carvings, one showing a man being baptised, another with three dogs, one leaping up playfully at a broken figure, and in the centre the Father with His crucified Son between his knees sitting beside Mary with the same Son as a babe on her lap, while a monk below sends up a prayer to them. The Madonna appears again over the piscina. On the wall is a triangle of stone with a worn carving of Christ found in a garden, and on an altar tomb lies a cross-legged knight in chain mail with a lion at his feet, probably one of the Leybournes of Berwick.

There are two other figures in the tower, Colonel Cureton, killed at Rhamnuggar in 1848, and the fine figure of the headmaster Samuel Butler, begun by Chantrey and finished at his death by E. H. Baily. Dr Butler became Bishop of Lichfield after achieving a great reputation for the school in his 38 years here; it was he who refronted the headmaster's house to match the school buildings, leaving his initials on the gateway. The font, with its carved bowl resting on angels, is over 500 years old; there is an Elizabethan chest; and in the vestry is a fragment of the medieval screen, elaborate Jacobean carving, and roundels of old Flemish glass.

The great wealth of St Mary's is in its glass, nearly every window being filled with Flemish paintings of the 15th and 16th centuries, all given by a rector. We could spend hours looking at these fascinating scenes and figures, which include the story of Tobit and the life of St Bernard. Several windows show the original donors of the glass kneeling with their patron saints, probably the oldest being the middle window in the north aisle, where the donors are identified by heraldry displayed by wild men and monsters, and their saints by emblems. There are dozens of Bible scenes and scores of saints, a Crucifixion scene in the north chapel showing Mary falling in the arms of John while Joseph of Arimathea and the centurion watch from horseback. A window in the west wall of the north aisle has a copy of the figure of St John from the great Crucifixion scene now in Lichfield Cathedral. All this is foreign glass, but the great Jesse window is English and of unique interest, made about 600 years ago and miraculously preserved, for it came from St Chad's after that church had fallen, and later the top of St Mary's spire endangered it again by crashing through the roof. The giant figure of Jesse lies at the bottom with David springing from his side and his descendants grouped all round him, while below are the Madonna and Child with a row of medieval English folk, Edward the Third, Sir John Charlton, his Welsh princess wife (Hawis of Powis Castle), and their children, for whose souls an inscription in Norman French begs us to pray.

Outside on the tower wall we read of a youth who in 1739 tried to glide down a rope fixed from the top of the spire to the other side of the river, but the rope snapped and he fell to his death while his wife was still collecting coppers from the crowd:

Let this small monument record the name
Of Cadman, and to future times proclaim
How by'n attempt to fly from this high spire
Across the Sabrine stream he did acquire
His fatal end. Twas not for want of skill
Or courage to perform the task he fell:
No, no, a faulty cord being drawn too tight
Hurried his soul on high to take her flight,
Which bid the body here beneath Good-Night.

There is a Roman Catholic church of last century by Edward Welby Pugin, overlooking the town walls, and from it we may cross the river for the two great sights outside the Severn Loop, the old Abbey and the new School.

Crossing the river by the English Bridge, we come upon the fine spectacle of the Abbey Church, its noble tower facing us with the great traceried west window and the wonderful doorway below. The church was saved from the destruction which overtook the rest of the abbey because the townsfolk had always worshipped in its nave. Edward the Third looks down from a canopied niche over the

14th century window which fills the lower Norman half of the tower with intricate tracery. The south and north doorways are Norman (the north with a two-storeyed medieval porch), and Norman also is the massive strength of the arcades, the round arches of the vanished central tower, the giant transept arches, and the stalwart shafts for vanished vaulting along the north and south walls. At the base of two north piers are reliefs of a dove and a serpent, and above the arcades are traces of the old triforium, with the double row of modern clerestory windows above. The black and white aisle roofs are 18th century.

Two remarkable possessions are the remains of the shrine of St Winifred and the great font hollowed out from the base of an ancient pillar. The remains of St Winifred were brought here from Holywell by the monks in 1136; five recesses in the shrine are empty, but three brought from a garden have broken figures of St Winifred between two saints. Besides the great font, which may be Roman, is a font bowl with owl-like heads linked with festoons, and near it is a little Norman pillar piscina carved with crude figures looking like a child's drawing of the horses of the Apocalypse. There are medieval tiles in the floor of the north chapel, and in the south chapel are fine oil paintings, a Jacobean altar table, and a Crucifixion in old glass.

At the west end of the nave is a remarkable collection of sculptured figures, some on altar tombs, and all but one having come here because their own churches threw them out. The odd one is the knight in a recess of the south aisle, said to be Roger de Montgomery, the Norman founder of the abbey; certain it is that the earl was buried here, having died in his own abbey three days after entering it as a monk. Close to him is a worn figure in high relief of a medieval priest of St Giles's church, a chalice, bell, book, and candle outlined beside him. Also in the south aisle are twin bearded figures of a 14th century man, two effigies of the same man, one in a long robe, the other showing his armour beneath the robe. These double figures are unique, but St Alkmund's, where they once lay head to feet on the same long tomb, threw them out at its rebuilding. Beside them now lies a dusty knight in chain mail of the 12th century, who came from Wombridge, his right hand ever ready on the hilt of his sword.

In the north aisle is another dusty figure, thought to be a 13th century judge, who came from old St Chad's; and in an alcove at the end of the aisle is a fascinating group of painted figures lying on altar tombs. William Charlton is here in alabaster with his wife, after lying in a churchyard for 30 years. He is a handsome fellow in the armour of 1524, with his sword buckled on; she is a pinched figure in a green dress with touches of red left on her cloak. Angels and friars are round their tomb, and what looks like the broken figure of a pilgrim is carved on the sole of his foot. There are only a few examples in all England of this old custom, a lesson in pride and humility; we see it in Westminster Abbey and again in St George's Chapel, Windsor. Next come Richard Onslow and his wife, a mild old man who was Speaker in Elizabeth's Parliament. He and his wife have their heads on elaborately-worked cushions, and he has what looks like a carving of the family Bible under his. His cap and her curious headdress are rarely seen on tombs. Their daughters, six prim figures, are round them, all with a trinket hanging from their girdles. This family came from old St Chad's. The handsome couple next to them are William Jones and his wife, of early Stuart days, he with touches of red on his alderman's robe, she wearing the curious felt headdress known as a Mary Queen of Scots cap. There are cherubs and shields round their tomb, which came from St Alkmund's. Another alderman has his painted bust on the wall, a queer hunchbacked figure; he is John Lloyd, who died two years before Charles went to the scaffold.

It is strange to find a monument of the old abbey standing alone and apart from all these. On the other side of the road, next to a coalyard, is the stone pulpit of the refectory, a 14th century gem with a beautiful boss of the Crucifixion on its vaulted roof and with figures in canopied niches. Here would stand one monk reading to the rest at their meals, but a man could stand here today and preach to coal-heavers on one side and garage men on the other, and to the crowds passing by in the street. A paved enclosure leads us to it, and nothing can take away the surprise of this solitary sentinel of the past looking on at the passing throng.

Down this road, leading out of Shrewsbury to Watling Street and the Roman Uriconium, we come to where Lord Hill stands high on his column, the tallest Doric pillar in the world, 132 feet, with his medals proudly glittering on his chest, and with four lions much

The Abbey Church of Shrewsbury

St Chad's Church

Medieval Abbey Pulpit

The Old School, now the Library and Museum

FAMOUS SIGHTS OF SHREWSBURY

Butcher Row

Fish Street

Council House Gateway

Tudor House in Dogpole

IN OLD SHREWSBURY

The English Bridge

The Famous School

SHREWSBURY BY THE SEVERN

inferior to Nelson's noble beasts at the base of his column, which can be climbed by 172 steps.

St Giles's church stands outside the walls because 800 years ago it was attached to a leper hospital. One would scarcely guess this, for it looks an uninteresting building, but when we look more closely we see that many of the stones are old, and inside is a perfect Norman font from another church, cut all over with zigzags and stiff figures. On a windowsill are worn fragments of the churchyard cross. The figure of St Giles in a chancel lancet is an excellent copy of medieval glass; yellow fragments and faces from real medieval glass are in other windows and the noble east window is to a brother of Bishop Walsham How, whose father also has a window here.

Not far from Lord Hill's Column is one of Shrewsbury's show places, the grand four-square gabled house which Richard Prynce, a cunning Elizabethan lawyer, was building for himself out of the abbey's old stones while all his friends were building their older-fashioned magpie houses within the city walls. He covered his house with three coats of whitewash, and so it came to be known as the White Hall, or Whitehall. It is delightful and dignified, with a gate-house fitted with the very clock which told the time to the lawyer's workmen and would tell it again with a bit of mending. Here, too, is the house he built for his doves, with an arcaded cornice and a cupola to match his own; inside is the original ladder, fitted to a centre beam and turning, still without a squeak, so that a man on it can put his hand into every one of the 600 nesting-niches. The house (which may be seen) has a staircase on which every tread is a solid block of oak, and an Elizabethan boudoir panelled in wood showing the axeman's marks and painted in rich panels of black and white. There are some delightful old Dutch tiles in another room.

It is well in this old town, with its roots so deep in our ancient story, to say farewell on the green slopes which rise from the river to the fine new home of Shrewsbury School, lately extended by a new block of scientific laboratories named after Darwin. It was towards the end of last century that the school moved into the massive red buildings of the 18th century Foundling Hospital. Shrewsbury School was 200 years old when the hospital was built, and by the time it changed its address had grown so that the hospital buildings were too small for it, and were developed into a great block of school houses and administrative buildings with a chapel, a fine library, and wide playing-fields on the height above the riverside. The Severn is delightful as it sweeps beside the grounds.

In a few years more the school will be celebrating its 400th anniversary, and it has a record of which any school may well be proud. The model rules drawn up by Thomas Ashton in 1578 are still shown in manuscript in the school library with the register of the pupils in which two famous names appear together, Philip Sidney and Fulke Greville. When the time came for one of these friends to die the other wrote of him two lines of poetry:

> *Knowledge his light hath lost, Valour hath slain her knight,*
> *Sidney is dead, dead is my friend, dead is the world's delight;*

and in course of time, when Fulke Greville died, these words, written by himself, were his epitaph: *Servant to Queen Elizabeth, Counsellor to King James and Friend to Sir Philip Sidney*.

The school had three famous headmasters last century who raised it to a very high standard: Samuel Butler, Benjamin Kennedy, and Henry Moss (who moved the school from the town to the hilltop across the river). There are two inspirations that greet us as we come to it—a piece of school wall brought from the town on which are cut names famous in England scholarship, and Mr A. G. Walker's noble peace memorial, a bronze figure of the school's most famous scholar, Philip Sidney. On the front of the high pedestal is a bronze relief of a scene in the Great War, with a Latin inscription attributing to Sidney the saying that he recognises as his own the pupils of his school; and on the back of the pedestal is the immortal scene at Zutphen with Sidney giving his last cup of water to one whose need was greater than his. On Empire Day in 1923, when this beautiful monument was unveiled, the splendid entrance gates hung on their handsome pillars were opened for the first time in memory of H. W. Moss, headmaster for 42 years.

For the new school chapel there was brought from the old school a handsome screen of 1617 with a frieze carved with monsters and faces, and at the same time came the 17th century pulpit, which has deep sunk panels let into it.

Separating the nave from the chancel is a richly carved Jacobean balustrade, and in front of it is a desk carved with the name of a master of the school in Elizabethan days. In the nave is a series of Kempe windows illustrating Virtues, each with an appropriate scene below a symbolical figure; among them is Sir Philip Sidney at Zutphen under the figure of Charity, Edward the Sixth granting the charter with Hope above him, and a scene from the Boer War accompanying the figure of Fortitude. There is a memorial to an Archbishop of York, William Thomson, a 16th century plaque of the Madonna and Child by an Italian artist; and another plaque sculptured by George Drinkwater has a stirring memory and must be a moving inspiration to every Shrewsbury boy, for it shows an Old Boy who followed faithfully in the line of Philip Sidney; he was Andrew Comyn Irvine, who went with George Leigh Mallory up Everest and with him disappeared into the clouds. The sculpture shows him looking up towards Everest.

As long as the heroic spirit lives in England the name of this scholar of Shrewsbury School must be remembered. Irvine was 15 years younger than Mallory, who chose him as his companion for his last journey to the top of Everest. The party had reached nearly 28,000 feet and come perilously near disaster when Mallory declared he would not give up. Irvine's good humour, and his marvellous energy, were wonderful, and for him "a shot at the summit" was the chance of a lifetime. They set out on the morning of June 6, 1924, reaching Camp Six and writing a note there saying that they were sorry to leave the camp in such a mess, and then climbing on. One of the lower party who followed to Camp Six saw the Peak of Everest unveiled and the whole ridge clear before him, and as he gazed he noticed, far away on a snow slope leading up to what seemed to him the last step but one to the final pyramid, a tiny object moving and approaching the rock step. A second figure followed, and then the first climbed to the top of the step. As the watcher stood spellbound the scene became enveloped in mist, and the figures disappeared from human sight. It was the last that was seen of these two, one of them this Shrewsbury boy who has not been seen by human eyes since he was lost in the clouds.

The library is housed in what is called the Moser Building, and was designed by William Forsyth, who gave it two wings and a central hall with a beautiful portico. On the wall of one wing is an elaborate monument copied from the old one with the figures of two boys under niches, the clumsy new boy and the finished scholar, a Greek inscription reading: "If you are a lover of learning you will become learned."

The rooms in this block have magnificent open roofs of old oak, and the reading room has oak settles about a wide brick fireplace. One room is a picture gallery with a lovely series of drawings by William Strang; a series of portraits of headmasters, and a sculpture by J. H. Monsel Furse of a cock and a snake enrich another room.

The library is proud as well as beautiful, for it has books printed by Caxton and Wynkyn de Worde, some of the first books printed in this country. In another case, among some beautifully bound books, is one by an Italian master which has been described as the most perfect example of his binding in the world. There is the manuscript of the earliest known miracle play in English (about 1400), recording a dialogue between two shepherds, and there are still a few chained books in the library, along with a library catalogue of 1596, when all the books were chained. There are sketches made in an atlas by Darwin in his schooldays at Shrewsbury, and a letter he wrote on his last birthday, saying, "I feel a very old man, and my course is nearly run." A caricature of the headmaster Dr Kennedy was done by Samuel Butler, author of Erewhon, the grandson of another headmaster. What may seem to some the greatest treasure of all in this interesting library we found hanging at the end of a bookcase, the original death-mask of Oliver Cromwell; it was presented by Mr J. B. Oldham, himself an authority of no mean fame on English bindings, who planned this delightful little treasure house in which we found him.

It is worth while before we leave this famous school to remember that two of its boys won the VC in the Great War. Captain Harold Ackroyd saved many lives by moving up and down No Man's Land for hours attending the wounded during heavy fire, and twice going out in a storm of bullets to carry in wounded men. Captain Thomas Pryce led a house-to-house attack in a village in France, and when under 40 of his company survived he held back an enemy battalion for ten hours and stopped a German advance. His trench was blown in and the last round of ammunition was spent, but with only 17 men left he led a charge and cheered on his little group of Philip Sidneys, fighting when last seen against overwhelming odds. They were

The Norman Arches of the Abbey

Two Norman Doorways of St Mary's

SHREWSBURY'S OLDEST CHURCHES

Charles Darwin Statue

The Shropshire Memorial

The Castle on the Hill

IN SHREWSBURY TOWN

worthy, these heroes, of the school which has given to this old town and to England so great an example of the English spirit.

Charles Darwin

CHARLES DARWIN, Shrewsbury's greatest son, spent seven years at school here, a born naturalist lost in a purely classical atmosphere, considered an unsatisfactory pupil of inferior intellect. Going from here to Edinburgh to study medicine, he was driven away in horror by the suffering of children in the days before anaesthetics, and continued his education at Cambridge with a view to entering the Church. More at home botanising or beetle-collecting than in the divinity schools, he was permitted after much opposition to sail in the Beagle as unpaid naturalist on a five-year cruise round the world.

With rare opportunities of observing life and fossils in many lands, he now gave 20 years to study and investigation which led him to the belief that the different species in Nature's families are not fixed, nor each the result of separate creation, but are the slowly evolved product of many species from few, resulting from slight variations in organisms, or in adaptation to environment, enabling plants or animals to survive changing conditions and perpetuate their kind, while the unchanged and less fit died without posterity. He never heard of Mendel, whose discoveries would have complemented his own, but he was startled by receiving from Alfred Russel Wallace a paper embodying results obtained in the East leading him to the same conclusions. Wallace's paper and a summary of Darwin's work were read the same night in 1858 before the Linnean Society, and in 1859 Darwin produced his Origin of Species.

It provoked such fierce controversy that he began to regret having begun his great task. He was no controversialist; he had against him all the conventional critics, true sons of bigotry and intolerance who in earlier days would have sent him to the stake. Fortunately he had a superb exponent in Professor Huxley, and a mighty German champion in Professor Haeckel, and his theories were accepted.

In 1839 Darwin had married his cousin Emma Wedgwood and settled at Downe in Kent, to remain there for the last 40 years of his life. The great voyage in the Beagle had ruined his health, and he was never afterwards free for a day from illness and suffering. Such were the sympathy and understanding of his wife and children, however, that he was spared all anxiety, and lived a beautiful and happy life. Squirrels would climb up him as he stood long motionless examining a tree. The gardener would talk of his "mooning and doing nothing" when he saw him rapt before a flower. His little boys would burst suddenly into his quiet study and promise him sixpence to go out and play with them.

The three boys who played with him became famous: Leonard, soldier, scientist, and political economist; George the astronomer and mathematician; Francis the botanist, biographer of his father and renowned in his own sphere for his profound investigations on the functions of plants. Charles died in 1882, and sleeps in Westminster Abbey, near Sir Isaac Newton.

Abraham and Isaac

SIDBURY. Its old black and white farmhouses peep out from the orchards, and the new church hides among the trees. The medieval church was burnt down in 1912, but the new one has much of its original herringbone masonry, and the richly carved font is a copy of its Norman predecessor. In the churchyard is a hollow yew 30 feet round, doubtless the oldest thing in the village. Not far off is a house (the Batche) with a secret hiding place and a 17th century wall painting of Abraham and Isaac over a mantelpiece.

SILVINGTON. It has a little valley of its own, an old manor house with 14th century windows, and a church with a Norman doorway. The doorway has a plain tympanum and shafts with scalloped capitals; the ironwork on its door is as old as the porch which shelters it, 300 years. The tower arch, with foliage and stars on its capitals, is 700 years old, and has above it a window of the same age with a modern figure of St Michael in it. The font is Norman, round and plain, and the altar table and the chancel panelling are 17th century. In those days Edward Mytton was lord of the manor, and his memorial tablet is adorned with heraldry, flowers, and two wreathed skulls.

The Panorama

SMETHCOTT. Its little church, high and solitary, has one of the most wonderful panoramas in the county. All round the compass it looks, seeing the great plain to the north, the Wrekin, rising magnificently, the swelling lines of the Lawley and Caradoc Hills, and the pastoral hills closer at hand. Its worshippers have been enjoying this noble view for eight centuries, and some of this very masonry was raised by Norman hands. Much has been rebuilt, but there is a blocked doorway through which the Normans walked, a small window which lit up their chancel, and stone fragments carved in their day. The fine little hammerbeam roof has some old timbers, and an unusual possession is an oblong font like a small bath, very ancient, and with a crude old oak cover. In a field opposite the church is a big mound said to be an old place of burial.

STANTON. Near this lonely village, at its manor house in a park on the hill, lived Mary Webb in the days before her marriage. She would look out over most of the county she was later to make famous in her books; she would see the black and white mill on the banks of the Roden; and she would know this Norman church with its ancient doorways, its two deeply splayed windows, its Tudor porch, and its pulpit with Jacobean panels. A lychgate stands in proud memory of those who did not come back from the war, four out of 64 who went.

Black and White Delight

STANTON LACY. Sheltered by hills and with the River Corve flowing by, it is a dreamland village of black and white cottages roofed with thatch and tile, and set among gardens and orchards. Its chief glory is the Saxon work in its little church, one of the few churches the imperious Normans suffered to remain in Shropshire while enriching so many other places in the county with their own splendid structures. In an outer wall of the chancel are two recesses with fine canopies, sheltering two 13th century figures supposed to be ancient lords of the manor, de Lacys. One, believed to be a Crusader, is nearly seven feet high, and under his tomb a huge skeleton has been found in a stone coffin. The central tower and its arches, with ballflower capitals, were built 600 years ago, but three walls have great irregular Saxon stones and long-and-short work. In the north wall is a narrow Saxon doorway, built up but with its round arch perfect, and above it is a Saxon cross with a Norman stone above it carved with balls as decoration.

The chancel is that in which the crusading de Lacy came to pray, and the five double lancets and the simple sanctuary window are as he saw them; a tiny window in a transept must have been already old when he was young.

Nearly 20 generations have been brought for christening to this font, and in the modern reredos are medieval panels painted with saints and Christ with a chalice. There are two old piscinas and a panelled Jacobean oak chest.

In the modernised manor house are parts of the massive 12th century foundation walls of the home of the de Lacys.

The Old Door

STANTON LONG. It has one of the things which will always thrill the traveller when he comes to a village church, an ancient door still opening and closing after five hundred years or more. Here, in a porch of stone and timber, is a doorway from the 13th century, and in it a door which may have been here all the time, still with its elaborate hinges and a small closing ring. The church is neat and well cared for, and has a wooden turret quaintly set on the high nave roof. There are 13th century lancet windows, some with trefoil heads; a filled-up priest's doorway; several ancient niches; and a fine old black and white roof with quatrefoil panels.

A Queen's Embroidery

STAPLETON. Its ancient church is something of a curiosity, a little building whose two storeys were long ago thrown into one. The lower part, with walls four feet thick, was built in early Norman times, and has kept its wide doorway, deep recesses in the chancel, and tiny narrow windows. Before the 12th century passed away another storey was added, turning the first building into a crypt; but in a few decades the two were made one. The priest's door was built between the storeys, and is reached by a flight of steps in the church. The windows and the piscina of the old upper level are left high up in the walls. The roofs are well timbered, the pulpit is handsomely carved, and there is a chair from Cromwell's time. The tall candlesticks with their elaborate carving and colour came from Nuremberg. But the thrilling possession of the church is a framed panel on the chancel wall, a piece of embroidery dull with age, but remarkable because it is thought to be the work of Mary Queen of Scots. It has been used here as a pulpit frontal.

A big mound to the south of the church is older than anything else we see. It may mark the site of a house before the Conqueror came.

STIRCHLEY. It has watched the march of Industrialism across its pleasant slopes but has seen Nature cover its scars with green again. The church, with its walls of brick built in the 18th century, gives no little hint of antiquity as we approach, but a great surprise awaits us, for the interior is dominated by a magnificent Norman chancel arch with three orders of carving, zigzag, chain, and rosettes. The arch has fine capitals. Two original Norman windows remain in the chancel, and a third has been refashioned with Norman stones. The children are christened at a modern font, but there is a tiny worn one which may very well have been here since the Norman days.

Stocks and Whipping-Post Forlorn

STOCKTON. A lovely place above the Severn with the village stocks and the whipping-post standing forlorn in the shade of an elm, it has a medieval church embowered in trees and a Georgian house in a lovely garden. The oldest possession of the church is the 14th century font; the lower part of the tower is 15th century; there is an Elizabethan altar table and a 17th century chest with excellent ironwork, and on the walls is some 17th century panelling. The best possession of the church is its Jacobean pulpit richly adorned with flowers and canopies.

The Proud Carpenter

STOKE-ST-MILBOROUGH. Enfolded in a leafy hollow of Clee Hills, its houses nestling in orchards clothing the hillside, it has magnificent views, with Titterstone Clee Hill a majestic pinnacle of its natural splendours.

From this hillside issue many brooks, chattering over the stones; one of them, springing from a bank near the church, is named St Milburga's Well, the legend being that Milburga, a granddaughter of King Penda, escaped a grave peril here, and the spring was revealed by a blow from her horse's hoof.

The church, one of four in England dedicated to her, has a fine 600-year-old tower. The quaint old porch, with a timber arch, herringbone, and stone seats, has in its floor an ancient coffin stone and Norman masonry in its inner doorway. The fine chancel arch, with stepped mouldings, is nearly as the Normans built it, one capital with their leaf carving, the other modern. The splendid tower arch, 700 years old, has five clustered shafts at either side, making a noble frame for the massive old font.

Cream walls light up the splendid beams and rafters of the high-pitched black and white roof with gables of open timbering, and one of the beams has the name of the man who carved it, for he proudly signed it as he finished it in 1707, Francis Hartar, carpenter.

The Ancient Castle

STOKESAY. It is one of the most charming survivals of medieval England, one of the pictures that do not pass from the traveller's mind. The ancient castle is worth coming far to see. Romantic and charming, it stands at the narrowing of a valley, grouped with its beautiful gatehouse and the sturdy church close by.

We came here when the moat was a riot of flowers, a perfect setting for this gatehouse with its gabled stone roof and overhanging storey. Black with age are its splendid timbers, finely carved by Tudor artists with grotesque men and women, dragons, and angels. On the archway running through to the courtyard we see Adam and Eve with the serpent and the forbidden fruit; and at the end is a great studded door with a wicket and five holes pierced for firearms.

The castle has a south tower and a north tower, and between them a banqueting hall and a handsome drawing-room. An old door opens to the banqueting hall, which is over 50 feet long and about 700 years old. It is lit by fine windows with simple tracery, and has a steep roof finely timbered. At one end a stairway with steps of solid oak leads to the rooms in the north tower, built by the Normans and capped in the 17th century with a black and white top. One room has a fireplace 700 years old, and another has ancient tiles in the floor.

Above a cellar and two small rooms at the other end of the hall is the drawing-room, reached by a flight of steps outside. It is a surprising place to come upon in these gaunt walls. From floor to ceiling it is panelled with Jacobean oak, and of the same age is its splendid chimney-piece, a mass of elaborate carving. On each side is a peephole into the hall below, and leading from the room is a little passage to an odd corner for a watcher in the south tower.

The south tower is a fine structure of three storeys, built by Lawrence de Ludlow in 1284. Its battlements are seven feet high, with loop-holes for bowmen; its walls are thick enough to enclose a staircase; and in it are two fine rooms, both oddly shaped, with lancet windows and sills on which we can sit.

No one has lived here since Queen Anne's time. The castle was garrisoned for Charles Stuart and escaped damage when it surrendered without a siege. Time was bringing it into decay when generous friends came forward to save it, and now it is all in fine repair.

Only the moat lies between the castle and the churchyard, where two elms stand by the lychgate. The church is a simple little place, with a low embattled tower, a Norman doorway, a tower arch probably 13th century, and a font about 300 years old. The nave is crowded with a gallery and much 17th century woodwork, including a three-decker pulpit and panelled box-pews. There are two unusual pews all in one in the chancel. There are two paintings of Moses and Aaron, and on the wall hangs an illuminated history of the church.

One of the nave windows is to a soldier of the Boer War, and shows the Angels appearing to the Shepherds; another shows Michael and Gabriel in memory of the first Shropshire man to lose his life by flying, Mr Hotchkiss, who fell in 1912 near Wolvercote in Oxfordshire, where a memorial is on the bridge close to the spot.

Up a steep hill is the oldest possession of Stokesay, Norton Camp, with two ditches perfectly preserved since the Romans dug them.

A Tudor Judge

STOKE-UPON-TERN. Its handsome church is not old, but it carries on an ancient story of worship here on the banks of the Tern, having a line of rectors back to the 12th century, and a group of Norman coffin lids on the grass by the tower. Within are good modern screens and an attractive pulpit, a long chest of 1631, and a fine window of archangels Michael and Gabriel in memory of two soldiers of the Great War. Saved from an earlier building are a small 18th century brass engraved with an angel and an alabaster tomb with figures of Sir Reginald Corbet and his wife, he in the robes of a

Tudor judge. Carved round the tomb are portraits of four sons and five daughters, and two figures in shrouds. The first Shropshire home of the Corbets was a castle here, but only a few traces of its moat have survived the centuries.

Saxon Sculpture

STOTTESDON. It has one of the oldest bridges in England, a tiny bridge of stone crossing the River Rea; it is said to be of Roman origin and is scheduled as an ancient monument. We may hope it has something Roman in it, for we find here Saxon, Norman, and Tudor too. The church has a Saxon tympanum, a Norman font, and something of the work of Tudor and Jacobean craftsmen.

We may easily miss the Saxon tympanum, for it is over the inner doorway under the tower and difficult to see. It appears to represent a hunting scene with three queer animals, two upside down and one with a human face. There are other queer carvings near them, one a grotesque head with a beard. The wall round this doorway is also Saxon, but the outer doorway and base of the tower are Norman. The tower was finished in the 16th century.

The nave and another doorway (now filled in) are Norman, and the nave has a grand Norman arcade with five arches on leafy capitals and a grotesque figure on one of the pillars. The porch and most of the south aisle are 14th century, and the chancel is one of the best 14th century structures in Shropshire. It has three canopied seats for priests, an ancient arch which may have covered an Easter sepulchre, a few medieval tiles, and an Elizabethan altar table. On the central pinnacle of the sedilia canopy are two little faces. The new screen has fragments of the old worked into it, and the Jacobean pulpit has fine quaint bearded figures.

The magnificent Norman font has been little touched since the Normans put it here. The great round bowl has strange animals and birds carved on it, one bird with a smaller bird in its claws, and there are seven faces, a figure holding a cross, and a deep border of scroll work. It is all splendid Norman craftsmanship, but the double rows of floral carving below the bowl were probably added in the 13th century. The windows glow with colour old and new. A south aisle window is filled with fragments of rich medieval glass, and another window near it has fragments of roses, shields, and a small face. Two 14th century medallions with faces in them were found buried under a yew in the churchyard and are now in a vestry window. In the modern windows is a charming Nativity with the Madonna in a rich blue cloak, the Wise Men in deep blue, green, and gold, the foreground starred with gentian and hyacinth, Jerusalem in the background, and a host of angels above. It is in memory of Arthur Grant, a civil servant in India. In memory of Charles Grant is a 19th century window with Christ with the doctors in the Temple, and the peace memorial window shows Christ in a cloak of red and gold riding a white horse at the head of armoured horsemen.

STOWE. It lies almost hidden in a deep fold of Stowe Hill, looking over the Teme Valley to the rolling hills of the Welsh border. Its 13th century church has kept its massive walls, with modern windows and a wooden bell turret; and it has a very fine 17th century roof, black and white with panelled sides. The chancel is attractive and colourful, with an east window of the Ascension, lancets showing Faith and Hope, and figures of St Michael and St George at the sides of the reredos. A small mosaic to a child shows three angel-children in blue and white, and there is a fine figure of Faith on a golden mosaic ground. A big oak beam divides the chancel from the nave, and the altar table is Jacobean.

Weeping Cross

SUTTON. It is scattered on the edge of Shrewsbury, and has seen its 13th century church come to ruin. Crumbling and desolate we find it in a field, with a wooden window in the modern west wall, nine old lancets, a Norman font, and traces of painting still on the walls. Some of the furniture has gone to Shrewsbury School, including a Tudor reading desk inscribed to Richard Atkys, who was a master and may have been rector here. Half a mile away is a traffic roundabout with a medieval memory. It is the site of Weeping Cross, to which the Trade Companies of Shrewsbury came in procession to bewail their sins on Corpus Christi day.

SUTTON MADDOCK. The Tudor tower was left when the church was made new last century, and stands like a stalwart sentinel. It has two ancient sculptured stones built into it, one of a grotesque animal over the south window, the other over the east window with two crude crosses rising from what looks like a wreath of flowers. The church has an Elizabethan table, and the pulpit and the reredos are carved in oak.

TASLEY. It had a wooden church with a thatched roof about a hundred years ago, high on a hill a mile from Bridgnorth, but the little church has gone and the new one keeps a few of its possessions—the beautiful 15th century chancel screen and a pulpit and reading desk made from the old carved oak. The screen has graceful tracery ending in a double cornice of delicately carved grapes on one side and vine leaves on the other.

Shropshire's Westminster Abbey

TONG. The traveller remembers it for the beauty of its ancient church, its wooded slopes, its thatched cottages, and the castle in the distance, and its people find delight in the assurance that Charles Dickens was thinking of it when he wrote The Old Curiosity Shop and the story of Little Nell. Tong Castle is a turreted building on the site of the ancient castle of the Vernons, and is an imposing sight from the churchyard; but it is 18th century, young compared with the ancient heritage of the historic church. It has been called the Westminster Abbey of the Midlands, and though the description is extravagant the church is full of age and beauty in carved stone and sculptured marble, richly wrought wood, and delicate glass. Its effigies and brasses are one of the sights of Shropshire. The church is a wife's tribute to her husband, and comes from the days before Agincourt, for it was built in 1410 by Lady Elizabeth Pembruge, who lies with her lord within. Some of the stones of the older church were used in the walls; it was originally a collegiate church, and the ruined masonry still seen on the slope below was part of the medieval college.

Battlemented and adorned with grotesque carvings, the church has a striking tower with a small spire, and its porch has an ancient roof and stone seats. On the north doorway are bullet marks from the Civil War, and we find them also on the wall. The priest's doorway into the chancel has a fine oak door, and the chancel has three stone seats for priests. The lovely Golden Chapel, with a wealth of gilding and painting and a grand array of monuments, was added 400 years ago; it has a fan-vaulted roof with grapes carved on the pendants.

There are ancient tiles in the chapel floor, and an old altar stone with five consecration crosses; and a soft light falls on the imposing monuments from the 16th century windows.

Sir Fulke de Pembruge, here with his wife Elizabeth, the builder of the church, is a splendid figure in armour, his head resting on a helmet and his feet on a lion; his wife is in widow's weeds with headless angels supporting her head and a fawn at her feet.

Sir Richard Vernon, Speaker of the Commons in 1426, also lies here in armour, with his head on a helmet, his feet on a lion, and his lovely wife beside him with angels at her pillow and small animals at her feet. Round the tomb are apostles and more angels, with a wealth of canopy-work. The memorial of their eldest son, Sir William Vernon, Treasurer of Calais and the last man to hold the office of Constable of England, is a fine brass showing him in armour with his wife beside him and a little row of children below. Sir William's grandson, Sir Henry Vernon, was linked with a pathetic chapter in English history, for he was guardian of Prince Arthur, whose death at Ludlow Castle when he was but 16 changed the course of history by opening up the way to the throne for Henry the Eighth. Sir Henry, who witnessed the marriage of the young prince to Catherine of Aragon, was the builder of the Golden Chapel, and has an imposing monument under its splendid arch, showing him in armour with a helmet of black plumes and a boar's head crest, and his wife with her hair about her shoulders and two dogs at her feet. His son Richard is on another tomb, armoured, with his feet on a lion and his wife at his side, a tall lady with two dogs holding the hem of her dress; on one end of their tomb is the small figure of their son George, the Peverel of the Peak in Scott's novel, and father of the famous Dorothy Vernon of Haddon Hall.

The portrait of Humphrey, another son of Sir Henry Vernon, is engraved on a stone with his wife's, their heads almost worn away. In a niche is a canopied stone figure of yet another member of this illustrious family, Sir Arthur Vernon, Warden of Tong College, who died in 1517. It shows him with one hand holding a book and the other raised as in preaching; he appears again on a fine brass in the chapel with a shield in each corner and a chalice above his head.

On a high 17th century tomb in the south transept are beautiful figures of Sir Thomas Stanley in plate armour, with his wife Margaret, sister of Dorothy Vernon, and below is a figure of their son Edwin in Commonwealth armour. On the end of the tomb are lines with a punning reference to the name of Stanley, attributed to Shakespeare but probably written by Richard Barnefield:

> *When all to tyme's consumption*
> *Shall be given*
> *Standly for whom this stands*
> *Shall stand in Heaven.*

Among the many other monuments here may be noted a tablet above the door of the chapel with an inscription to Daniel Higgs, which tells us there were "few so honest, none more so"; a 17th century monument in the chancel with a kneeling figure of Anne Wylde, who died at 16; and a 17th century tablet (over the vestry door) to Elizabeth Pierrepont, 11-year-old daughter of Lord Pierrepont, the "ornament of her friends, the delight of her family, the most pleasing hope of both."

From memorials of those who worshipped here we turn to other treasures. There are carved stalls with misereres that have been in use for over 500 years. Some have graceful floral ornament, others show a winged man holding a smaller one, a face with foliage coming from the mouth, a head of Christ; one of the Annunciation is remarkable for having a lily leaf engraved with the Crucifixion. Behind the stalls is panelling enriched with grapes and flying birds and other lovely carving. There is also a group of 15th century deskends, one carved with the Resurrection and another with the Ascension, showing 13 small figures around Our Lord.

Here are three splendid medieval screens. The oldest, in the south aisle, has delicate tracery, a cornice with acorns and foliage, and a stringcourse of laurel leaves and vine. The north aisle screen has fine tracery and Tudor cresting. The chancel screen has lovely carving of oak leaves, acorns, vine, and birds. To this catalogue of grand old woodwork must be added the Jacobean pulpit, an Elizabethan chair, two ancient chests, and all the roofs, the nave roof having a splendid array of angels.

The font is 500 years old and the west window has an assembly of 15th century glass showing angels and figures of St Edmund and St Bartholomew, the Madonna and Child, and emblems of the

Tong   **Shropshire's Westminster Abbey**

The Castle Walls and Village Church

The Oak Staircase of the Banqueting Hall

MEDIEVAL STOKESAY

The Beautiful Tudor Gatehouse

The North Tower of the Castle

STOKESAY CASTLE

Uffington   **The Ruined Walls of Haughmond Abbey**

Uffington   **Norman Doorways of Haughmond Chapter House**

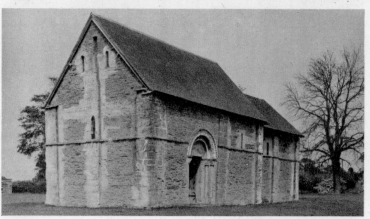

Heath   **The Little Norman Church**

Passion. One very rare possession is in the vestry, an exquisite silver ciborium, a sacramental vessel enriched with gems and said to have been designed by Holbein. It has been exhibited at the British Museum, and is kept locked behind a door which a wise ingenuity has made it possible to open by the insertion of a shilling. In a glass case also in the vestry is a medieval altar cloth embroidered with cherubs, flowers, and a variety of designs; it is said to have been made by the nuns of Whiteladies, near Boscobel, and was given to the church in Charles Stuart's day by the ladies of Tong Castle.

With these treasures in the vestry is a collection of ancient church records and rare old books, including 37 volumes of records of Church Councils from AD 34 to the Council of Trent. One book is said to have belonged to Queen Elizabeth. Here are also some lovely medieval missals which the verger will show to interested visitors. In the belfry is the little 13th century sanctus bell and the great bell (weighing 52 cwts) given to the church by Sir Henry Vernon in thanksgiving for having been guided home one night in 1518 by the sound of the bells of Tong.

The Quaint Men by the Door

TUGFORD. Narrow and unfrequented ways bring us to it among the orchards, sheltering in a deep fold of the hill where a stream comes down on its way to the River Corve. Its church is old and simple, with leaning walls, no aisles, and no chancel arch; it has fine recesses in the outside walls, all with cinquefoil arches and one with capitals of slender leaves. The tower is of three ages and three stages; it was begun in the 13th century, carried on in the 14th, and battlemented in the 18th.

The finest possession of the church, and the oldest, is a splendid Norman doorway. Hiding in the shadows in the top corners of it inside the church are two little men, one with his tongue out and the other lying on his back with his hand over his mouth. Outside the doorway the roll moulding of the round arch runs down to the ground, while the beautiful outer moulding, like a chain of diamonds, rests on shafts with foliage capitals. There is another Norman doorway which has been blocked up and a little Norman window in the nave. The flower-like font resting on a circle of foliage is perhaps a little too late for the Normans.

The east window has three 14th century glass roundels, two of them with heads. The altar table and altar rails are Jacobean, and along the front of a little choir gallery at the west end are panels of 15th century carving. At the side of the gallery is a quaint dormer clerestory. A brass plate tells of Hugh Pugh, who was rector here for 58 years until 1722, and a brass cross is in memory of Richard Woodhouse who was rector for 57 years, dying in 1918; the first rector was born while Charles Stuart was fighting for his crown and lived under five sovereigns and two protectors; the second saw the birth of railways and lived into our Wireless Age.

Broncroft Castle, a mile away, is a 14th century castle transformed into a beautiful house with embattled towers. It is charmingly set among orchards and trees, with lawns and flower-decked walls round the gardens and wide views over the hills and Corve Dale.

The Ruined Abbey

UFFINGTON. Its great attraction for lovers of old buildings is the ruined Abbey of Haughmond about a mile away; but it has a small church of its own, rebuilt in the eighteen-fifties, with several old things to see. There is a perfect example of an old pitch-pipe used for the village choir; a group of medieval tiles; and a remarkable collection of old Flemish and German glass, seven panels being richly coloured, and 22 plain. Among scenes from the Bible and the Apocrypha is one of Christ walking in a city, dated 1575. Another of 1633 shows the baptism in Jordan; and most human of all perhaps is the appearance to Mary Magdalene in the garden, a scene in which Our Lord is wearing a Flemish hat and carrying a wooden spade.

The abbey ruins are set against a richly wooded hill, and are in the safe keeping of the Office of Works. We found smoke coming out of chimneys built here 600 years ago, those of the caretaker's cottage having belonged originally to the kitchen of the monks.

We come first to the old Guest Hall, with its great fireplace and seats below the windows, a 14th century building altered after the Reformation when the abbey became a private house. A doorway at the east leads to another building with a lofty 15th century window, thought to have been the abbot's lodging, and beyond is the chapter house with the magnificent timbers of its ceiling still in place after six centuries. Its ancient west front has an elaborate Norman doorway, with a smaller doorway on each side and between their columns are canopies with small figures of saints and bishops.

Little of the abbey church is standing save part of a wall and a Norman doorway which led to the cloisters. Beside the doorway are 14th century sculptures of Peter and Paul. High windows and a doorway remind us of the refectory, and many scattered fragments tell of those who worked here and the beauty they saw. Two Norman tombstones are among the oldest, inscribed to John Fitzalan and his wife, who must have known the abbey's founder, William Fitzalan, in the 12th century.

In the woods is a little 14th century well-house, ten feet by seven, with a roof of flat stone. It is like a tiny oratory.

The Lost Roman Temple

UPPINGTON. It has grown lovely through the centuries and has not been spoilt; it has had a long time to grow lovely in, for here we came upon a fragment of a Roman altar dug up in the churchyard years ago and standing now like a symbol of a forgotten past. It is about four feet high with a small circle carved on one side, and it would seem that there may have been a Roman temple here and that it was succeeded by a Saxon church, for built up in the wall of the nave is a Norman doorway with a crude dragon chiselled in the tympanum looking like the work of a Saxon craftsman.

Another Norman doorway is still used, the light falls through a Norman window, and in the refashioning of the church last century the Norman chancel arch was preserved and heightened. The walls on both sides of the arch have rows of carvings. In the chancel is a small 17th century brass in memory of John Stanier, steward of the Earl of Bradford, of his wife Rachael, and of his son; the brass tells us that he was faithful to his master, his friend, and his God, and that his son, though he lived but few years, had the blessing of many. His wife Rachael was the sister of Richard Allestree, a famous theologian of his day.

Allestree was born here and lived through the decisive years of the 17th century, a Royalist. It is recorded that the Parliamentary Army, breaking into Christ Church, Oxford, and finding nothing there but a groat and a halter, went to the deanery, collected all they could, and locked up their treasure before going to bed. In the morning it had gone, Allestree having seized it and put it safely away. He was imprisoned for some weeks, during which his health was broken, and after the Restoration he was made provost of Eton College, and when he died he was buried there, and has a monument.

A fine bronze tablet tells us of a villager of wide renown, an Anglesey tinker's son who became one of the national poets of Wales. He was Gronow Owen, and became curate here in the middle of the 18th century. The tablet set up in 1930 tells us that he was a lover of Wales and her languages and that his genius enshrined in mortal verse the language of his native land. He lies at Northolt, Middlesex.

In the churchyard, on which two queer heads look down from one of the windows, is a yew with a hollow trunk 30 feet round.

Norman and Tudor Days

UPTON CRESSETT. It is as remote a spot as Shropshire has. Rough tracks lead to it across the fields and the main road is miles away. The fine old hall (now a farmhouse) and the rare little church stand together, good neighbours through the centuries, lovely and unspoilt. The house is Tudor, with mellow walls of warm red brick and splendid groups of twisted chimneys. It has a staircase of solid oak blocks, and one of the fine rooms has a rich oak frieze, another has its original timber roof, and in a third it is said the dashing Prince Rupert once slept. The line of the moat can be traced, and the gatehouse, with its original towers, fine gables, and patterned walls of brick and stone, stand foursquare to all the winds that blow.

The church is more than twice as old as this Tudor gateway. For centuries men and women have passed through the charming porch, have rested on the stone seats covered with oak, and have passed under the zigzag arch of the Norman doorway. They have looked at this lovely spire borne on massive timbers, and have baptised their children at this Norman font. The little girl we found sitting here waiting for evensong, was looking on a scene such as Norman children looked on. The light falls through Norman windows, and the great chancel arch has four orders of Norman carving and traces of a fifth resting on its sturdy capitals. The little Norman chancel into which it leads us has a narrow east window with three little panels of old glass which look at a distance like delicate engravings, and show the Crucifixion, the Descent from the Cross, and what appears to be the Resurrection; there is a fourth panel in another window showing the Procession to Calvary. The age of the glass is unknown, but the wealth of detail and the vigorous drawing of the figures suggest it was the work of the school of Albert Durer. There is a Jacobean altar table, a Jacobean pulpit, and a simple chest, and through the wide arch leading from the chancel into the Cressett chapel we come upon traces of ancient wall-paintings and a brass of the 17th century, showing Richard Cressett and his wife kneeling at prayer with their five children.

A mile or so away towards Morville the lane narrows so that the hedgerows almost touch, and we pass a farmhouse with grand timbered walls and Tudor chimneys.

Thomas Telford's Ironworks

UPTON MAGNA. It gathers round a green where four roads meet, a pump in the middle and at each corner a black and white house. Its imposing tower is 500 years old, the guardian of a church with panelled buttresses, four Norman windows in the chancel, and 13th century lancets in the east wall. In the tower is a medieval chest made from a single block of wood, and near the 300-year-old font is a big modern wall-painting of the Baptism. A window showing New Testament scenes is in memory of George Corbet, who was vicar for half a century. There is an elaborate monument to William Barker of Haughmond Abbey, set up when the Civil War was troubling England. It shows him on a gilt mattress, leaning on his elbow, and is enriched with coloured shields, an eagle, and hanging drapery of stone.

Not far from the village is a farm called The Forge, its name reminding us that here stood the ironworks which fashioned the links for Thomas Telford's suspension bridge over Menai Straits.

WATERS UPTON. Its church was refashioned in 1864 by George Edmund Street, architect of the London Law Courts, and has two good coloured windows, one of the Three Marys in memory of a Mary who died in 1917, the other showing Peter and John in memory of two officers who fell in the Great War. A brass tablet proudly records the names of forty men who went to fight from this small village with only about forty homes.

From the Top of the Old Volcano

WELLINGTON. It is the modern town of the ancient Wrekin, the famous hill which throws its shadow far across this fair landscape. A few old houses remain of the village from which the town sprang, but the Wrekin has come into the life and legend of Shropshire folk for ages. Its fame is old beyond reckoning, and its shape, its isolated grandeur, must have stirred the people here with something of the feeling the Psalmist had for the hill of Hermon. Its waters, its green slopes, its rocks weirdly cleft, its Gate of Heaven and Gate of Hell, the Raven's Bowl on its summit holding water in the hollow of the rock, and the riven rock called Needle's Eye, have all come into legend, and all delight the traveller's eye.

The summit of the Wrekin is only 1335 feet above the sea, but the view commands all Wales, from Snowdon to the Sugar Loaf of Monmouth. The Welsh mountains, the Hawkstone and the Parkgate Hills in Cheshire, Mow Cop in Staffordshire, the Peak Hills in Derbyshire, Bardon Hill in Leicestershire, Radnor Forest, the Malverns and the Abberley Hills in Worcestershire, the Cotswolds of Gloucestershire, Edge Hill in Warwickshire, and even the Banbury Hills nearly 70 miles away may all be seen on a clear day in this wonderful panorama. Ages back beyond human memory the Wrekin was on fire, a blazing volcano, and here fire blazed again in Armada Year when, as Macaulay tells us, "Streamed in crimson on the wind the Wrekin's crest of light." Its little foot-hill Ercall, which has traces of an old fort, is also remarkable for its wooded beauty.

Wellington in the midst of its modern developments, has a touch of ancient beauty in timbered dwellings peeping out between the shops. The long timbered Old Hall flanking Watling Street has seen the tide of travellers flow by for centuries. It was the home of the Foresters of the Royal Forest of Wrekin.

The modern Christ Church has a lofty tower and a striking oak screen with a great figure of the Prince of Peace between angels, enriched in canopy and tracery with the rose, shamrock, thistle, and leek, and painted regimental badges; the screen and the chapel beside it (beautifully panelled in oak) form the peace memorial. The finely carved pulpit has canopied figures of Christ preaching and of

Peter and Paul. The Children's Corner has two charming windows given by children, one with Christ standing in a wood, the other with the Madonna receiving children who bring flowers. A window with a richly coloured group of angels is in memory of William Smith who was blind; he did what he could and was organ blower here for 33 years.

The church of All Saints is 18th century, and has a fine brass eagle lectern, a marble pulpit with a figure of Our Lord, and a window of St Cecilia with musical angels about her in memory of an organist and choirmaster for 37 years, Malcolm Allison. There is a marble monument with an angel in memory of a vicar's wife, Helen Banning, and another monument with a girl sitting in memory of Elizabeth Oliver, of whom we read that in her, from the earliest dawn of reason, a bud of sweetest promise was unfolded.

Here were born two people who have found their way to fame, William Withering, and Sarah Smith. Withering was the son of an 18th century surgeon and made a reputation as a physician and botanist and mineralogist; he was also one of the earliest advocates of the abolition of the slave trade. He was a friend of Joseph Priestley, and towards the end of his life, in 1791, he felt himself to be in danger at the time when Priestley's house was sacked by rioters after a dinner to commemorate the French Revolution. Withering loaded up his books and specimens on wagons covered with hay in order to protect them, but he escaped peril and himself afterwards lived in Priestley's house at Edgbaston for the last five years of his life. When he died it was wittily said that "the flower of physicians was Withering."

Sarah Smith is probably unknown by that familiar name, but as Hesba Stretton, author of Jessica's First Prayer, she was a best-seller in her day. She was a bookseller's daughter and attended school at the Old Hall in Wellington, beginning early to write little tales with no thought of printing them. One of them was sent to Dickens by her sister, all unknown to Sarah, and Dickens sent her £5 for it and asked for more. She felt that the name of Sarah Smith would not do, and made up Hesba out of the initials of her brothers and sisters and adopted Stretton from the name of a Shropshire village. In 1866 she wrote the tale of a poor girl's awakening to the understanding of religion and called it Jessica's First Prayer. It appeared in the

Sunday at Home and has since been printed everywhere. The story was set in the slums and interested Lord Shaftesbury, and Alexander the Second of Russia ordered it to be read in Russian schools. Hesba Stretton became a woman of importance, helping the Baroness Burdett-Coutts with her charities, and helping also to found the Society for the Prevention of Cruelty to Children. She loved travel and had a host of friends, old and young; she worked hard and hated publicity, and she made her living entirely by her pen. She scorned fine dresses and jewellry, and was never in a theatre.

The Chieftain's Son

WELSHAMPTON. A strange little story we came upon here on the fringe of Shropshire's lake country, for in the shade of a great Wellingtonia by the little church lies the son of an African chief. We have searched in vain for the reason why Moshueshue lies here, but here they laid him in 1863, a young man of 24 whose father ruled in Basutoland and sent his son to learn our ways in England and to study in a missionary college. He must have been much esteemed, for we see him in a window in the church robed in white and being baptised in a river by a saint, with a chariot and servant standing by, as befitted his high rank.

The trim little church has a chancel with an apse and was designed by Sir Gilbert Scott in 13th century style. The porch has a fine arch with a king and a queen at the sides, and the nave has four bays with pillars of black veined marble and splendid little sculptures of foliage between the arches. In one a bird is feeding its young, in another a bird is pecking an insect off a leaf, and there are birds eating berries.

The fine chancel arch has four slender shafts of black marble on each side with capitals of flowers. The elaborate reredos has a beautiful panel of the Crucifixion with the four women and John at the foot of the Cross: elaborate, too, are the stone pulpit and font, both set on stems crowned with flowers. The fine nave roof has round arches rising from 76 small wooden pillars.

The Brute

WEM. It seems a pity that its name should be coupled with the name of a brute, for Judge Jeffreys called himself Baron

Wem from Grinshill Hill

Whitchurch with its Stately Church Tower

TWO OLD SHROPSHIRE TOWNS

The Famous Wrekin From Wenlock Edge

A Delightful Vista Near Wellington

THE WREKIN COUNTRY

Jeffreys of Wem, though he was a Welshman and might have saved the village from this indignity.

A mound near the churchyard takes the story of Wem back to the days when it had a Norman castle, of which no trace is left, but it has kept the 14th century tower of the church. It had its own great fire a few years after London was burned down, and it knew the tragic days of the Civil War, when it was among the first towns to declare for Parliament, the great Puritan Richard Baxter helping to garrison its defence. It has a grammar school which was founded in 1650, a neat little town hall of our own century, the 17th century house (Lowe Hall) in which Jeffreys lived some time, and a charming little white house which was one of the boyhood homes of William Hazlitt; it is in Noble Street.

The founder of the grammar school was a lord mayor of London during the Civil War, Sir Thomas Adams, and was sent to prison for his loyalty to the king; but his reward came when he was invited to go with General Monk to Breda, to bring back Charles the Second to the throne.

High above the sycamores rise the pinnacles of the church, and leading to the churchyard are two 18th century gateways with ornamental vases crowning their posts. The tower has a 13th century doorway, and a canopied niche with a figure of a saint, his feet on a corbel carved with a head. All round the interior are galleries, and from the massive roof hangs a brass chandelier with a dove above the candles.

Hereabouts in the 18th century were born two boys whose names were not soon to be forgotten: John Astley, the portrait painter who went to Rome with Sir Joshua Reynolds and grew rich from his art; and John Ireland who came to London as a watchmaker and is remembered as the biographer of Hogarth. He was born at what is now a farmhouse which has still medieval woodwork in it.

A mile away on the Welshampton road we come to a beautiful black and white house with a hiding-hole in the attic, and with a door-handle made in Shakespeare's day.

Judge Jeffreys, who lived at Lowe Hall and linked his name with Wem, was a coarse, hard-drinking fellow who sought Court favour and became a judge. Degraded for corruptly preventing the summoning of Parliament, he was saved from banishment, and Charles the Second made him a baronet and a Prosecutor for the Crown. It was his delight to bully and browbeat poor peasants, and he took bribes for acquitting the innocent. He sent Alice Lisle to death for giving food and shelter to starving fugitives, and he went from town to town sentencing men and boys to death—hundreds of them he sent to the gallows, and hundreds more transported. He himself had a fee of £10 a head for many prisoners he sent abroad to the planters. Though he was made Lord Chancellor by the last of our Stuart kings, the time came when he tried to escape to France to save himself from being torn to pieces; he was caught, however, and thrown into the Tower, where he died a victim of disease and drink, execrated by the nation.

A more pleasant association with Wem was that of our great essayist, Hazlitt. He came here as a boy of eight, his father being a preacher. Young Hazlitt received most of his education in his father's house, and was so well-informed that he was only just in his teens when he wrote a letter to the Shrewsbury Chronicle concerning the persecution of Joseph Priestley at Birmingham. Until he was thirty he spent most of his time either in London or at Wem, and here he must have gained most of the wide knowledge he reveals in his essays. It was here that he first met Coleridge, who visited the father and invited the son to visit him at Stowey.

A Splendid Vista

WENTNOR. A windswept village under the ridge of the Long-mynd, it looks out to the splendour of line upon line of hills and to the peace of the sheltered valley. In the churchyard what is known as the Hurricane Gravestone is a sad witness to the storms that have brought tragic consequences in their train, an inscription telling of a blizzard which struck a house at Asterton close by in the winter of 1772, sweeping it bodily away and killing seven people.

The Norman church has been largely made new, but not all its ancient glories are gone. One of the corner-stones is an old sculptured head upside down, and in a splendid modern porch, shaded by a stately yew, is a doorway with work by the Norman masters who built the north doorway and the little round window in the nave. Most of the woodwork is from the old church. There are 15th century beams and carved panels in the nave roof, the altar table and pulpit are Jacobean, and there is old carving in the seats. Four oak corner-posts supporting the belfry are 25 feet high and 15 inches square, and the arrangement of them suggests a delightful ingle nook. The clock was made by a village blacksmith 150 years ago. On the walls hangs a beautiful illuminated parchment telling the story of the church.

The Norman Knight

WESTBURY. By one of its quiet roads stands a quaint 18th century tower, the sentry of a long and spacious church with leaning walls. It has a north arcade 700 years old, and a window 500 years old, but much of it has been made new. There are handsome modern roofs, and a bright east window with ten panels including scenes of Moses and Joseph, Lazarus, the Baptism, and the Crucifixion. We come here upon a famous Shropshire family, the Corbets; and a mile or two away stands what is left of the fortress built by Roger Fitz-Corbet, who came with the Conqueror to fight at Hastings. Its great days ended with the Civil War, and little is left save earthworks. But after eight centuries the name of Cause Castle still reminds us of Pays de Caux, the birthplace a Norman knight loved to remember when he made his home in a strange land.

The Holy Well

WEST FELTON. Its old manor house, with a moated mound close by, stands near the church and the rectory; and another of its old houses, The Nursery, has in its grounds a fine yew, a curious sundial of Shakespeare's day with several dials, and an old font carved with the Greek palindrome (reading the same both ways) meaning Wash not my face alone, but wash my sins also. It was cast out of Kinnerley church, and its base is said to be 12th century. Here in 1782 was born the writer and poet John Freeman Dovaston, and here, after the death of his father in 1808, he settled down to his hobbies, the study of natural history and the writing of verse popular in its day but now forgotten.

By the busy highway stands a graceful cross in memory of those who died for peace; and walking in the village we were intrigued by the sight of a little wooden pulpit perched on the edge of a garden high above the road, not a preaching pulpit as it seemed, but a safe place for the children to see traffic going by.

The church has a great roof over its nave and aisles, and has mostly been built in the last 200 years. Its old possessions are two Norman arcades, a good Jacobean chest, an ornate memorial of the Restoration period, and a sundial of 1700 mounted on three steps which may be from a medieval cross.

One of the modern windows is a fine triple lancet, another has lovely Kempe glass of the Angel appearing to the Shepherds, a third shows the Women at the Tomb and Christ appearing to Peter, and a fourth is very charming with St Francis among his little friends the birds. It is a happy tribute to a maid of 14, who, like Francis, was in tune with Nature.

A few minutes away at Woolston is a little black and white house built over St Winifred's holy well. Here her body rested on its way from Holywell to Shrewsbury. The water springs up in an alcove and runs into two stone basins, sparkling and clear, an unfailing supply for the hamlet.

WHEATHILL. It is one of the small Clee villages, seeming to dream away its days unmindful of the world. Its church has a Norman doorway high and narrow with cable moulding, and a tympanum carved in diamond shapes. The chancel arch is Norman with carved capitals and zigzag, and the chancel has one Norman window left. In another chancel window, 600 years old, are fragments of its original glass. The open timbers of the roofs are 300 years old, and the altar table and altar rails and a chair in the sanctuary are all 17th century. The oak lectern is carved with ivy, oak leaves, and acorns. Above a tablet to a 17th century rector is a curious egg-shaped head with staring eyes and wings where the ears should be, probably a symbol of fleeting mortality.

Music, Shakespeare, and Antiquity

WHITCHURCH. Whatever else it may have to entitle it to a place in fame and history, it has three great honours that can never be taken away. It was one of its sons who opened up for us our famous Saxon history; another son of Whitchurch has given us music beloved by millions; and a third man linked forever with its name is that John Talbot who sleeps here and lives in Shakespeare as

The scourge of France,
The Talbot so much feared abroad
That with his name the mothers still their babes.

Here also for some time lived Bishop Heber, who wrote Greenland's Icy Mountains, and here were spent some years of the youth of that popular and humorous artist Randolph Caldecott, whose pictures Whitchurch is proud to hang on its walls. The old castle is gone, but there are black and white houses. The old church has gone, but the 18th century church is full of interest. The old grammar school is going, but it has remained on its old site for 300 years, and is moving outside because it grows bigger and better.

We read of the great John Talbot in the porch of the magnificent 18th century church, and behind the organ (still in its fine case of 1755) lies another John Talbot who died in 1550 after giving Whitchurch its grammar school; he was rector here and is sculptured in his robes. The great John Talbot, Earl of Shrewsbury, sleeps here and has a tablet telling us how he fell near Bordeaux in 1453, an old warrior of 80, and how he asked his bodyguard to bury him in the church porch here, so that, as they had fought and strode over his body while he lived, so should they and his children for ever pass over it and guard it in death. Hanging on the vestry wall is a photograph of his skull, which was picked up on the battlefield with the mark of the battle axe that struck him down still on it. In the lady chapel the brave man lies on his canopied tomb, wearing his armour with the mantle and Order of the Garter over it.

But even without its monuments this church would attract the traveller, for its stately tower is a landmark far and wide. Dedicated to the 8th century saint, Alkmund, it follows a Saxon church and a Norman White Church which gave the town its name. With classical pillars, handsome galleries, and brass candelabra the interior is inspiring, leading up to a reredos with oak pillars and carvings of four saints. Even the vestry is full of things to see, a big table made from the sounding board of a three-decker pulpit, an old painting of the medieval church which fell in 1711, and, best of all, a little keepsake from the Mother of Parliaments, the silken royal arms which formerly hung behind the Speaker's chair.

There is a Restoration font with a handsome Queen Anne cover, a peace memorial figure of St Michael in brilliant colour on the west wall, and a magnificent screen in Jacobean style enclosing a chapel in memory of William Henry Egerton, who was rector for 62 years. The chapel has a reredos with scenes in relief of the early life of

Jesus, and in the centre a lovely roundel of the Madonna surrounded by angels.

A brass on the floor tells of a rector's little son 200 years ago, and another brass is to a rector of the 17th century. On a plain wall tablet we read of one of the early Nonconformist ministers, Philip Henry, who began his life in Whitehall and lies buried here. As a child he had played with the royal princes; as a boy he had watched Charles Stuart walking to his trial and seen his last moments on the scaffold; as a man he preached Nonconformity in Flintshire, losing his position when the Restoration came. He left diaries covering 22 years, of great interest for the light they shed on the days of religious persecution in England. There are letters from him and relics relating to himself and his son Matthew Henry (famous for his Bible Commentaries) in the museum in High Street.

Here the library, reading-room, museum, and art gallery are all found together, and the museum has fine collections of birds and geological specimens, three fine Roman urns and a bronze Roman lamp, Roman coins, and ancient deeds and records of the neighbourhood in medieval days. Here also are pictures by local artists, the original of the Prodigal Son by Sir William Etty, RA, Maldraeth Bay by J. W. Oakes, ARA, and a collection of about 30 paintings and drawings by Randolph Caldecott, whose pictures of nursery rhymes were so familiar to the last generation. The artist lived at Whitchurch in his youth, working as a bank clerk. Also hanging on the walls are portraits of Sir Edward German, and kept here are examples of musical scores written by him.

The son of Whitchurch who interested himself in Saxon England was Abraham Wheelocke, a poor scholar who made himself one of the best students of Oriental languages in England, with an unrivalled knowledge of Arabic and Persian. He became a librarian at Cambridge at £10 a year, and first professor of Arabic at £40. He made a Persian translation of the Bible, but did not live to finish his printing of it. He busied himself with Anglo-Saxon manuscripts and translated Bede and the Anglo-Saxon Chronicle, which had lain for centuries as unreadable as the Arabic of which he made himself the master. Wheelocke translated the Chronicle into the language of his day; it was his crowning work, but he was not satisfied, for he associated himself with the scholars who produced the Polyglot

Bible, the Bible in eight languages side by side. He worked on struggling against ill-health and poverty until the end came, finding him in 1653 still immersed in his self-appointed tasks.

The musical genius of Whitchurch who became a national figure will hardly be recognised if we give his name as Mr E. G. Jones, but all the world knows him by the name the initials stand for, Edward German. Jones Senior was organist at the Congregational Chapel here and his son came up to London to play in theatre orchestras. Few days go by when somewhere in England there are not heard certain gay tuneful melodies which long familiarity never makes less welcome. They are the tunes of Edward German's Merrie England, his delightful opera. He wrote tunes for Shakespeare's Much Ado and dances for Nell Gwynn; and the light operas of A Princess of Kensington and Tom Jones were also his. He was of the school of Gilbert and Sullivan opera, and when Sir Arthur Sullivan died it was thought the mantle might fall on him. He finished the music for the Emerald Isle, for which Sullivan had left only a sketch, and he did it admirably, but Sir Arthur's mantle was a giant's robe too big for him to wear, and we are sure he knew it; yet in his unassuming way he went on to write the light tuneful music that captures the ear of millions. All his life of 74 years he kept out of the limelight, known and admired among a small circle of fellow musicians but hardly more than a name to the public which listened to him.

Whatever he achieved he won without advertisement, and possibly was never so well known as now. But we might say of him, remembering the epitaph to Sir Christopher Wren in St Paul's, that if you seek his monument, *Listen, and you shall hear*.

He Met Joan on the Battlefield

JOHN TALBOT, first Earl of Shrewsbury, who sleeps at Whitchurch, was virtually the hero of the first part of Shakespeare's Henry the Sixth. He was born towards the close of the 14th century, fought against Owen Glendower, and twice governed Ireland, where, opposing violence to violence, he caused it to be said that, "there came not from the time of Herod anyone so wicked in evil deeds."

His fame was made in France, where his deeds were legendary in his own day and his name was King Talbot. From 1420 onwards he was foremost in the fighting, not a great general but a born leader, who by his courage and high spirit seemed to personify the England of his age. At Joan of Arc's siege of Orleans he held the Bastille, and when he was driven out Joan, impressed by his renown, thought she had beaten the English leader. It was due entirely to his rashness that his force was defeated at Patay, where he was taken prisoner. For four years he remained in captivity, an immense ransom being demanded for his release.

It was during this time that Joan was captured. Had she had a single friend she might have been given her liberty in exchange for Talbot—though possibly he would not have consented, for, like the entire English army and its allies, he never doubted that Joan was a witch and an emissary of Satan, and might have regarded such an exchange as disgraceful and impious. Exchanged in 1433, he was mainly responsible for delaying the final overthrow of English rule in France. He strides resplendent through the pages of Shakespeare, never more proudly heroic than when he hastened to the relief of beleaguered Castillon, accompanied by his gallant son. He beat off the besiegers, and then, without waiting for his artillery, made a reckless assault with a handful of men on the enemy's camp. It was the courage of a madman. His little force was practically annihilated by cannon-fire. Seeing death for himself inevitable, he begged his son to flee, but the young hero refused to leave him, and was mortally wounded before the eyes of his father, who, clasping him to his breast, exclaimed:

> *Soldiers, adieu! I have what I would have*
> *Now my old arms are young John Talbot's grave.*

So father and son died together; a father mourned his son and England mourned a great and well-loved captain. His body was recovered after the battle and brought here, and here he lies in peace after his long wars, among his kindred.

The Children's Bishop

WHITTINGTON. A big village with a story centuries old, it had its fortress in Saxon England and has something of its castle still, making a charming picture with the church and the proud swans sailing on a wayside moat. At the other end of the village is a fine old house in black and white, near the Three Trees which make a triangle in the middle of the road.

The Saxon fortress was rebuilt by Norman hands, and here are portions of two of its seven towers, impressively strong even in their ruin. With them are grassy mounds and banks, a courtyard with a little garden, and a fine 13th century gatehouse still used to live in. A 600-year-old window in one of the towers is said to be the only relic of Whittington's medieval church.

Very familiar must it all have been to one of the best-known parsons of last century, William Walsham How. Here he was rector for 28 years, living at the rectory with its fine old yew, and here he was laid to rest in 1897, a flat stone marking his grave in the burial-ground opposite the church. A fine cross, carved with the Good Shepherd and the bishop's staff and mitre, reminds us of him by the wayside.

His devotional writings gained for him a wide reputation, and he received offers of several bishoprics, all of which he declined. But in 1879 he accepted the post of suffragan to the Bishop of London and became the leader of a crusade to raise the spiritual level of the East End. He won the interest of rich Londoners, of public schools, and of universities, and everywhere he went the more spiritually-minded people were attracted to him. Particularly he loved his title of Children's Bishop.

After his wife's death he accepted the bishopric of Wakefield, and became as popular in Yorkshire as he had been in London. He died in 1897, and though his splendid memorial was the enlargement of Wakefield Cathedral he was buried here, where he worked so long. We gather something of his life and character from the hymns he wrote: his belief in practical religion from *Soldiers of the Cross, arise*; his geniality and zest for life from *Summer suns are glowing*. Finest of all perhaps is his solemn and inspiring hymn, *For all the saints who from their labours rest*.

The church is a 19th century building, like a great hall inside; and Bishop How, when he came here, found it so ugly that he said of Mr Davies the rector and Mr Harrison the architect:

> *We will not censure Mr Davies,*
> *Now good man he in his grave is:*
> *Nevertheless the church you gave us*
> *Ugly is past all comparison,*
> *O, you dreadful Mr Harrison.*

It has been enriched since those days, and has attractive choir-seats and a screen in memory of the bishop himself. A striking feature is the fine flat roof with its big panels, spanning 60 feet and resting only on the walls; and striking too is the fine new glass in the east window, a Jesse Tree on a clear background, with coloured figures in the branches leading up to the Madonna at the top. Another window shows the Annunciation, with St Martin and St Hubert. Two faithful servants of the church are remembered on these walls, Thomas Scriven who sang in the choir for nearly half a century, and John Beckett who sang for no less than 68 years.

The churchyard has an 18th century sundial and an old yew. Its handsome iron gates are a peace memorial to those who fell.

Burne-Jones Windows

WHITTON. Secluded among the hills, it is reached by deep-cut lanes with a splendid landscape of the Teme valley. Whitton Court, lying back above the village, is mainly Elizabethan, but has some 15th century timbers and Jacobean gables. For 600 years the low tapering tower has beckoned the people to the Norman church. Much has changed, but in the timber porch is a Norman doorway with a tympanum, and a Norman window remains in the nave. Some 20 generations have been christened at the font, charmingly framed in the baptistry under the tower, where the sturdy little arch and the oak seats round the walls form a delightful picture lighted by a deeply splayed old window. Six centuries have passed since the sculptor carved the sanctuary window, which, after waiting 500 years, was enriched with Burne-Jones glass in red, blue, and green showing Mary and John in rich draperies, and miniature scenes of the Annunciation, the Wise Men, and the Nativity, with Mary and Joseph gazing raptly on the Child. A chancel window has the priest's seat set in it, and there is old linenfold in the choir-stalls.

WHIXALL. A big and scattered village, it is close to a wide tract of peat bog, where its people still cut the peat for fuel. Its brick church was built in the eighteen-sixties by George Edmund Street, who built the Law Courts in London, and a delightful little place it is, with Doré engravings round the walls.

A Romantic Spot

WILLEY. It is a romantic spot, far from busy roads, among gentle slopes clad with some of the most magnificent trees (beech, chestnut, and fir) to be seen in Shropshire. In the heart of all this beauty is the Tudor manor house, old home of the Weld family, and for miles between this and the new hall the paths wander through enchanting scenery. The old house has many gables, and in the gardens are ruined walls. The church is old and new, with three Norman windows and a Norman font, and a pulpit, reading desk, and pews of Jacobean oak. There is a high pew above the nave in which the great family would sit. In a chapel designed by Sir Arthur Blomfield is an imposing monument to John George Weld, second Baron Forester. It shows in white marble, delicately carved by Sir Edgar Boehm, a Resurrection scene in which Mary stands at the empty tomb, a graceful figure with flowing hair, two angels and two women with her. A white marble monument to Sir John Weld, a town clerk of London who died in the year of the Great Fire, has Corinthian columns and 13 small coats-of-arms round the epitaph.

In the churchyard lies Major Wolstan Weld-Forester, whose name is on the peace memorial. Wounded while leading the Grenadier Guards at the first Battle of Ypres, he died in his own village and was buried among his own people.

Named after a King's Son

WISTANSTOW. It has in its name the echo of a pitiful tragedy and in its history a beautiful romance.

It takes its name from St Wystan, the fatherless heir to Wiglaf, a 9th century king of Mercia. It is said that at a Council of Peace his uncle, professing to give Wystan an affectionate embrace, drew his sword and killed him.

Much more pleasant is the tale behind one of the windows in the Norman and medieval church. The window, like the oak pulpit carved with the Four Evangelists, is a memorial to the Hoggins family, to one of whom there came in 1791 a man who begged that she would be his bride. He was a stranger and declared himself as John Jones and he had means for which none could account, so that he was thought to be a highwayman or a smuggler.

He bought land and began to build a house, and while the house was rising he lodged with the Hoggins family at Bolas Magna, fell in love with Sarah, and married her. One day he set out with her for a holiday, and they came into Lincolnshire and found themselves at Stamford, looking at the stately Burghley House which we may all see there. Sarah was enraptured with the beauty of it; it was the loveliest spot she had ever seen, she said. "Then it is yours," he said, "and you are Marchioness of Exeter."

The church to which she used to come was built by the Normans on the site of a Saxon church. It is approached by splendid pines. Its tower was raised in the days of Richard Lionheart, but its bold arches and its battlements are 14th century. The priest comes into the chancel by a doorway built when our English builders were succeeding the Normans; it has a big grotesque on a capital and a head at either side. From the same days comes the font. There are 17th century dates on a lock in the porch and on a beam in the chancel but the splendid roof of the nave, with its carved bosses and its quatrefoils in diamond panels, is as old as the roof of Westminster Hall, which Richard the Second built. The raftered roofs of a transept are little younger, and there is a fine medieval chest. In the nave are many old box-pews. St Wystan stands in a window as a golden-haired boy in a red cloak taking the crown from his mother, who is dressed in purple, white, and gold.

A mile away is a farm which was once a castle, with remnants of its moat and walls pierced for archers when Roger Cheney built his fortified manor here 500 years ago. The spring which served the fortress now supplies the dairy. In one of the fields are earthworks thrown up when the house was besieged in the Civil War, and on Wart Hill is an ancient camp.

Chaplain to the Tragic Princes

WITHINGTON. It has quaint cottages, a neat Georgian vicarage, and a modern church with a reredos of the Crucifixion by George Edmund Street. Two Tudor brasses the church has, one of John Olney with his wife and seven sons, the other of Adam Grafton, who was priest here, Dean of St Mary's College at Shrewsbury, and a well-known figure at Court when the Tudor Age began. He was chaplain to the unhappy boy king Edward the Fifth, murdered with his brother in the Tower, and to Henry the Seventh's eldest son Prince Arthur, whose death at 16 changed the course of our history. His arms are with his name on the tower he built at Battlefield, and we read that he was the most worshipful priest living in his days.

Humphrey Cotes of Bosworth Field

WOODCOTE. Its modern hall stands in a great park on a hill with glorious views. Behind it is a Norman chapel altered in Elizabethan times, but still keeping its Norman doorway with carved capitals. It has an 18th century pulpit, a good kingpost roof, and handsome chancel fittings in memory of two men killed in the war. There are many memorials to the Cotes family, who were for centuries at the hall, and best of them all is an old stone engraved with lifesize portraits of Humphrey Cotes and his wife. We see him as a warrior, and are reminded of his last fight at the dawn of the Tudor Age, when, gathering his tenants and friends at a hill still called Muster Hill, he led them to Bosworth Field, where he was slain in the great fight which ended the reign of the House of York and ushered in the Tudors of our Golden Age.

The Rector Lost in the Snow

WOOLSTASTON. It has fine views, a moated earthwork covering nearly an acre, and a pretty gathering of buildings round the green. Its hall has become a farm, and has at the back a massive porch, once the chief entrance. An old black and white house is charming with gables and a balcony.

The church is quaint and old, with ancient tiles on the roof, a fine yew for company, and a doorway through which the priest was walking before the seals were set on Magna Carta. There are walls and windows of the 13th century, and just as old is the people's doorway with its beautiful modern door. In the north wall is a 12th century tympanum, with a carving of scales thought to be by a later hand. The interior is dim but homely, and has an effective touch of colour in its eastern lancets, where we see Michael and Gabriel and the Light of the World. A roof-beam at the west end rests on wooden pillars and forms an arch. There are bench-backs and panelling from the 18th century, and a chest of the same period is used as an altar table. The font is a curiosity put together from two old fonts, one on the other. The top one is thought to be the original font of the church; the other was brought from the destroyed chapel at Womerton.

All who come will admire the carving of the pulpit and the reading desk, which, with that of the lectern and altar rails, was fashioned last century by a local man, William Hill. He was paid with the money the rector received from the sale of a true story called A Night in the Snow, telling of the rector's wonderful escape when, after taking a service at Ratlinghope, he was for 27 hours lost in the snow on the Longmynd. He was Edmund Donald Carr, and he turned his perilous adventure to good account for this church, which he loved and restored.

The Time in Mexico

WORFIELD. It is set in quiet watermeadows, with old gabled houses and a noble church by a wooded hill. A crouching stone lion and the stone head of a man staring up behind it must be from an older church or an ancient tomb; they lie by the gate like phantoms of the past. There is a lovely clipped yew tree, with a trunk about 13 feet round and wooden seats beneath it where for generations men have sat to gossip pleasantly on long summer days. A charming old sundial with a slender shaft and a metal top gives times at Worfield and Jerusalem, and curiously, for some unknown reason, for Mexico as well.

The pinnacled tower and spire rise nearly 200 feet from a base 700 years old, and the porch door has been opened and shut by 20 generations. It is grooved by wind and rain and bound with iron bands, wrought in scrolls and fantastic likenesses of birds and beast. The inner door has good tracery, and there is more fine old woodwork inside the church. The lofty screen across the 13th century chancel arch is enriched with quatrefoils, rosettes, and a beautiful canopy; it is 500 years old. There is a grand chest eight feet long with ancient ironwork, and a quaint almsbox inscribed "Be sure as you remember the poor." In the vestry are three old carved wood panels, showing Christ carrying the Cross, a Roman soldier, and a woman's head.

A gem of 14th century glass gleams in a south aisle window, showing the Crucifixion, and to the right of this, among modern glass, is a group of kings, monks, and a bishop in old glass, all with their eyes turned towards the Cross. Two more windows in this aisle have medieval glass in their tracery, one showing a dark bearded head, the white face of a woman, and the brown face of a child; the other with an angel whose fingers pluck a stringed instrument in her lap.

In the floor is a stone engraved with a worn figure of John de Worfield, a 15th century priest, and on an imposing Jacobean tomb are figures of Sir Edward Bromley and his wife, under a great canopy resting on seven columns. The reredos is beautifully carved in alabaster, and shows the Ascension, St Peter, the Madonna, St John, and St Chad.

At the hamlet of Chesterton, two miles away, are cottages said to have been partly built from the ruins of a 15th century chapel, and a wooded knoll close by has earthworks of a Roman camp.

The Lost Garrison

WORTHEN. It lies half way between Shrewsbury and Montgomery, its back to the Long Mountain and its southern outlook to the Devil's Chair on the jagged crest of Stiperstones, made memorable by Mary Webb in The Golden Arrow.

The church is set back from the road, and has a stolid tower built in the 13th and 15th centuries with an odd assortment of stones, some of them unusually long. A quaint 18th century porch protects a richly moulded doorway 400 years older.

Most striking inside is the woodwork of the pews and the roof of the nave. There are three long lines of very fine seats with bobbin ends, Jacobean box-pews with carved panels, and a block of stout Elizabethan benches. The squire's pew has a coat-of-arms, and is near a low two-decker pulpit. Our own generation has seen the uncovering of the fine 14th century timbers in the roof, and the old chancel arch came to light at the same time. But the most curious discovery of the restorers was a sealed vault containing 13 skeletons, buried without a clue to their identity or the time of their burial. It is possible that they were members of the last garrison at Cause Castle, men who met a violent end when the castle was taken in 1646.

The medieval font is unusually shaped like a globe with eight sides. There is an attractive reredos below a window showing the Angels at the Tomb and Christ in Glory. In another window we see Christ and Mary in the garden; and a third is striking with the Ascension and figures of five Disciples. A brass inscription tells of a Dean of Hereford who was rector here and chaplain to the first two Stuarts, preaching often at Court.

A mile away at Leigh stands Hampton Hall, a 17th century house with a fine porch; and a moat reminds us of Leigh Hall which held out for the King in Cromwell's day. In another direction at Aston Rogers is The Pound House, a timbered home of 500 years ago with part of its ancient moat.

Queen Margaret and the Robber

WROCKWARDINE. A lonely lane from Watling Street brings us to this tranquil place, where for 600 years men have been able to climb this tower and look across to Staffordshire and Derbyshire or the peaks of Wales, or to mark the changing light on the Clee Hills and the Wrekin. Here Nature is magnificent.

And man too is magnificent, for these mighty arches of the tower are Norman and they rest on Saxon stones. Everywhere about us is something from old days. The bowl of the little font is believed to have been made by a Saxon craftsman; it has still his carvings at the corners, worn by wind and rain while the bowl lay in a garden. There is a perfect Norman window in the chancel with a copy of Holman Hunt's Light of the World in it, and a Norman doorway with its carved capitals but without their pillars. The door is ancient and of thickly studded oak. A Norman arch in a transept has been blocked up, and in both nave and chancel are Norman and medieval windows blocked up in the 14th century. The oak pulpit and the chancel rails are 17th century, and behind the altar is a lovely piece of ancient tapestry with flowers and scrolls in a soft harmony of colour. The chancel roof looking down on it is 14th century.

In the chancel is a grand old chair with a delightful carving of Queen Margaret and the Robber, those words being carved underneath. There are lions on the arms, and the queen is shown protecting the little prince, while the robber, with one hand raised and the other seizing his sword, is about to attack her. There is a fine little ironbound chest, and among the monuments is a fashionable one of the 18th century to William Cludde; it has cherubs, scrolls, an urn, and a painted shield.

A window in the nave pays tribute to a woman who gave her life for England, Edith Leake, who died in nursing wounded soldiers during the influenza epidemic of 1918. The window has delicately-coloured figures of Joan of Arc and St Margaret of Scotland, with a host of angels above and flowers below. Another lovely window is

Whittington   **Castle Gatehouse and Moat**

Tudor Tower of Church

Bases of Forum Pillars

The Ruined Basilica of Uriconium

ROMAN WROXETER

in memory of Robert Newhill, a churchwarden; it was designed by his daughter to illustrate the Psalm, "He bringeth them to the haven where they would be," and in a little panel is a ship in harbour and two children kneeling below with peacocks, owls, rabbits and goats. About two miles to the west of Wrockwardine is the hamlet of Charlton with a fragment of an ancient castle surrounded by a dry moat, little remaining but a mound lonely in a field.

Watling Street Loses Itself

WROXETER. Here, by the church, old Watling Street loses itself in a grassy lane ending at the River Severn, where is a ford used by the Romans and fragments of a bridge they built.

But it is the church itself that makes Wroxeter an exciting place for those who are thrilled by old things, for parts of it were built by the Saxons with huge stones taken from the old Roman town of Uriconium. We enter the churchyard between Roman pillars, Roman stones form an arch in a garden by the church, and the great font is fashioned from the base of a Roman pillar, brought from the basilica of Uriconium and turned upside down. Round the top of it is a moulding thought to be Saxon.

Nearly as rare as these Roman relics are several examples of Saxon carving. A long cross-shaft in the south wall is decorated with spiral ornament and an animal like a giraffe; two other stones are carved with animals, probably dogs; and a plinth stone in the 12th century chancel arch has a Saxon carving of birds feeding on worms.

In the walls of the Tudor tower are moulded stones from Haughmond Abbey. Four figures in long robes make excellent gargoyles, and in niches on the tower are three figures including St Peter. The chancel is Norman, with a priest's doorway which has a double row of zigzags above a double row of 13th century ornament.

There are three fine arches carved on the choir-stalls by Elizabethan craftsmen, a long chest with ironwork 700 years old, and a beautiful recess adorned with ballflower and traces of painting. The altar table, the pulpit, and the altar rails are Jacobean.

On fine tombs in the chancel lie six people who lived in the Tudor Age, three husbands and three wives. Sir Thomas Bromley, who sat on Edward the Sixth's Council of Regency, is here in his robes as Lord Chief Justice, with his wife beside him and their daughter carved on the front of the tomb. Opposite lie Sir Richard Newport and his Margaret, both holding books, he in Elizabethan armour and she with a bird at the hem of her frock. Their children carved below are fully coloured, holding gloves and posies and shields-of-arms. On the third tomb lies John Berker who lived about 17 days after losing his wife; still on his hands are the iron gauntlets he wore when Shakespeare was alive, and his lady, we noticed, is the only one of the three to have heels on her shoes.

A huge white monument with cherubs and heads of horses tells of Francis Newport, first Earl of Bradford, who as a young man sat in the Short and Long Parliaments, living on through the Civil War, the Commonwealth, the Restoration, and the coming of William of Orange, and dying when Queen Anne was on the throne.

The Birmingham of Roman Britain

FROM the road between Wellington and Shrewsbury we see standing above the cornfields a rugged mass of masonry, pierced by an arch. At the nearest point to it a byway turns towards it; it is Watling Street, changing its direction to cross the Severn and run south to link the Roman outposts on the border of Wales. The mass of masonry is all that is left standing, higher than a man, of Uriconium, fourth city of Roman Britain.

This huge fragment was part of the south wall of a basilica of which the foundations have been traced in the field to the north, revealing that it was 229 feet long and 67 feet wide. This basilica, built about AD 140 and probably used as the law court, was in the centre of a city surrounded by a wall two miles long, protected by wide ditches of which traces remain.

South of the basilica on either side of Watling Street (here a narrow country road), are the buildings which have been excavated and left open for all to see. Stepping down from the street on the steps trodden by Romans and British, we find ourselves in a court-yard partly paved with small bricks laid herringbone fashion. Round three sides are a dozen cells, each formerly a shop, the sill of its wooden door still visible. Across a passage are the foundation walls of two bigger buildings, one the factory of a bronze-worker, his furnace still here, the other, joined to the outer wall of the basilica, the workshop of a smith. These workshops and other discoveries show that Uriconium was an industrial centre, a veritable Birmingham of Roman Britain.

Behind the workshops are perfect double walls which held water tanks for cleansing lavatories beyond, evidence of the high state of civilisation reached here 1800 years ago. The greater part of the excavated area shows the public baths, but some of the coal and charcoal which warmed them has been found in a storehouse. The foundations of part of the covered passage round them have been revealed, and most of the lower walls of the rooms, with some of the pillars supporting the floors. Steps lead down to a tiny doorway through which a man could just creep in to clear out ashes. Between the pillars under the floor of one of the hot-air rooms was found a skeleton which told something of the tragic fate of Uriconium. The man had crept into this hiding-place when the city was attacked, and he had with him his savings—132 coins. The baths were burned over his head, he was suffocated, and remained here with the portraits of six Roman Emperors in his hand for 14 centuries; his skull with those of two women found hiding near him are in the museum.

On the other side of Watling Street is a field which has been excavated during this century and covered again except for the bases of 12 columns which are seen in a trench parallel with the street. These are in their original position on a continuous base of huge stones with an open gutter for rain in front. The colonnade runs under the soil for an equal distance to the north, so that it was 132 yards long, forming two sides of the forum of between nearly two and three acres; the other two sides had broad corridors under tiled roofs, which protected the market stalls. Hundreds of pieces of pottery were found, many perfect, having fallen when the stalls collapsed, and in one pile were 80 whetstones with the marks of the saw still on them, the stock of some unlucky shopkeeper.

The most remarkable find in this field was a collection of pieces of a tablet which had been fixed over the main entrance to the forum. It has been pieced together and is now in Shrewsbury Museum with most of the other important finds at Uriconium; it is 12 feet long and 4 feet high, and the inscription, bold and clear, states that the building was erected by the Community of the Cornovii in honour of the Emperor Hadrian in AD 130. Other finds in this field were the foundations of other baths, a silver mirror a foot wide with a lovely twisted handle, water-pipes of lead and wood, and a bronze diploma granting a Roman soldier his discharge and citizenship; dated 135, this was the seventh of these diplomas found in England.

One other group of stones lies exposed in this field to tell a story, dragged here from the banks of the Severn where they helped to support a bridge the Romans built beside the old ford. In a museum beside the excavations are a number of the coins, ornaments, and other objects used by the Romans and British who lived in this city, which appears to have been a national workshop rather than a garrison town. Remains of legionaries are few, but there is ample evidence to prove that here was a contented and active population until the Romans left our land and the Welsh, or some other foes, swept suddenly down, slaughtering the people and burning their homes so that the only use of Uriconium after that was a quarry for builders.

YOCKLETON. Its 19th century church, sheltered in limes, has a tower and spire 75 feet high and stands by the rectory with cedars, firs, and oaks in its grounds, and a stream running by a fine avenue down to the road. Behind the rectory is a great mound overgrown with trees, a lookout in the old, old, far-off days. The three lancets of the east window has a Crucifixion in memory of the village men who died for peace; St George and St Chad in memory of a rector and a major; St Nicholas with his ship and St Oswald with his kingly sceptre in memory of a captain.

SHROPSHIRE
IN 5-MILE SQUARES

SHROPSHIRE TOWNS AND VILLAGES

In this key to our map of Shropshire are all the towns and villages treated in this book. If a place is not on the map by name, its square is given here, so that the way to it is easily found, each square being five miles. One or two hamlets are in the book with their neighbouring villages ; for these see Index.

INDEX

This index includes all notable subjects and people likely to be sought for, and a special index of pictures appears at the beginning of this volume.

INDEX

INDEX

251

INDEX